George D. Rise

Note-Maturity and Date-Differential Tables

George D. Rise

Note-Maturity and Date-Differential Tables

ISBN/EAN: 9783337811709

Printed in Europe, USA, Canada, Australia, Japan

Cover: Foto ©Suzi / pixelio.de

More available books at **www.hansebooks.com**

Note-Maturity and Date-Differential Tables.

By Geo. D. Rise, Lebanon, Pa.

—:o:—

The Note-Maturity Tables show, at a glance, the exact day of maturity (the last day of grace) of Notes dated any day in the year, whether the notes are made payable from five days to one hundred days after date, or from one month to twelve months after date; giving also the changes when the Notes are dated, or mature, in Leap-Year. Perpetual.

—:o:—

The Date-Differential Tables show the number of days from any date in the year to any other date in the year, the result in every case including both dates, as is banking custom.

For Banks, Bankers and Business Men generally.

Price, postpaid, One Dollar; Six copies for Five Dollars.

Note-Maturity Tables, without grace.

For use in States where Three Days' Grace are NOT ALLOWED.

Several States of the Union have abolished the allowance of "three days' grace;" it is likely that other States will adopt the same custom, and the subject of recommending such action is being seriously considered by the American Bankers' Association and by some of the State Bankers' Associations. In view of possible changes by reason of such legislation, I have added to this book a set of Maturity Tables [pages 115 to 209 inclusive] giving the maturity of notes dated any day in the year, including Leap-Year changes, for use in such States as do not allow three days' grace.

PRESS OF
THE REPORT PUBLISHING CO.,
LEBANON, PA.

NOTE-MATURITY .
and
DATE-DIFFERENTIAL
TABLES.

—:o:—

The use of these Tables will save Bankers and other business men much labor and time in reckoning the date of maturity of notes, and also in calculating the number of days from any day in the year to any other day in the year, (the result including both dates, as is banking custom.)

The tables give these points at a glance, without any chance of error. The busy man has scarcely the time to spare to make the calculations necessary to obtain results, and tables that are accurate, that are conveniently arranged, and that contain the information that is wanted, are always in demand.

It is a well-known fact that Banks often suffer loss by reason of protesting notes on the wrong day—not the exact day of maturity—through errors made in reckoning.

A note protested in error, before its exact day of maturity, makes the offender liable to an action for damages ; on the other hand, if the note is protested a day too late, the endorser is relieved from liability for payment thereof. The object of this work is to save all the labor of making the reckonings, (and the consequent chance of errors,) to save much time to a busy class of workers, and to save the risk of damage or loss by reason of errors.

Geo. D. Rise.

Lebanon, Pa., 1891.

The Note-Maturity tables give all changes that occur by reason of Leap-Year.

The day of maturity given is, in every case, the last day of grace.

Examples :

A note dated January 9th, at 75 days after date, will be due March 28th (see page 8) ; in leap-year the same note will be due on March 27th (see page 9).

A note dated April 26th, at 40 days, matures on June 8th; if dated April 26th, at 10 months, it matures on March 1st ; if dated April 26th, at 10 months, and the note should mature in leap-year, the date of maturity will be February 29th (see page 41).

INDEX.

Note-Maturity for notes dated in January, Pages 6 to 19
   do.   do.   February, " 18 to 29
   do.   do.   March, " 28 to 35
   do.   do.   April, " 36 to 41
   do.   do.   May, " 42 to 48
   do.   do.   June, " 48 to 54
   do.   do.   July, " 54 to 60
   do.   do.   August, " 60 to 66
   do.   do.   September, " 66 to 72
   do.   do.   October, " 72 to 78
   do.   do.   November, " 78 to 87
   do.   do.   December, " 86 to 99
No. of days from any day in January,   Page 102
   do.   do.   February, " 103
   do.   do.   March, " 104
   do.   do.   April, " 105
   do.   do.   May, " 106
   do.   do.   June, " 107
   do.   do.   July, " 108
   do.   do.   August, " 109
   do.   do.   September, " 110
   do.   do.   October. " 111
   do.   do.   November, " 112
   do.   do.   December. " 113

Note-Maturity Tables.

The dates of notes are given at the top of each page ; the time of the note in the first column ; and the date of maturity at the intersecting point of the date column and the time line.

Time.	January 1.	January 2.	January 3.	January 4.	January 5.
5 days.	Jan. 9	Jan. 10	Jan. 11	Jan. 12	Jan. 13
10 days.	Jan. 14	Jan. 15	Jan. 16	Jan. 17	Jan. 18
15 days.	Jan. 19	Jan. 20	Jan. 21	Jan. 22	Jan. 23
20 days.	Jan. 24	Jan. 25	Jan. 26	Jan. 27	Jan. 28
25 days.	Jan. 29	Jan. 30	Jan. 31	Feb. 1	Feb. 2
30 days.	Feb. 3	Feb. 4	Feb. 5	Feb. 6	Feb. 7
35 days.	Feb. 8	Feb. 9	Feb. 10	Feb. 11	Feb. 12
40 days.	Feb. 13	Feb. 14	Feb. 15	Feb. 16	Feb. 17
45 days.	Feb. 18	Feb. 19	Feb. 20	Feb. 21	Feb. 22
50 days.	Feb. 23	Feb. 24	Feb. 25	Feb. 26	Feb. 27
55 days.	Feb. 28	Mar. 1	Mar. 2	Mar. 3	Mar. 4
60 days.	Mar. 5	Mar. 6	Mar. 7	Mar. 8	Mar. 9
65 days.	Mar. 10	Mar. 11	Mar. 12	Mar. 13	Mar. 14
70 days.	Mar. 15	Mar. 16	Mar. 17	Mar. 18	Mar. 19
75 days.	Mar. 20	Mar. 21	Mar. 22	Mar. 23	Mar. 24
80 days.	Mar. 25	Mar. 26	Mar. 27	Mar. 28	Mar. 29
85 days.	Mar. 30	Mar. 31	Apr. 1	Apr. 2	Apr. 3
90 days.	Apr. 4	Apr. 5	Apr. 6	Apr. 7	Apr. 8
95 days.	Apr. 9	Apr. 10	Apr. 11	Apr. 12	Apr. 13
100 days.	Apr. 14	Apr. 15	Apr. 16	Apr 17	Apr. 18
1 month.	Feb. 4	Feb. 5	Feb. 6	Feb. 7	Feb. 8
2 months.	Mar. 4	Mar. 5	Mar. 6	Mar. 7	Mar. 8
3 months.	Apr. 4	Apr. 5	Apr. 6	Apr. 7	Apr. 8
4 months.	May 4	May 5	May 6	May 7	May 8
5 months.	Jun 4	Jun. 5	Jun. 6	Jun. 7	Jun. 8
6 months.	Jul. 4	Jul. 5	Jul. 6	Jul. 7	Jul. 8
7 months.	Aug. 4	Aug. 5	Aug. 6	Aug. 7	Aug. 8
8 months.	Sep. 4	Sep. 5	Sep. 6	Sep. 7	Sep. 8
9 months.	Oct. 4	Oct. 5	Oct. 6	Oct. 7	Oct. 8
10 months.	Nov. 4	Nov. 5	Nov. 6	Nov. 7	Nov. 8
11 months.	Dec. 4	Dec. 5	Dec. 6	Dec. 7	Dec. 8
12 months.	Jan. 4	Jan. 5	Jan. 6	Jan. 7	Jan. 8

For Leap-Year changes, see next page.

Changes when Notes mature in Leap-Year.

Time.	Janu'ry 1.	Janu'ry 2.	Janu'ry 3.	Janu'ry 4.	Janu'ry 5.
55 days.	Feb. 28	Feb. 29	Mar. 1	Mar. 2	Mar. 3
60 days.	Mar. 4	Mar. 5	Mar. 6	Mar. 7	Mar. 8
65 days.	Mar. 9	Mar. 10	Mar. 11	Mar. 12	Mar. 13
70 days.	Mar. 14	Mar. 15	Mar. 16	Mar. 17	Mar. 18
75 days.	Mar. 19	Mar. 20	Mar. 21	Mar. 22	Mar. 23
80 days.	Mar. 24	Mar. 25	Mar. 26	Mar. 27	Mar. 28
85 days.	Mar. 29	Mar. 30	Mar. 31	Apr. 1	Apr. 2
90 days.	Apr. 3	Apr. 4	Apr. 5	Apr. 6	Apr. 7
95 days.	Apr. 8	Apr. 9	Apr. 10	Apr. 11	Apr. 12
100 days.	Apr. 13	Apr. 14	Apr. 15	Apr. 16	Apr. 17

Time.	January 6.	January 7.	January 8.	January 9.	January 10.
5 days.	Jan. 14	Jan. 15	Jan. 16	Jan. 17	Jan. 18
10 days.	Jan. 19	Jan. 20	Jan. 21	Jan. 22	Jan. 23
15 days.	Jan. 24	Jan. 25	Jan. 26	Jan. 27	Jan. 28
20 days.	Jan. 29	Jan. 30	Jan. 31	Feb. 1	Feb. 2
25 days.	Feb. 3	Feb. 4	Feb. 5	Feb. 6	Feb. 7
30 days.	Feb. 8	Feb. 9	Feb. 10	Feb. 11	Feb. 12
35 days.	Feb. 13	Feb. 14	Feb. 15	Feb. 16	Feb. 17
40 days.	Feb. 18	Feb. 19	Feb. 20	Feb. 21	Feb. 22
45 days.	Feb. 23	Feb. 24	Feb. 25	Feb. 26	Feb. 27
50 days.	Feb. 28	Mar. 1	Mar. 2	Mar. 3	Mar. 4
55 days.	Mar. 5	Mar. 6	Mar. 7	Mar. 8	Mar. 9
60 days.	Mar. 10	Mar. 11	Mar. 12	Mar. 13	Mar. 14
65 days.	Mar. 15	Mar. 16	Mar. 17	Mar. 18	Mar. 19
70 days.	Mar. 20	Mar. 21	Mar. 22	Mar. 23	Mar. 24
75 days.	Mar. 25	Mar. 26	Mar. 27	Mar. 28	Mar. 29
80 days.	Mar. 30	Mar. 31	Apr. 1	Apr. 2	Apr. 3
85 days.	Apr. 4	Apr. 5	Apr. 6	Apr. 7	Apr. 8
90 days.	Apr. 9	Apr. 10	Apr. 11	Apr. 12	Apr. 13
95 days.	Apr. 14	Apr. 15	Apr. 16	Apr. 17	Apr. 18
100 days.	Apr. 19	Apr. 20	Apr. 21	Apr. 22	Apr. 23
1 month.	Feb. 9	Feb. 10	Feb. 11	Feb. 12	Feb. 13
2 months.	Mar. 9	Mar. 10	Mar. 11	Mar. 12	Mar. 13
3 months.	Apr. 9	Apr. 10	Apr. 11	Apr. 12	Apr. 13
4 months.	May 9	May 10	May 11	May 12	May 13
5 months.	Jun. 9	Jun. 10	Jun. 11	Jun. 12	Jun. 13
6 months.	Jul. 9	Jul. 10	Jul. 11	Jul. 12	Jul. 13
7 months.	Aug. 9	Aug. 10	Aug. 11	Aug. 12	Aug. 13
8 months.	Sep. 9	Sep. 10	Sep. 11	Sep. 12	Sep. 13
9 months.	Oct. 9	Oct. 10	Oct. 11	Oct. 12	Oct. 13
10 months.	Nov. 9	Nov. 10	Nov. 11	Nov. 12	Nov. 13
11 months.	Dec. 9	Dec. 10	Dec. 11	Dec. 12	Dec. 13
12 months.	Jan. 9	Jan. 10	Jan. 11	Jan. 12	Jan. 13

For Leap-Year changes, see next page.

Changes when Notes mature in Leap-Year.

Time.	Janu'ry 6.	Janu'ry 7.	Janu'ry 8.	Janu'ry 9.	Janu'ry 10.
50 days.	Feb. 28	Feb. 29	Mar. 1	Mar. 2	Mar. 3
55 days.	Mar. 4	Mar. 5	Mar. 6	Mar. 7	Mar. 8
60 days.	Mar. 9	Mar. 10	Mar. 11	Mar. 12	Mar. 13
65 days.	Mar. 14	Mar. 15	Mar. 16	Mar. 17	Mar. 18
70 days.	Mar. 19	Mar. 20	Mar. 21	Mar. 22	Mar. 23
75 days.	Mar. 24	Mar. 25	Mar. 26	Mar. 27	Mar. 28
80 days.	Mar. 29	Mar. 30	Mar. 31	Apr. 1	Apr. 2
85 days.	Apr. 3	Apr. 4	Apr. 5	Apr. 6	Apr. 7
90 days.	Apr. 8	Apr. 9	Apr. 10	Apr. 11	Apr. 12
95 days.	Apr. 13	Apr. 14	Apr. 15	Apr. 16	Apr. 17
100 days.	Apr. 18	Apr. 19	Apr. 20	Apr. 21	Apr. 22

Time.	January 11.	January 12.	January 13.	January 14.	January 15.
5 days.	Jan. 19	Jan. 20	Jan. 21	Jan. 22	Jan. 23
10 days.	Jan. 24	Jan. 25	Jan. 26	Jan. 27	Jan. 28
15 days.	Jan. 29	Jan. 30	Jan. 31	Feb. 1	Feb. 2
20 days.	Feb. 3	Feb. 4	Feb. 5	Feb. 6	Feb. 7
25 days.	Feb. 8	Feb. 9	Feb. 10	Feb. 11	Feb. 12
30 days.	Feb. 13	Feb. 14	Feb. 15	Feb. 16	Feb. 17
35 days.	Feb. 18	Feb. 19	Feb. 20	Feb. 21	Feb. 22
40 days.	Feb. 23	Feb. 24	Feb. 25	Feb. 26	Feb. 27
45 days.	Feb. 28	Mar. 1	Mar. 2	Mar. 3	Mar. 4
50 days.	Mar. 5	Mar. 6	Mar. 7	Mar. 8	Mar. 9
55 days.	Mar. 10	Mar. 11	Mar. 12	Mar. 13	Mar. 14
60 days.	Mar. 15	Mar. 16	Mar. 17	Mar. 18	Mar. 19
65 days.	Mar. 20	Mar. 21	Mar. 22	Mar. 23	Mar. 24
70 days.	Mar. 25	Mar. 26	Mar. 27	Mar. 28	Mar. 29
75 days.	Mar. 30	Mar. 31	Apr. 1	Apr. 2	Apr. 3
80 days.	Apr. 4	Apr. 5	Apr. 6	Apr. 7	Apr. 8
85 days.	Apr. 9	Apr. 10	Apr. 11	Apr. 12	Apr. 13
90 days.	Apr. 14	Apr. 15	Apr. 16	Apr. 17	Apr. 18
95 days.	Apr. 19	Apr. 20	Apr. 21	Apr. 22	Apr. 23
100 days.	Apr. 24	Apr. 25	Apr. 26	Apr. 27	Apr. 28
1 month.	Feb. 14	Feb. 15	Feb. 16	Feb. 17	Feb. 18
2 months.	Mar. 14	Mar. 15	Mar. 16	Mar. 17	Mar. 18
3 months.	Apr. 14	Apr. 15	Apr. 16	Apr. 17	Apr. 18
4 months.	May 14	May 15	May 16	May 17	May 18
5 months.	Jun. 14	Jun. 15	Jun. 16	Jun. 17	Jun. 18
6 months.	Jul. 14	Jul. 15	Jul. 16	Jul. 17	Jul. 18
7 months.	Aug. 14	Aug. 15	Aug. 16	Aug. 17	Aug. 18
8 months.	Sep. 14	Sep. 15	Sep. 16	Sep. 17	Sep. 18
9 months.	Oct. 14	Oct. 15	Oct. 16	Oct. 17	Oct. 18
10 months.	Nov. 14	Nov. 15	Nov. 16	Nov. 17	Nov. 18
11 months.	Dec. 14	Dec. 15	Dec. 16	Dec. 17	Dec. 18
12 months.	Jan. 14	Jan. 15	Jan. 16	Jan. 17	Jan. 18

For Leap-Year changes, see next page.

Changes when Notes mature in Leap-Year.

Time.	Janu'ry 11.	Janu'ry 12.	Janu'ry 13.	Janu'ry 14.	Janu'ry 15.
45 days.	Feb. 28	Feb. 29	Mar. 1	Mar. 2	Mar. 3
50 days.	Mar. 4	Mar. 5	Mar. 6	Mar. 7	Mar. 8
55 days.	Mar. 9	Mar. 10	Mar. 11	Mar. 12	Mar. 13
60 days.	Mar. 14	Mar. 15	Mar. 16	Mar. 17	Mar. 18
65 days.	Mar. 19	Mar. 20	Mar. 21	Mar. 22	Mar. 23
70 days.	Mar. 24	Mar. 25	Mar. 26	Mar. 27	Mar. 28
75 days.	Mar. 29	Mar. 30	Mar. 31	Apr. 1	Apr. 2
80 days.	Apr. 3	Apr. 4	Apr. 5	Apr. 6	Apr. 7
85 days.	Apr. 8	Apr. 9	Apr. 10	Apr. 11	Apr. 12
90 days.	Apr. 13	Apr. 14	Apr. 15	Apr. 16	Apr. 17
95 days.	Apr. 18	Apr. 19	Apr. 20	Apr. 21	Apr. 22
100 days.	Apr. 23	Apr. 24	Apr. 25	Apr. 26	Apr. 27

Time.	January 16.	January 17.	January 18.	January 19.	January 20.
5 days.	Jan. 24	Jan. 25	Jan. 26	Jan. 27	Jan. 28
10 days.	Jan. 29	Jan. 30	Jan. 31	Feb. 1	Feb. 2
15 days.	Feb. 3	Feb. 4	Feb. 5	Feb. 6	Feb. 7
20 days.	Feb. 8	Feb. 9	Feb. 10	Feb. 11	Feb. 12
25 days.	Feb. 13	Feb. 14	Feb. 15	Feb. 16	Feb. 17
30 days.	Feb. 18	Feb. 19	Feb. 20	Feb. 21	Feb. 22
35 days.	Feb. 23	Feb. 24	Feb. 25	Feb. 26	Feb. 27
40 days.	Feb. 28	Mar. 1	Mar. 2	Mar. 3	Mar. 4
45 days.	Mar. 5	Mar. 6	Mar. 7	Mar. 8	Mar. 9
50 days.	Mar. 10	Mar. 11	Mar. 12	Mar. 13	Mar. 14
55 days.	Mar. 15	Mar. 16	Mar. 17	Mar. 18	Mar. 19
60 days.	Mar. 20	Mar. 21	Mar. 22	Mar. 23	Mar. 24
65 days.	Mar. 25	Mar. 26	Mar. 27	Mar. 28	Mar. 29
70 days.	Mar. 30	Mar. 31	Apr. 1	Apr. 2	Apr. 3
75 days.	Apr. 4	Apr. 5	Apr. 6	Apr. 7	Apr. 8
80 days.	Apr. 9	Apr. 10	Apr. 11	Apr. 12	Apr. 13
85 days.	Apr. 14	Apr. 15	Apr. 16	Apr. 17	Apr. 18
90 days.	Apr. 19	Apr. 20	Apr. 21	Apr. 22	Apr. 23
95 days.	Apr. 24	Apr. 25	Apr. 26	Apr. 27	Apr. 28
100 days.	Apr. 29	Apr. 30	May 1	May 2	May 3
1 month.	Feb. 19	Feb. 20	Feb. 21	Feb. 22	Feb. 23
2 months.	Mar. 19	Mar. 20	Mar. 21	Mar. 22	Mar. 23
3 months.	Apr. 19	Apr. 20	Apr. 21	Apr. 22	Apr. 23
4 months.	May 19	May 20	May 21	May 22	May 23
5 months.	Jun. 19	Jun. 20	Jun. 21	Jun. 22	Jun. 23
6 months.	Jul. 19	Jul. 20	Jul. 21	Jul. 22	Jul. 23
7 months.	Aug. 19	Aug. 20	Aug. 21	Aug. 22	Aug. 23
8 months.	Sep. 19	Sep. 20	Sep. 21	Sep. 22	Sep. 23
9 months.	Oct. 19	Oct. 20	Oct. 21	Oct. 22	Oct. 23
10 months.	Nov. 19	Nov. 20	Nov. 21	Nov. 22	Nov. 23
11 months.	Dec. 19	Dec. 20	Dec. 21	Dec. 22	Dec. 23
12 months.	Jan. 19	Jan. 20	Jan. 21	Jan. 22	Jan. 23

For Leap-Year changes, see next page.

Changes when Notes mature in Leap-Year.

Time.	Janu'ry 16.	Janu'ry 17.	Janu'rv 18.	Janu'ry 19.	Janu'ry 20.
40 days.	Feb. 28	Feb. 29	Mar. 1	Mar. 2	Mar. 3
45 days.	Mar. 4	Mar. 5	Mar. 6	Mar. 7	Mar. 8
50 days.	Mar. 9	Mar. 10	Mar. 11	Mar. 12	Mar. 13
55 days.	Mar. 14	Mar. 15	Mar. 16	Mar. 17	Mar. 18
60 days.	Mar. 19	Mar. 20	Mar. 21	Mar. 22	Mar. 23
65 days.	Mar. 24	Mar. 25	Mar. 26	Mar. 27	Mar. 28
70 days.	Mar. 29	Mar. 30	Mar. 31	Apr. 1	Apr. 2
75 days.	Apr. 3	Apr. 4	Apr. 5	Apr. 6	Apr. 7
80 days.	Apr. 8	Apr. 9	Apr. 10	Apr. 11	Apr. 12
85 days.	Apr. 13	Apr. 14	Apr. 15	Apr. 16	Apr. 17
90 days.	Apr. 18	Apr. 19	Apr. 20	Apr. 21	Apr. 22
95 days.	Apr. 23	Apr. 24	Apr. 25	Apr. 26	Apr. 27
100 days.	Apr. 28	Apr. 29	Apr. 30	May 1	May 2

Time.	January 21.	January 22.	January 23.	January 24.	January 25.
5 days.	Jan. 29	Jan. 30	Jan. 31	Feb. 1	Feb. 2
10 days.	Feb. 3	Feb. 4	Feb. 5	Feb. 6	Feb. 7
15 days.	Feb. 8	Feb. 9	Feb. 10	Feb. 11	Feb. 12
20 days.	Feb. 13	Feb. 14	Feb. 15	Feb. 16	Feb. 17
25 days.	Feb. 18	Feb. 19	Feb. 20	Feb. 21	Feb. 22
30 days.	Feb. 23	Feb. 24	Feb. 25	Feb. 26	Feb. 27
35 days.	Feb. 28	Mar. 1	Mar. 2	Mar. 3	Mar. 4
40 days.	Mar. 5	Mar. 6	Mar. 7	Mar. 8	Mar. 9
45 days.	Mar. 10	Mar. 11	Mar. 12	Mar. 13	Mar. 14
50 days.	Mar. 15	Mar. 16	Mar. 17	Mar. 18	Mar. 19
55 days.	Mar. 20	Mar. 21	Mar. 22	Mar. 23	Mar. 24
60 days.	Mar. 25	Mar. 26	Mar. 27	Mar. 28	Mar. 29
65 days.	Mar. 30	Mar. 31	Apr. 1	Apr. 2	Apr. 3
70 days.	Apr. 4	Apr. 5	Apr. 6	Apr. 7	Apr. 8
75 days.	Apr. 9	Apr. 10	Apr. 11	Apr. 12	Apr. 13
80 days.	Apr. 14	Apr. 15	Apr. 16	Apr. 17	Apr. 18
85 days.	Apr. 19	Apr. 20	Apr. 21	Apr. 22	Apr. 23
90 days.	Apr. 24	Apr. 25	Apr. 26	Apr. 27	Apr. 28
95 days.	Apr. 29	Apr. 30	May 1	May 2	May 3
100 days.	May 4	May 5	May 6	May 7	May 8
1 month.	Feb. 24	Feb. 25	Feb. 26	Feb. 27	Feb. 28
2 months.	Mar. 24	Mar. 25	Mar. 26	Mar. 27	Mar. 28
3 months.	Apr. 24	Apr. 25	Apr. 26	Apr. 27	Apr. 28
4 months.	May 24	May 25	May 26	May 27	May 28
5 months.	Jun. 24	Jun. 25	Jun. 26	Jun. 27	Jun. 28
6 months.	Jul. 24	Jul. 25	Jul. 26	Jul. 27	Jul. 28
7 months.	Aug. 24	Aug. 25	Aug. 26	Aug. 27	Aug. 28
8 months.	Sep. 24	Sep. 25	Sep. 26	Sep. 27	Sep. 28
9 months.	Oct. 24	Oct. 25	Oct. 26	Oct. 27	Oct. 28
10 months.	Nov. 24	Nov. 25	Nov. 26	Nov. 27	Nov. 28
11 months.	Dec. 24	Dec. 25	Dec. 26	Dec. 27	Dec. 28
12 months.	Jan. 24	Jan. 25	Jan. 26	Jan. 27	Jan. 28

For Leap-Year changes, see next page.

Changes when Notes mature in Leap-Year.

Time.	Janu'ry 21.	Janu'ry 22.	Janu'ry 23.	Janu'ry 24.	Janu'ry 25.
35 days.	Feb. 28	Feb. 29	Mar. 1	Mar. 2	Mar. 3
40 days.	Mar. 4	Mar. 5	Mar. 6	Mar. 7	Mar. 8
45 days.	Mar. 9	Mar. 10	Mar. 11	Mar. 12	Mar. 13
50 days.	Mar. 14	Mar. 15	Mar. 16	Mar. 17	Mar. 18
55 days.	Mar. 19	Mar. 20	Mar. 21	Mar. 22	Mar. 23
60 days.	Mar. 24	Mar. 25	Mar. 26	Mar. 27	Mar. 28
65 days.	Mar. 29	Mar. 30	Mar. 31	Apr. 1	Apr. 2
70 days.	Apr. 3	Apr. 4	Apr. 5	Apr. 6	Apr. 7
75 days.	Apr. 8	Apr. 9	Apr. 10	Apr. 11	Apr. 12
80 days.	Apr. 13	Apr. 14	Apr. 15	Apr. 16	Apr. 17
85 days.	Apr. 18	Apr. 19	Apr. 20	Apr. 21	Apr. 22
90 days.	Apr. 23	Apr. 24	Apr. 25	Apr. 26	Apr. 27
95 days.	Apr. 28	Apr. 29	Apr. 30	May 1	May 2
100 days.	May 3	May 4	May 5	May 6	May 7

Time.	January 26.	January 27.	January 28.	January 29.	January 30.
5 days.	Feb. 3	Feb. 4	Feb. 5	Feb. 6	Feb. 7
10 days.	Feb. 8	Feb. 9	Feb. 10	Feb. 11	Feb. 12
15 days.	Feb. 13	Feb. 14	Feb. 15	Feb. 16	Feb. 17
20 days.	Feb. 18	Feb. 19	Feb. 20	Feb. 21	Feb. 22
25 days.	Feb. 23	Feb. 24	Feb. 25	Feb. 26	Feb. 27
30 days.	Feb. 28	Mar. 1	Mar. 2	Mar. 3	Mar. 4
35 days.	Mar. 5	Mar. 6	Mar. 7	Mar. 8	Mar. 9
40 days.	Mar. 10	Mar. 11	Mar. 12	Mar. 13	Mar. 14
45 days.	Mar. 15	Mar. 16	Mar. 17	Mar. 18	Mar. 19
50 days.	Mar. 20	Mar. 21	Mar. 22	Mar. 23	Mar. 24
55 days.	Mar. 25	Mar. 26	Mar. 27	Mar. 28	Mar. 29
60 days.	Mar. 30	Mar. 31	Apr. 1	Apr. 2	Apr. 3
65 days.	Apr. 4	Apr. 5	Apr. 6	Apr. 7	Apr. 8
70 days.	Apr. 9	Apr. 10	Apr. 11	Apr. 12	Apr. 13
75 days.	Apr. 14	Apr. 15	Apr. 16	Apr. 17	Apr. 18
80 days.	Apr. 19	Apr. 20	Apr. 21	Apr. 22	Apr. 23
85 days.	Apr. 24	Apr. 25	Apr. 26	Apr. 27	Apr. 28
90 days.	Apr. 29	Apr. 30	May 1	May 2	May 3
95 days.	May 4	May 5	May 6	May 7	May 8
100 days.	May 9	May 10	May 11	May 12	May 13
1 month.	Mar. 1	Mar. 2	Mar. 3	Mar. 3	Mar. 3
2 months.	Mar. 29	Mar. 30	Mar. 31	Apr. 1	Apr. 2
3 months.	Apr. 29	Apr. 30	May 1	May 2	May 3
4 months.	May 29	May 30	May 31	Jun. 1	Jun. 2
5 months.	Jun. 29	Jun. 30	Jul. 1	Jul. 2	Jul. 3
6 months.	Jul. 29	Jul. 30	Jul. 31	Aug. 1	Aug. 2
7 months.	Aug. 29	Aug. 30	Aug. 31	Sep. 1	Sep. 2
8 months.	Sep. 29	Sep. 30	Oct. 1	Oct. 2	Oct. 3
9 months.	Oct. 29	Oct. 30	Oct. 31	Nov. 1	Nov. 2
10 months.	Nov. 29	Nov. 30	Dec. 1	Dec. 2	Dec. 3
11 months.	Dec. 29	Dec. 30	Dec. 31	Jan. 1	Jan. 2
12 months.	Jan. 29	Jan. 30	Jan. 31	Feb. 1	Feb. 2

For Leap-Year changes, see next page.

Changes when Notes mature in Leap-Year.

Time.	Janu'ry 26.	Janu'ry 27.	Janu'ry 28.	Janu'ry 29.	Janu'ry 30.
30 days.	Feb. 28	Feb. 29	Mar. 1	Mar. 2	Mar. 3
35 days.	Mar. 4	Mar. 5	Mar. 6	Mar. 7	Mar. 8
40 days.	Mar. 9	Mar. 10	Mar. 11	Mar. 12	Mar. 13
45 days.	Mar. 14	Mar. 15	Mar. 16	Mar. 17	Mar. 18
50 days.	Mar. 19	Mar. 20	Mar. 21	Mar. 22	Mar. 23
55 days.	Mar. 24	Mar. 25	Mar. 26	Mar. 27	Mar. 28
60 days.	Mar. 29	Mar. 30	Mar. 31	Apr. 1	Apr. 2
65 days.	Apr. 3	Apr. 4	Apr. 5	Apr. 6	Apr. 7
70 days.	Apr. 8	Apr. 9	Apr. 10	Apr. 11	Apr. 12
75 days.	Apr. 13	Apr. 14	Apr. 15	Apr. 16	Apr. 17
80 days.	Apr. 18	Apr. 19	Apr. 20	Apr. 21	Apr. 22
85 days.	Apr. 23	Apr. 24	Apr. 25	Apr. 26	Apr. 27
90 days.	Apr. 28	Apr. 29	Apr. 30	May 1	May 2
95 days.	May 3	May 4	May 5	May 6	May 7
100 days.	May 8	May 9	May 10	May 11	May 12
1 month.	Feb. 29	Mar. 1	Mar. 2	Mar. 3	Mar. 3

Time.	January 31.	Febr'y 1.	Febr'y 2.	Febr'y 3.	Febr'y 4.
5 days.	Feb. 8	Feb. 9	Feb. 10	Feb. 11	Feb. 12
10 days.	Feb. 13	Feb. 14	Feb. 15	Feb. 16	Feb. 17
15 days.	Feb. 18	Feb. 19	Feb. 20	Feb. 21	Feb. 22
20 days.	Feb. 23	Feb. 24	Feb. 25	Feb. 26	Feb. 27
25 days.	Feb. 28	Mar. 1	Mar. 2	Mar. 3	Mar. 4
30 days.	Mar. 5	Mar. 6	Mar. 7	Mar. 8	Mar. 9
35 days.	Mar. 10	Mar. 11	Mar. 12	Mar. 13	Mar. 14
40 days.	Mar. 15	Mar. 16	Mar. 17	Mar. 18	Mar. 19
45 days.	Mar. 20	Mar. 21	Mar. 22	Mar. 23	Mar. 24
50 days.	Mar. 25	Mar. 26	Mar. 27	Mar. 28	Mar. 29
55 days.	Mar. 30	Mar. 31	Apr. 1	Apr. 2	Apr. 3
60 days.	Apr. 4	Apr. 5	Apr. 6	Apr. 7	Apr. 8
65 days.	Apr. 9	Apr. 10	Apr. 11	Apr. 12	Apr. 13
70 days.	Apr. 14	Apr. 15	Apr. 16	Apr. 17	Apr. 18
75 days.	Apr. 19	Apr. 20	Apr. 21	Apr. 22	Apr. 23
80 days.	Apr. 24	Apr. 25	Apr. 26	Apr. 27	Apr. 28
85 days.	Apr. 29	Apr. 30	May 1	May 2	May 3
90 days.	May 4	May 5	May 6	May 7	May 8
95 days.	May 9	May 10	May 11	May 12	May 13
100 days.	May 14	May 15	May 16	May 17	May 18
1 month.	Mar. 3	Mar. 4	Mar. 5	Mar. 6	Mar. 7
2 months.	Apr. 3	Apr. 4	Apr. 5	Apr. 6	Apr. 7
3 months.	May 3	May 4	May 5	May 6	May 7
4 months.	Jun. 3	Jun. 4	Jun. 5	Jun. 6	Jun. 7
5 months.	Jul. 3	Jul. 4	Jul. 5	Jul. 6	Jul. 7
6 months.	Aug. 3	Aug. 4	Aug. 5	Aug. 6	Aug. 7
7 months.	Sep. 3	Sep. 4	Sep. 5	Sep. 6	Sep. 7
8 months.	Oct. 3	Oct. 4	Oct. 5	Oct. 6	Oct. 7
9 months.	Nov. 3	Nov. 4	Nov. 5	Nov. 6	Nov. 7
10 months.	Dec. 3	Dec. 4	Dec. 5	Dec. 6	Dec. 7
11 months.	Jan. 3	Jan. 4	Jan. 5	Jan. 6	Jan. 7
12 months.	Feb. 3	Feb. 4	Feb. 5	Feb. 6	Feb. 7

For Leap-Year changes, see next page.

Changes when Notes mature in Leap-Year.

Time.	Janu'ry 31.	Febr'y 1.	Febr'y 2.	Febr'y 3.	Febr'y 4.
25 days.	Feb. 28	Feb. 29	Mar. 1	Mar. 2	Mar. 3
30 days.	Mar. 4	Mar. 5	Mar. 6	Mar. 7	Mar. 8
35 days.	Mar. 9	Mar. 10	Mar. 11	Mar. 12	Mar. 13
40 days.	Mar. 14	Mar. 15	Mar. 16	Mar. 17	Mar. 18
45 days.	Mar. 19	Mar. 20	Mar. 21	Mar. 22	Mar. 23
50 days.	Mar. 24	Mar. 25	Mar. 26	Mar. 27	Mar. 28
55 days.	Mar. 29	Mar. 30	Mar. 31	Apr. 1	Apr. 2
60 days.	Apr. 3	Apr. 4	Apr. 5	Apr. 6	Apr. 7
65 days.	Apr. 8	Apr. 9	Apr. 10	Apr. 11	Apr. 12
70 days.	Apr. 13	Apr. 14	Apr. 15	Apr. 16	Apr. 17
75 days.	Apr. 18	Apr. 19	Apr. 20	Apr. 21	Apr. 22
80 days.	Apr. 23	Apr. 24	Apr. 25	Apr. 26	Apr. 27
85 days.	Apr. 28	Apr. 29	Apr. 30	May 1	May 2
90 days.	May 3	May 4	May 5	May 6	May 7
95 days.	May 8	May 9	May 10	May 11	May 12
100 days.	May 13	May 14	May 15	May 16	May 17

Time.	Febr'y 5.	Febr'y 6.	Febr'y 7.	Febr'y 8.	Febr'y 9.
5 days.	Feb. 13	Feb. 14	Feb. 15	Feb. 16	Feb. 17
10 days.	Feb. 18	Feb. 19	Feb. 20	Feb. 21	Feb. 22
15 days.	Feb. 23	Feb. 24	Feb. 25	Feb. 26	Feb. 27
20 days.	Feb. 28	Mar. 1	Mar. 2	Mar. 3	Mar. 4
25 days.	Mar. 5	Mar. 6	Mar. 7	Mar. 8	Mar. 9
30 days.	Mar. 10	Mar. 11	Mar. 12	Mar. 13	Mar. 14
35 days.	Mar. 15	Mar. 16	Mar. 17	Mar. 18	Mar. 19
40 days.	Mar. 20	Mar. 21	Mar. 22	Mar. 23	Mar. 24
45 days.	Mar. 25	Mar. 26	Mar. 27	Mar. 28	Mar. 29
50 days.	Mar. 30	Mar. 31	Apr. 1	Apr. 2	Apr. 3
55 days.	Apr. 4	Apr. 5	Apr. 6	Apr. 7	Apr. 8
60 days.	Apr. 9	Apr. 10	Apr. 11	Apr. 12	Apr. 13
65 days.	Apr. 14	Apr. 15	Apr. 16	Apr. 17	Apr. 18
70 days.	Apr. 19	Apr. 20	Apr. 21	Apr. 22	Apr. 23
75 days.	Apr. 24	Apr. 25	Apr. 26	Apr. 27	Apr. 28
80 days.	Apr. 29	Apr. 30	May 1	May 2	May 3
85 days.	May 4	May 5	May 6	May 7	May 8
90 days.	May 9	May 10	May 11	May 12	May 13
95 days.	May 14	May 15	May 16	May 17	May 18
100 days.	May 19	May 20	May 21	May 22	May 23
1 month.	Mar. 8	Mar. 9	Mar. 10	Mar. 11	Mar. 12
2 months.	Apr. 8	Apr. 9	Apr. 10	Apr. 11	Apr. 12
3 months.	May 8	May 9	May 10	May 11	May 12
4 months.	Jun. 8	Jun. 9	Jun. 10	Jun. 11	Jun. 12
5 months.	Jul. 8	Jul. 9	Jul. 10	Jul. 11	Jul. 12
6 months.	Aug. 8	Aug. 9	Aug. 10	Aug. 11	Aug. 12
7 months.	Sep. 8	Sep. 9	Sep. 10	Sep. 11	Sep. 12
8 months.	Oct. 8	Oct. 9	Oct. 10	Oct. 11	Oct. 12
9 months.	Nov. 8	Nov. 9	Nov. 10	Nov. 11	Nov. 12
10 months.	Dec. 8	Dec. 9	Dec. 10	Dec. 11	Dec. 12
11 months.	Jan. 8	Jan. 9	Jan. 10	Jan. 11	Jan. 12
12 months.	Feb. 8	Feb. 9	Feb. 10	Feb. 11	Feb. 12

For Leap-Year changes, see next page.

Changes when Notes mature in Leap-Year.

Time.	Febr'y 5.	Febr'y 6.	Febr'y 7.	Febr'y 8.	Febr'y 9.
20 days.	Feb. 28	Feb. 29	Mar. 1	Mar. 2	Mar. 3
25 days.	Mar. 4	Mar. 5	Mar. 6	Mar. 7	Mar. 8
30 days.	Mar. 9	Mar. 10	Mar. 11	Mar. 12	Mar. 13
35 days.	Mar. 14	Mar. 15	Mar. 16	Mar. 17	Mar. 18
40 days.	Mar. 19	Mar. 20	Mar. 21	Mar. 22	Mar. 23
45 days.	Mar. 24	Mar. 25	Mar. 26	Mar. 27	Mar. 28
50 days.	Mar. 29	Mar. 30	Mar. 31	Apr. 1	Apr. 2
55 days.	Apr. 3	Apr. 4	Apr. 5	Apr. 6	Apr. 7
60 days.	Apr. 8	Apr. 9	Apr. 10	Apr. 11	Apr. 12
65 days.	Apr. 13	Apr. 14	Apr. 15	Apr. 16	Apr. 17
70 days.	Apr. 18	Apr. 19	Apr. 20	Apr. 21	Apr. 22
75 days.	Apr. 23	Apr. 24	Apr. 25	Apr. 26	Apr. 27
80 days.	Apr. 28	Apr. 29	Apr. 30	May 1	May 2
85 days.	May 3	May 4	May 5	May 6	May 7
90 days.	May 8	May 9	May 10	May 11	May 12
95 days.	May 13	May 14	May 15	May 16	May 17
100 days.	May 18	May 19	May 20	May 21	May 22

Time.	Febr'y 10.	Febr'y 11.	Febr'y 12.	Febr'y 13.	Febr'y 14.
5 days.	Feb. 18	Feb. 19	Feb. 20	Feb. 21	Feb. 22
10 days.	Feb. 23	Feb. 24	Feb. 25	Feb. 26	Feb. 27
15 days.	Feb. 28	Mar. 1	Mar. 2	Mar. 3	Mar. 4
20 days.	Mar. 5	Mar. 6	Mar. 7	Mar. 8	Mar. 9
25 days.	Mar. 10	Mar. 11	Mar. 12	Mar. 13	Mar. 14
30 days.	Mar. 15	Mar. 16	Mar. 17	Mar. 18	Mar. 19
35 days.	Mar. 20	Mar. 21	Mar. 22	Mar. 23	Mar. 24
40 days.	Mar. 25	Mar. 26	Mar. 27	Mar. 28	Mar. 29
45 days.	Mar. 30	Mar. 31	Apr. 1	Apr. 2	Apr. 3
50 days.	Apr. 4	Apr. 5	Apr. 6	Apr. 7	Apr. 8
55 days.	Apr. 9	Apr. 10	Apr. 11	Apr. 12	Apr. 13
60 days.	Apr. 14	Apr. 15	Apr. 16	Apr. 17	Apr. 18
65 days.	Apr. 19	Apr. 20	Apr. 21	Apr. 22	Apr. 23
70 days.	Apr. 24	Apr. 25	Apr. 26	Apr. 27	Apr. 28
75 days.	Apr. 29	Apr. 30	May 1	May 2	May 3
80 days.	May 4	May 5	May 6	May 7	May 8
85 days.	May 9	May 10	May 11	May 12	May 13
90 days.	May 14	May 15	May 16	May 17	May 18
95 days.	May 19	May 20	May 21	May 22	May 23
100 days.	May 24	May 25	May 26	May 27	May 28
1 month.	Mar. 13	Mar. 14	Mar. 15	Mar. 16	Mar. 17
2 months.	Apr. 13	Apr. 14	Apr. 15	Apr. 16	Apr. 17
3 months.	May 13	May 14	May 15	May 16	May 17
4 months.	Jun. 13	Jun. 14	Jun. 15	Jun. 16	Jun. 17
5 months.	Jul. 13	Jul. 14	Jul. 15	Jul. 16	Jul. 17
6 months.	Aug. 13	Aug. 14	Aug. 15	Aug. 16	Aug. 17
7 months.	Sep. 13	Sep. 14	Sep. 15	Sep. 16	Sep. 17
8 months.	Oct. 13	Oct. 14	Oct. 15	Oct. 16	Oct. 17
9 months.	Nov. 13	Nov. 14	Nov. 15	Nov. 16	Nov. 17
10 months.	Dec. 13	Dec. 14	Dec. 15	Dec. 16	Dec. 17
11 months.	Jan. 13	Jan. 14	Jan. 15	Jan. 16	Jan. 17
12 months.	Feb. 13	Feb. 14	Feb. 15	Feb. 16	Feb. 17

For Leap-Year changes, see next page.

Changes when Notes mature in Leap-Year.

Time.	Febr'y 10.	Febr'y 11.	Febr'y 12.	Febr'y 13.	Febr'y 14.
15 days.	Feb. 28	Feb. 29	Mar. 1	Mar. 2	Mar. 3
20 days.	Mar. 4	Mar. 5	Mar. 6	Mar. 7	Mar. 8
25 days.	Mar. 9	Mar. 10	Mar. 11	Mar. 12	Mar. 13
30 days.	Mar. 14	Mar. 15	Mar. 16	Mar. 17	Mar. 18
35 days.	Mar. 19	Mar. 20	Mar. 21	Mar. 22	Mar. 23
40 days.	Mar. 24	Mar. 25	Mar. 26	Mar. 27	Mar. 28
45 days.	Mar. 29	Mar. 30	Mar. 31	Apr. 1	Apr. 2
50 days.	Apr. 3	Apr. 4	Apr. 5	Apr. 6	Apr. 7
55 days.	Apr. 8	Apr. 9	Apr. 10	Apr. 11	Apr. 12
60 days.	Apr. 13	Apr. 14	Apr. 15	Apr. 16	Apr. 17
65 days.	Apr. 18	Apr. 19	Apr. 20	Apr. 21	Apr. 22
70 days.	Apr. 23	Apr. 24	Apr. 25	Apr. 26	Apr. 27
75 days.	Apr. 28	Apr. 29	Apr. 30	May 1	May 2
80 days.	May 3	May 4	May 5	May 6	May 7
85 days.	May 8	May 9	May 10	May 11	May 12
90 days.	May 13	May 14	May 15	May 16	May 17
95 days.	May 18	May 19	May 20	May 21	May 22
100 days.	May 23	May 24	May 25	May 26	May 27

Time.	Febr'y 15.	Febr'y 16.	Febr'y 17.	Febr'y 18.	Febr'y 19.
5 days.	Feb. 23	Feb. 24	Feb. 25	Feb. 26	Feb. 27
10 days.	Feb. 28	Mar. 1	Mar. 2	Mar. 3	Mar. 4
15 days.	Mar. 5	Mar. 6	Mar. 7	Mar. 8	Mar. 9
20 days.	Mar. 10	Mar. 11	Mar. 12	Mar. 13	Mar. 14
25 days.	Mar. 15	Mar. 16	Mar. 17	Mar. 18	Mar. 19
30 days.	Mar. 20	Mar. 21	Mar. 22	Mar. 23	Mar. 24
35 days.	Mar. 25	Mar. 26	Mar. 27	Mar. 28	Mar. 29
40 days.	Mar. 30	Mar. 31	Apr. 1	Apr. 2	Apr. 3
45 days.	Apr. 4	Apr. 5	Apr. 6	Apr. 7	Apr. 8
50 days.	Apr. 9	Apr. 10	Apr. 11	Apr. 12	Apr. 13
55 days.	Apr. 14	Apr. 15	Apr. 16	Apr. 17	Apr. 18
60 days.	Apr. 19	Apr. 20	Apr. 21	Apr. 22	Apr. 23
65 days.	Apr. 24	Apr. 25	Apr. 26	Apr. 27	Apr. 28
70 days.	Apr. 29	Apr. 30	May 1	May 2	May 3
75 days.	May 4	May 5	May 6	May 7	May 8
80 days.	May 9	May 10	May 11	May 12	May 13
85 days.	May 14	May 15	May 16	May 17	May 18
90 days.	May 19	May 20	May 21	May 22	May 23
95 days.	May 24	May 25	May 26	May 27	May 28
100 days.	May 29	May 30	May 31	Jun. 1	Jun. 2
1 month.	Mar. 18	Mar. 19	Mar. 20	Mar. 21	Mar. 22
2 months.	Apr. 18	Apr. 19	Apr. 20	Apr. 21	Apr. 22
3 months.	May 18	May 19	May 20	May 21	May 22
4 months.	Jun. 18	Jun. 19	Jun. 20	Jun. 21	Jun. 22
5 months.	Jul. 18	Jul. 19	Jul. 20	Jul. 21	Jul. 22
6 months.	Aug. 18	Aug. 19	Aug. 20	Aug. 21	Aug. 22
7 months.	Sep. 18	Sep. 19	Sep. 20	Sep. 21	Sep. 22
8 months.	Oct. 18	Oct. 19	Oct. 20	Oct. 21	Oct. 22
9 months.	Nov. 18	Nov. 19	Nov. 20	Nov. 21	Nov. 22
10 months.	Dec. 18	Dec. 19	Dec. 20	Dec. 21	Dec. 22
11 months.	Jan. 18	Jan. 19	Jan. 20	Jan. 21	Jan. 22
12 months.	Feb. 18	Feb. 19	Feb. 20	Feb. 21	Feb. 22

For Leap-Year changes, see next page.

Changes when Notes mature in Leap-Year.

Time.	Febr'y 15.	Febr'y 16.	Febr'y 17.	Febr'y 18.	Febr'y 19.
10 days.	Feb. 28	Feb. 29	Mar. 1	Mar. 2	Mar. 3
15 days.	Mar. 4	Mar. 5	Mar. 6	Mar. 7	Mar. 8
20 days.	Mar. 9	Mar. 10	Mar. 11	Mar. 12	Mar. 13
25 days.	Mar. 14	Mar. 15	Mar. 16	Mar. 17	Mar. 18
30 days.	Mar. 19	Mar. 20	Mar. 21	Mar. 22	Mar. 23
35 days.	Mar. 24	Mar. 25	Mar. 26	Mar. 27	Mar. 28
40 days.	Mar. 29	Mar. 30	Mar. 31	Apr. 1	Apr. 2
45 days.	Apr. 3	Apr. 4	Apr. 5	Apr. 6	Apr. 7
50 days.	Apr. 8	Apr. 9	Apr. 10	Apr. 11	Apr. 12
55 days.	Apr. 13	Apr. 14	Apr. 15	Apr. 16	Apr. 17
60 days.	Apr. 18	Apr. 19	Apr. 20	Apr. 21	Apr. 22
65 days.	Apr. 23	Apr. 24	Apr. 25	Apr. 26	Apr. 27
70 days.	Apr. 28	Apr. 29	Apr. 30	May 1	May 2
75 days.	May 3	May 4	May 5	May 6	May 7
80 days.	May 8	May 9	May 10	May 11	May 12
85 days.	May 13	May 14	May 15	May 16	May 17
90 days.	May 18	May 19	May 20	May 21	May 22
95 days.	May 23	May 24	May 25	May 26	May 27
100 days.	May 28	May 29	May 30	May 31	June 1

Time.	Febr'y 20.	Febr'y 21.	Febr'y 22.	Febr'y 23.	Febr'y 24.
5 days.	Feb. 28	Mar. 1	Mar. 2	Mar. 3	Mar. 4
10 days.	Mar. 5	Mar. 6	Mar. 7	Mar. 8	Mar. 9
15 days.	Mar. 10	Mar. 11	Mar. 12	Mar. 13	Mar. 14
20 days.	Mar. 15	Mar. 16	Mar. 17	Mar. 18	Mar. 19
25 days.	Mar. 20	Mar. 21	Mar. 22	Mar. 23	Mar. 24
30 days.	Mar. 25	Mar. 26	Mar. 27	Mar. 28	Mar. 29
35 days.	Mar. 30	Mar. 31	Apr. 1	Apr. 2	Apr. 3
40 days.	Apr. 4	Apr. 5	Apr. 6	Apr. 7	Apr. 8
45 days.	Apr. 9	Apr. 10	Apr. 11	Apr. 12	Apr. 13
50 days.	Apr. 14	Apr. 15	Apr. 16	Apr. 17	Apr. 18
55 days.	Apr. 19	Apr. 20	Apr. 21	Apr. 22	Apr. 23
60 days.	Apr. 24	Apr. 25	Apr. 26	Apr. 27	Apr. 28
65 days.	Apr. 29	Apr. 30	May 1	May 2	May 3
70 days.	May 4	May 5	May 6	May 7	May 8
75 days.	May 9	May 10	May 11	May 12	May 13
80 days.	May 14	May 15	May 16	May 17	May 18
85 days.	May 19	May 20	May 21	May 22	May 23
90 days.	May 24	May 25	May 26	May 27	May 28
95 days.	May 29	May 30	May 31	Jun. 1	Jun. 2
100 days.	June 3	June 4	June 5	June 6	June 7
1 month.	Mar. 23	Mar. 24	Mar. 25	Mar. 26	Mar. 27
2 months.	Apr. 23	Apr. 24	Apr. 25	Apr. 26	Apr. 27
3 months.	May 23	May 24	May 25	May 26	May 27
4 months.	Jun. 23	Jun. 24	Jun. 25	Jun. 26	Jun. 27
5 months.	Jul. 23	Jul. 24	Jul. 25	Jul. 26	Jul. 27
6 months.	Aug. 23	Aug. 24	Aug. 25	Aug. 26	Aug. 27
7 months.	Sep. 23	Sep. 24	Sep. 25	Sep. 26	Sep. 27
8 months.	Oct. 23	Oct. 24	Oct. 25	Oct. 26	Oct. 27
9 months.	Nov. 23	Nov. 24	Nov. 25	Nov. 26	Nov. 27
10 months.	Dec. 23	Dec. 24	Dec. 25	Dec. 26	Dec. 27
11 months.	Jan. 23	Jan. 24	Jan. 25	Jan. 26	Jan. 27
12 months.	Feb. 23	Feb. 24	Feb. 25	Feb. 26	Feb. 27

For Leap-Year changes, see next page.

Changes when Notes mature in Leap-Year.

Time.	Febr'y 20.	Febr'y 21.	Febr'y 22.	Febr'y 23.	Febr'y 24.
5 days.	Feb. 28	Feb. 29	Mar. 1	Mar. 2	Mar. 3
10 days.	Mar. 4	Mar. 5	Mar. 6	Mar. 7	Mar. 8
15 days.	Mar. 9	Mar. 10	Mar. 11	Mar. 12	Mar. 13
20 days.	Mar. 14	Mar. 15	Mar. 16	Mar. 17	Mar. 18
25 days.	Mar. 19	Mar. 20	Mar. 21	Mar. 22	Mar. 23
30 days.	Mar. 24	Mar. 25	Mar. 26	Mar. 27	Mar. 28
35 days.	Mar. 29	Mar. 30	Mar. 31	Apr. 1	Apr. 2
40 days.	Apr. 3	Apr. 4	Apr. 5	Apr. 6	Apr. 7
45 days.	Apr. 8	Apr. 9	Apr. 10	Apr. 11	Apr. 12
50 days.	Apr. 13	Apr. 14	Apr. 15	Apr. 16	Apr. 17
55 days.	Apr. 18	Apr. 19	Apr. 20	Apr. 21	Apr. 22
60 days.	Apr. 23	Apr. 24	Apr. 25	Apr. 26	Apr. 27
65 days.	Apr. 28	Apr. 29	Apr. 30	May 1	May 2
70 days.	May 3	May 4	May 5	May 6	May 7
75 days.	May 8	May 9	May 10	May 11	May 12
80 days.	May 13	May 14	May 15	May 16	May 17
85 days.	May 18	May 19	May 20	May 21	May 22
90 days.	May 23	May 24	May 25	May 26	May 27
95 days.	May 28	May 29	May 30	May 31	June 1
100 days.	June 2	June 3	June 4	June 5	June 6

Time.	Febr'y 25.	Febr'y 26.	Febr'y 27.	Febr'y 28.	March 1.
5 days.	Mar. 5	Mar. 6	Mar. 7	Mar. 8	Mar. 9
10 days.	Mar. 10	Mar. 11	Mar. 12	Mar. 13	Mar. 14
15 days.	Mar. 15	Mar. 16	Mar. 17	Mar. 18	Mar. 19
20 days.	Mar. 20	Mar. 21	Mar. 22	Mar. 23	Mar. 24
25 days.	Mar. 25	Mar. 26	Mar. 27	Mar. 28	Mar. 29
30 days.	Mar. 30	Mar. 31	Apr. 1	Apr. 2	Apr. 3
35 days.	Apr. 4	Apr. 5	Apr. 6	Apr. 7	Apr. 8
40 days.	Apr. 9	Apr. 10	Apr. 11	Apr. 12	Apr. 13
45 days.	Apr. 14	Apr. 15	Apr. 16	Apr. 17	Apr. 18
50 days.	Apr. 19	Apr. 20	Apr. 21	Apr. 22	Apr. 23
55 days.	Apr. 24	Apr. 25	Apr. 26	Apr. 27	Apr. 28
60 days.	Apr. 29	Apr. 30	May 1	May 2	May 3
65 days.	May 4	May 5	May 6	May 7	May 8
70 days.	May 9	May 10	May 11	May 12	May 13
75 days.	May 14	May 15	May 16	May 17	May 18
80 days.	May 19	May 20	May 21	May 22	May 23
85 days.	May 24	May 25	May 26	May 27	May 28
90 days.	May 29	May 30	May 31	Jun. 1	Jun. 2
95 days.	June 3	June 4	June 5	June 6	June 7
100 days.	June 8	June 9	June 10	June 11	June 12
1 month.	Mar. 28	Mar. 29	Mar. 30	Mar. 31	Apr. 4
2 months.	Apr. 28	Apr. 29	Apr. 30	May 1	May 4
3 months.	May 28	May 29	May 30	May 31	Jun. 4
4 months.	Jun. 28	Jun. 29	Jun. 30	July 1	Jul. 4
5 months.	Jul. 28	Jul. 29	Jul. 30	Jul. 31	Aug. 4
6 months.	Aug. 28	Aug. 29	Aug. 30	Aug. 31	Sep. 4
7 months.	Sep. 28	Sep. 29	Sep. 30	Oct. 1	Oct. 4
8 months.	Oct. 28	Oct. 29	Oct. 30	Oct. 31	Nov. 4
9 months.	Nov. 28	Nov. 29	Nov. 30	Dec. 1	Dec. 4
10 months.	Dec. 28	Dec. 29	Dec. 30	Dec. 31	Jan. 4
11 months.	Jan. 28	Jan. 29	Jan. 30	Jan. 31	Feb. 4
12 months.	Feb. 28	Mar. 1	Mar. 2	Mar. 3	Mar. 4

For Leap-Year changes, see next page.

Changes when notes are DATED in Leap-Year.

Time.	Febr'y 25.	Febr'y 26.	Febr'y 27.	Febr'y 28.	Febr'y 29.
5 days.	Mar. 4	Mar. 5	Mar. 6	Mar. 7	Mar. 8
10 days.	Mar. 9	Mar. 10	Mar. 11	Mar. 12	Mar. 13
15 days.	Mar. 14	Mar. 15	Mar. 16	Mar. 17	Mar. 18
20 days.	Mar. 19	Mar. 20	Mar. 21	Mar. 22	Mar. 23
25 days.	Mar. 24	Mar. 25	Mar. 26	Mar. 27	Mar. 28
30 days.	Mar. 29	Mar. 30	Mar. 31	Apr. 1	Apr. 2
35 days.	Apr. 3	Apr. 4	Apr. 5	Apr. 6	Apr. 7
40 days.	Apr. 8	Apr. 9	Apr. 10	Apr. 11	Apr. 12
45 days.	Apr. 13	Apr. 14	Apr. 15	Apr. 16	Apr. 17
50 days.	Apr. 18	Apr. 19	Apr. 20	Apr. 21	Apr. 22
55 days.	Apr. 23	Apr. 24	Apr. 25	Apr. 26	Apr. 27
60 days.	Apr. 28	Apr. 29	Apr. 30	May 1	May 2
65 days.	May 3	May 4	May 5	May 6	May 7
70 days.	May 8	May 9	May 10	May 11	May 12
75 days.	May 13	May 14	May 15	May 16	May 17
80 days.	May 18	May 19	May 20	May 21	May 22
85 days.	May 23	May 24	May 25	May 26	May 27
90 days.	May 28	May 29	May 30	May 31	June 1
95 days.	June 2	June 3	June 4	June 5	June 6
100 days.	June 7	June 8	June 9	June 10	June 11
1 month.	Mar. 28	Mar. 29	Mar. 30	Mar. 31	Apr. 1
2 months.	Apr. 28	Apr. 29	Apr. 30	May 1	May 2
3 months.	May 28	May 29	May 30	May 31	June 1
4 months.	June 28	June 29	June 30	July 1	July 2
5 months.	July 28	July 29	July 30	July 31	Aug. 1
6 months.	Aug. 28	Aug. 29	Aug. 30	Aug. 31	Sep. 1
7 months.	Sep. 28	Sep. 29	Sep. 30	Oct. 1	Oct. 2
8 months.	Oct. 28	Oct. 29	Oct. 30	Oct. 31	Nov. 1
9 months.	Nov. 28	Nov. 29	Nov. 30	Dec. 1	Dec. 2
10 months.	Dec. 28	Dec. 29	Dec. 30	Dec. 31	Jan. 1
11 months.	Jan. 28	Jan. 29	Jan. 30	Jan. 31	Feb. 1
12 months.	Feb. 28	Mar. 1	Mar. 2	Mar. 3	Mar. 3
*12 mo's,L.Y	Feb. 28	Feb. 29	Mar. 1	Mar. 2	

*Use this line for notes dated in an ordinary year, and maturing in Leap Year.

Time.	March 2.	March 3.	March 4.	March 5.	March 6.
5 days.	Mar. 10	Mar. 11	Mar. 12	Mar. 13	Mar. 14
10 days.	Mar. 15	Mar. 16	Mar. 17	Mar. 18	Mar. 19
15 days.	Mar. 20	Mar. 21	Mar. 22	Mar. 23	Mar. 24
20 days.	Mar. 25	Mar. 26	Mar. 27	Mar. 28	Mar. 29
25 days.	Mar. 30	Mar. 31	Apr. 1	Apr. 2	Apr. 3
30 days.	Apr. 4	Apr. 5	Apr. 6	Apr. 7	Apr. 8
35 days.	Apr. 9	Apr. 10	Apr. 11	Apr. 12	Apr. 13
40 days.	Apr. 14	Apr. 15	Apr. 16	Apr. 17	Apr. 18
45 days.	Apr. 19	Apr. 20	Apr. 21	Apr. 22	Apr. 23
50 days.	Apr. 24	Apr. 25	Apr. 26	Apr. 27	Apr. 28
55 days.	Apr. 29	Apr. 30	May 1	May 2	May 3
60 days.	May 4	May 5	May 6	May 7	May 8
65 days.	May 9	May 10	May 11	May 12	May 13
70 days.	May 14	May 15	May 16	May 17	May 18
75 days.	May 19	May 20	May 21	May 22	May 23
80 days.	May 24	May 25	May 26	May 27	May 28
85 days.	May 29	May 30	May 31	Jun. 1	Jun. 2
90 days.	June 3	June 4	June 5	June 6	June 7
95 days.	June 8	June 9	June 10	June 11	June 12
100 days.	June 13	June 14	June 15	June 16	June 17
1 month.	Apr. 5	Apr. 6	Apr. 7	Apr. 8	Apr. 9
2 months.	May 5	May 6	May 7	May 8	May 9
3 months.	Jun. 5	Jun. 6	Jun. 7	June 8	Jun. 9
4 months.	Jul. 5	Jul. 6	Jul. 7	July 8	Jul. 9
5 months.	Aug. 5	Aug. 6	Aug. 7	Aug. 8	Aug. 9
6 months.	Sep. 5	Sep. 6	Sep. 7	Sep. 8	Sep. 9
7 months.	Oct. 5	Oct. 6	Oct. 7	Oct. 8	Oct. 9
8 months.	Nov. 5	Nov. 6	Nov. 7	Nov. 8	Nov. 9
9 months.	Dec. 5	Dec. 6	Dec. 7	Dec. 8	Dec. 9
10 months.	Jan. 5	Jan. 6	Jan. 7	Jan. 8	Jan. 9
11 months.	Feb. 5	Feb. 6	Feb. 7	Feb. 8	Feb. 9
12 months.	Mar. 5	Mar. 6	Mar. 7	Mar. 8	Mar. 9

Time.	March 7.	March 8.	March 9.	March 10.	March 11.
5 days.	Mar. 15	Mar. 16	Mar. 17	Mar. 18	Mar. 19
10 days.	Mar. 20	Mar. 21	Mar. 22	Mar. 23	Mar. 24
15 days.	Mar. 25	Mar. 26	Mar. 27	Mar. 28	Mar. 29
20 days.	Mar. 30	Mar. 31	Apr. 1	Apr. 2	Apr. 3
25 days.	Apr. 4	Apr. 5	Apr. 6	Apr. 7	Apr. 8
30 days.	Apr. 9	Apr. 10	Apr. 11	Apr. 12	Apr. 13
35 days.	Apr. 14	Apr. 15	Apr. 16	Apr. 17	Apr. 18
40 days.	Apr. 19	Apr. 20	Apr. 21	Apr. 22	Apr. 23
45 days.	Apr. 24	Apr. 25	Apr. 26	Apr. 27	Apr. 28
50 days.	Apr. 29	Apr. 30	May 1	May 2	May 3
55 days.	May 4	May 5	May 6	May 7	May 8
60 days.	May 9	May 10	May 11	May 12	May 13
65 days.	May 14	May 15	May 16	May 17	May 18
70 days.	May 19	May 20	May 21	May 22	May 23
75 days.	May 24	May 25	May 26	May 27	May 28
80 days.	May 29	May 30	May 31	Jun. 1	Jun. 2
85 days.	June 3	June 4	June 5	June 6	June 7
90 days.	June 8	June 9	June 10	June 11	June 12
95 days.	June 13	June 14	June 15	June 16	June 17
100 days.	June 18	June 19	June 20	June 21	June 22
1 month.	Apr. 10	Apr. 11	Apr. 12	Apr. 13	Apr. 14
2 months.	May 10	May 11	May 12	May 13	May 14
3 months.	Jun. 10	Jun. 11	Jun. 12	June 13	Jun. 14
4 months.	Jul. 10	Jul. 11	Jul. 12	July 13	Jul. 14
5 months.	Aug. 10	Aug. 11	Aug. 12	Aug. 13	Aug. 14
6 months.	Sep. 10	Sep. 11	Sep. 12	Sep. 13	Sep. 14
7 months.	Oct. 10	Oct. 11	Oct. 12	Oct. 13	Oct. 14
8 months.	Nov. 10	Nov. 11	Nov. 12	Nov. 13	Nov. 14
9 months.	Dec. 10	Dec. 11	Dec. 12	Dec. 13	Dec. 14
10 months.	Jan. 10	Jan. 11	Jan. 12	Jan. 13	Jan. 14
11 months.	Feb. 10	Feb. 11	Feb. 12	Feb. 13	Feb. 14
12 months.	Mar. 10	Mar. 11	Mar. 12	Mar. 13	Mar. 14

Time.	March 12.	March 13.	March 14.	March 15.	March 16.
5 days.	Mar. 20	Mar. 21	Mar. 22	Mar. 23	Mar. 24
10 days.	Mar. 25	Mar. 26	Mar. 27	Mar. 28	Mar. 29
15 days.	Mar. 30	Mar. 31	Apr. 1	Apr. 2	Apr. 3
20 days.	Apr. 4	Apr. 5	Apr. 6	Apr. 7	Apr. 8
25 days.	Apr. 9	Apr. 10	Apr. 11	Apr. 12	Apr. 13
30 days.	Apr. 14	Apr. 15	Apr. 16	Apr. 17	Apr. 18
35 days.	Apr. 19	Apr. 20	Apr. 21	Apr. 22	Apr. 23
40 days.	Apr. 24	Apr. 25	Apr. 26	Apr. 27	Apr. 28
45 days.	Apr. 29	Apr. 30	May 1	May 2	May 3
50 days.	May 4	May 5	May 6	May 7	May 8
55 days.	May 9	May 10	May 11	May 12	May 13
60 days.	May 14	May 15	May 16	May 17	May 18
65 days.	May 19	May 20	May 21	May 22	May 23
70 days.	May 24	May 25	May 26	May 27	May 28
75 days.	May 29	May 30	May 31	Jun. 1	Jun. 2
80 days.	June 3	June 4	June 5	June 6	June 7
85 days.	June 8	June 9	June 10	June 11	June 12
90 days.	June 13	June 14	June 15	June 16	June 17
95 days.	June 18	June 19	June 20	June 21	June 22
100 days.	June 23	June 24	June 25	June 26	June 27
1 month.	Apr. 15	Apr. 16	Apr. 17	Apr. 18	Apr. 19
2 months.	May 15	May 16	May 17	May 18	May 19
3 months.	Jun. 15	Jun. 16	Jun. 17	June 18	Jun. 19
4 months.	Jul. 15	Jul. 16	Jul. 17	July 18	Jul. 19
5 months.	Aug. 15	Aug. 16	Aug. 17	Aug. 18	Aug. 19
6 months.	Sep. 15	Sep. 16	Sep. 17	Sep. 18	Sep. 19
7 months.	Oct. 15	Oct. 16	Oct. 17	Oct. 18	Oct. 19
8 months.	Nov. 15	Nov. 16	Nov. 17	Nov. 18	Nov. 19
9 months.	Dec. 15	Dec. 16	Dec. 17	Dec. 18	Dec. 19
10 months.	Jan. 15	Jan. 16	Jan. 17	Jan. 18	Jan. 19
11 months.	Feb. 15	Feb. 16	Feb. 17	Feb. 18	Feb. 19
12 months.	Mar. 15	Mar. 16	Mar. 17	Mar. 18	Mar. 19

Time.	March 17.	March 18.	March 19.	March 20.	March 21.
5 days.	Mar. 25	Mar. 26	Mar. 27	Mar. 28	Mar. 29
10 days.	Mar. 30	Mar. 31	Apr. 1	Apr. 2	Apr. 3
15 days.	Apr. 4	Apr. 5	Apr. 6	Apr. 7	Apr. 8
20 days.	Apr. 9	Apr. 10	Apr. 11	Apr. 12	Apr. 13
25 days.	Apr. 14	Apr. 15	Apr. 16	Apr. 17	Apr. 18
30 days.	Apr. 19	Apr. 20	Apr. 21	Apr. 22	Apr. 23
35 days.	Apr. 24	Apr. 25	Apr. 26	Apr. 27	Apr. 28
40 days.	Apr. 29	Apr. 30	May 1	May 2	May 3
45 days.	May 4	May 5	May 6	May 7	May 8
50 days.	May 9	May 10	May 11	May 12	May 13
55 days.	May 14	May 15	May 16	May 17	May 18
60 days.	May 19	May 20	May 21	May 22	May 23
65 days.	May 24	May 25	May 26	May 27	May 28
70 days.	May 29	May 30	May 31	Jun. 1	Jun. 2
75 days.	June 3	June 4	June 5	June 6	June 7
80 days.	June 8	June 9	June 10	June 11	June 12
85 days.	June 13	June 14	June 15	June 16	June 17
90 days.	June 18	June 19	June 20	June 21	June 22
95 days.	June 23	June 24	June 25	June 26	June 27
100 days.	June 28	June 29	June 30	July 1	July 2
1 month.	Apr. 20	Apr. 21	Apr. 22	Apr. 23	Apr. 24
2 months.	May 20	May 21	May 22	May 23	May 24
3 months.	Jun. 20	Jun. 21	Jun. 22	June 23	Jun. 24
4 months.	Jul. 20	Jul. 21	Jul. 22	July 23	Jul. 24
5 months.	Aug. 20	Aug. 21	Aug. 22	Aug. 23	Aug. 24
6 months.	Sep. 20	Sep. 21	Sep. 22	Sep. 23	Sep. 24
7 months.	Oct. 20	Oct. 21	Oct. 22	Oct. 23	Oct. 24
8 months.	Nov. 20	Nov. 21	Nov. 22	Nov. 23	Nov. 24
9 months.	Dec. 20	Dec. 21	Dec. 22	Dec. 23	Dec. 24
10 months.	Jan. 20	Jan. 21	Jan. 22	Jan. 23	Jan. 24
11 months.	Feb. 20	Feb. 21	Feb. 22	Feb. 23	Feb. 24
12 months.	Mar. 20	Mar. 21	Mar. 22	Mar. 23	Mar. 24

Time.	March 22.	March 23.	March 24.	March 25.	March 26.
5 days.	Mar. 30	Mar. 31	Apr. 1	Apr. 2	Apr. 3
10 days.	Apr. 4	Apr. 5	Apr. 6	Apr. 7	Apr. 8
15 days.	Apr. 9	Apr. 10	Apr. 11	Apr. 12	Apr. 13
20 days.	Apr. 14	Apr. 15	Apr. 16	Apr. 17	Apr. 18
25 days.	Apr. 19	Apr. 20	Apr. 21	Apr. 22	Apr. 23
30 days.	Apr. 24	Apr. 25	Apr. 26	Apr. 27	Apr. 28
35 days.	Apr. 29	Apr. 30	May 1	May 2	May 3
40 days.	May 4	May 5	May 6	May 7	May 8
45 days.	May 9	May 10	May 11	May 12	May 13
50 days.	May 14	May 15	May 16	May 17	May 18
55 days.	May 19	May 20	May 21	May 22	May 23
60 days.	May 24	May 25	May 26	May 27	May 28
65 days.	May 29	May 30	May 31	Jun. 1	June 2
70 days.	June 3	June 4	June 5	June 6	June 7
75 days.	June 8	June 9	June 10	June 11	June 12
80 days.	June 13	June 14	June 15	June 16	June 17
85 days.	June 18	June 19	June 20	June 21	June 22
90 days.	June 23	June 24	June 25	June 26	June 27
95 days.	June 28	June 29	June 30	July 1	July 2
100 days.	July 3	July 4	July 5	July· 6	July 7
1 month.	Apr. 25	Apr. 26	Apr. 27	Apr. 28	Apr. 29
2 months.	May 25	May 26	May 27	May 28	May 29
3 months.	Jun. 25	Jun. 26	Jun. 27	June 28	June 29
4 months.	Jul. 25	Jul. 26	Jul. 27	July 28	July 29
5 months.	Aug. 25	Aug. 26	Aug. 27	Aug. 28	Aug. 29
6 months.	Sep. 25	Sep. 26	Sep. 27	Sep. 28	Scp. 29
7 months.	Oct. 25	Oct. 26	Oct. 27	Oct. 28	Oct. 29
8 months.	Nov. 25	Nov. 26	Nov. 27	Nov. 28	Nov. 29
9 months.	Dec. 25	Dec. 26	Dec. 27	Dec. 28	Dec. 29
10 months.	Jan. 25	Jan. 26	Jan. 27	Jan. 28	Jan. 29
11 months.	Feb. 25	Feb. 26	Feb. 27	Feb. 28	Mar. 1
*11 mo's, L.Y	Feb. 25	Feb. 26	Feb. 27	Feb. 28	Feb. 29
12 months.	Mar. 25	Mar. 26	Mar. 27	Mar. 28	Mar. 29

*Use this line for notes maturing in Leap Year.

Time.	March 27.	March 28.	March 29.	March 30.	March 31.
5 days.	Apr. 4	Apr. 5	Apr. 6	Apr. 7	Apr. 8
10 days.	Apr. 9	Apr. 10	Apr. 11	Apr. 12	Apr. 13
15 days.	Apr. 14	Apr. 15	Apr. 16	Apr. 17	Apr. 18
20 days.	Apr. 19	Apr. 20	Apr. 21	Apr. 22	Apr. 23
25 days.	Apr. 24	Apr. 25	Apr. 26	Apr. 27	Apr. 28
30 days.	Apr. 29	Apr. 30	May 1	May 2	May 3
35 days.	May 4	May 5	May 6	May 7	May 8
40 days.	May 9	May 10	May 11	May 12	May 13
45 days.	May 14	May 15	May 16	May 17	May 18
50 days.	May 19	May 20	May 21	May 22	May 23
55 days.	May 24	May 25	May 26	May 27	May 28
60 days.	May 29	May 30	May 31	Jun. 1	June 2
65 days.	June 3	June 4	June 5	June 6	June 7
70 days.	June 8	June 9	June 10	June 11	June 12
75 days.	June 13	June 14	June 15	June 16	June 17
80 days.	June 18	June 19	June 20	June 21	June 22
85 days.	June 23	June 24	June 25	June 26	June 27
90 days.	June 28	June 29	June 30	July 1	July 2
95 days.	July 3	July 4	July 5	July 6	July 7
100 days.	July 8	July 9	July 10	July 11	July 12
1 month.	Apr. 30	May 1	May 2	May 3	May 3
2 months.	May 30	May 31	Jun. 1	June 2	June 3
3 months.	Jun. 30	Jul. 1	Jul. 2	July 3	July 3
4 months.	Jul. 30	July 31	Aug. 1	Aug. 2	Aug. 3
5 months.	Aug. 30	Aug. 31	Sep. 1	Sep. 2	Sep. 3
6 months.	Sep. 30	Oct. 1	Oct. 2	Oct. 3	Oct. 3
7 months.	Oct. 30	Oct. 31	Nov. 1	Nov. 2	Nov. 3
8 months.	Nov. 30	Dec. 1	Dec. 2	Dec. 3	Dec. 3
9 months.	Dec. 30	Dec. 31	Jan. 1	Jan. 2	Jan. 3
10 months.	Jan. 30	Jan. 31	Feb. 1	Feb. 2	Feb. 3
11 months.	Mar. 2	Mar. 3	Mar. 3	Mar. 3	Mar. 3
*11 mo's, L.Y	Mar. 1	Mar. 2	Mar. 3	Mar. 3	Mar. 3
12 months.	Mar. 30	Mar. 31	Apr. 1	Apr. 2	Apr. 3

*Use this line for notes maturing in Leap Year.

Time.	April 1.	April 2.	April 3.	April 4.	April 5.
5 days.	Apr. 9	Apr. 10	Apr. 11	Apr. 12	Apr. 13
10 days.	Apr. 14	Apr. 15	Apr. 16	Apr. 17	Apr. 18
15 days.	Apr. 19	Apr. 20	Apr. 21	Apr. 22	Apr. 23
20 days.	Apr. 24	Apr. 25	Apr. 26	Apr. 27	Apr. 28
25 days.	Apr. 29	Apr. 30	May 1	May 2	May 3
30 days.	May 4	May 5	May 6	May 7	May 8
35 days.	May 9	May 10	May 11	May 12	May 13
40 days.	May 14	May 15	May 16	May 17	May 18
45 days.	May 19	May 20	May 21	May 22	May 23
50 days.	May 24	May 25	May 26	May 27	May 28
55 days.	May 29	May 30	May 31	Jun. 1	June 2
60 days.	June 3	June 4	June 5	June 6	June 7
65 days.	June 8	June 9	June 10	June 11	June 12
70 days.	June 13	June 14	June 15	June 16	June 17
75 days.	June 18	June 19	June 20	June 21	June 22
80 days.	June 23	June 24	June 25	June 26	June 27
85 days.	June 28	June 29	June 30	July 1	July 2
90 days.	July 3	July 4	July 5	July 6	July 7
95 days.	July 8	July 9	July 10	July 11	July 12
100 days.	July 13	July 14	July 15	July 16	July 17
1 month.	May 4	May 5	May 6	May 7	May 8
2 months.	Jun. 4	June 5	Jun. 6	June 7	June 8
3 months.	Jul. 4	July 5	Jul. 6	July 7	July 8
4 months.	Aug. 4	Aug. 5	Aug. 6	Aug. 7	Aug. 8
5 months.	Sep. 4	Sep. 5	Sep. 6	Sep. 7	Sep. 8
6 months.	Oct. 4	Oct. 5	Oct. 6	Oct. 7	Oct. 8
7 months.	Nov. 4	Nov. 5	Nov. 6	Nov. 7	Nov. 8
8 months.	Dec. 4	Dec. 5	Dec. 6	Dec. 7	Dec. 8
9 months.	Jan. 4	Jan. 5	Jan. 6	Jan. 7	Jan. 8
10 months.	Feb. 4	Feb. 5	Feb. 6	Feb. 7	Feb. 8
11 months.	Mar. 4	Mar. 5	Mar. 6	Mar. 7	Mar. 8
12 months.	Apr. 4	Apr. 5	Apr. 6	Apr. 7	Apr. 8

Time.	April 6.	April 7.	April 8.	April 9.	April 10.
5 days.	Apr. 14	Apr. 15	Apr. 16	Apr. 17	Apr. 18
10 days.	Apr. 19	Apr. 20	Apr. 21	Apr. 22	Apr. 23
15 days.	Apr. 24	Apr. 25	Apr. 26	Apr. 27	Apr. 28
20 days.	Apr. 29	Apr. 30	May 1	May 2	May 3
25 days.	May 4	May 5	May 6	May 7	May 8
30 days.	May 9	May 10	May 11	May 12	May 13
35 days.	May 14	May 15	May 16	May 17	May 18
40 days.	May 19	May 20	May 21	May 22	May 23
45 days.	May 24	May 25	May 26	May 27	May 28
50 days.	May 29	May 30	May 31	Jun. 1	June 2
55 days.	June 3	June 4	June 5	June 6	June 7
60 days.	June 8	June 9	June 10	June 11	June 12
65 days.	June 13	June 14	June 15	June 16	June 17
70 days.	June 18	June 19	June 20	June 21	June 22
75 days.	June 23	June 24	June 25	June 26	June 27
80 days.	June 28	June 29	June 30	July 1	July 2
85 days.	July 3	July 4	July 5	July 6	July 7
90 days.	July 8	July 9	July 10	July 11	July 12
95 days.	July 13	July 14	July 15	July 16	July 17
100 days.	July 18	July 19	July 20	July 21	July 22
1 month.	May 9	May 10	May 11	May 12	May 13
2 months.	Jun. 9	June 10	Jun. 11	June 12	June 13
3 months.	Jul. 9	July 10	Jul. 11	July 12	July 13
4 months.	Aug. 9	Aug. 10	Aug. 11	Aug. 12	Aug. 13
5 months.	Sep. 9	Sep. 10	Sep. 11	Sep. 12	Sep. 13
6 months.	Oct. 9	Oct. 10	Oct. 11	Oct. 12	Oct. 13
7 months.	Nov. 9	Nov. 10	Nov. 11	Nov. 12	Nov. 13
8 months.	Dec. 9	Dec. 10	Dec. 11	Dec. 12	Dec. 13
9 months.	Jan. 9	Jan. 10	Jan. 11	Jan. 12	Jan. 13
10 months.	Feb. 9	Feb. 10	Feb. 11	Feb. 12	Feb. 13
11 months.	Mar. 9	Mar. 10	Mar. 11	Mar. 12	Mar. 13
12 months.	Apr. 9	Apr. 10	Apr. 11	Apr. 12	Apr. 13

Time.	April 11.	April 12.	April 13.	April 14.	April 15.
5 days.	Apr. 19	Apr. 20	Apr. 21	Apr. 22	Apr. 23
10 days.	Apr. 24	Apr. 25	Apr. 26	Apr. 27	Apr. 28
15 days.	Apr. 29	Apr. 30	May 1	May 2	May 3
20 days.	May 4	May 5	May 6	May 7	May 8
25 days.	May 9	May 10	May 11	May 12	May 13
30 days.	May 14	May 15	May 16	May 17	May 18
35 days.	May 19	May 20	May 21	May 22	May 23
40 days.	May 24	May 25	May 26	May 27	May 28
45 days.	May 29	May 30	May 31	Jun. 1	June 2
50 days.	June 3	June 4	June 5	June 6	June 7
55 days.	June 8	June 9	June 10	June 11	June 12
60 days.	June 13	June 14	June 15	June 16	June 17
65 days.	June 18	June 19	June 20	June 21	June 22
70 days.	June 23	June 24	June 25	June 26	June 27
75 days.	June 28	June 29	June 30	July 1	July 2
80 days.	July 3	July 4	July 5	July 6	July 7
85 days.	July 8	July 9	July 10	July 11	July 12
90 days.	July 13	July 14	July 15	July 16	July 17
95 days.	July 18	July 19	July 20	July 21	July 22
100 days.	July 23	July 24	July 25	July 26	July 27
1 month.	May 14	May 15	May 16	May 17	May 18
2 months.	Jun. 14	June 15	Jun. 16	June 17	June 18
3 months.	Jul. 14	July 15	Jul. 16	July 17	July 18
4 months.	Aug. 14	Aug. 15	Aug. 16	Aug. 17	Aug. 18
5 months.	Sep. 14	Sep. 15	Sep. 16	Sep. 17	Sep. 18
6 months.	Oct. 14	Oct. 15	Oct. 16	Oct. 17	Oct. 18
7 months.	Nov. 14	Nov. 15	Nov. 16	Nov. 17	Nov. 18
8 months.	Dec. 14	Dec. 15	Dec. 16	Dec. 17	Dec. 18
9 months.	Jan. 14	Jan. 15	Jan. 16	Jan. 17	Jan. 18
10 months.	Feb. 14	Feb. 15	Feb. 16	Feb. 17	Feb. 18
11 months.	Mar. 14	Mar. 15	Mar. 16	Mar. 17	Mar. 18
12 months.	Apr. 14	Apr. 15	Apr. 16	Apr. 17	Apr. 18

Time.	April 16.	April 17.	April 18.	April 19.	April 20.
5 days.	Apr. 24	Apr. 25	Apr. 26	Apr. 27	Apr. 28
10 days.	Apr. 29	Apr. 30	May 1	May 2	May 3
15 days.	May 4	May 5	May 6	May 7	May 8
20 days.	May 9	May 10	May 11	May 12	May 13
25 days.	May 14	May 15	May 16	May 17	May 18
30 days.	May 19	May 20	May 21	May 22	May 23
35 days.	May 24	May 25	May 26	May 27	May 28
40 days.	May 29	May 30	May 31	Jun. 1	June 2
45 days.	June 3	June 4	June 5	June 6	June 7
50 days.	June 8	June 9	June 10	June 11	June 12
55 days.	June 13	June 14	June 15	June 16	June 17
60 days.	June 18	June 19	June 20	June 21	June 22
65 days.	June 23	June 24	June 25	June 26	June 27
70 days.	June 28	June 29	June 30	July 1	July 2
75 days.	July 3	July 4	July 5	July 6	July 7
80 days.	July 8	July 9	July 10	July 11	July 12
85 days.	July 13	July 14	July 15	July 16	July 17
90 days.	July 18	July 19	July 20	July 21	July 22
95 days.	July 23	July 24	July 25	July 26	July 27
100 days.	July 28	July 29	July 30	July 31	Aug. 1
1 month.	May 19	May 20	May 21	May 22	May 23
2 months.	Jun. 19	June 20	Jun. 21	June 22	June 23
3 months.	Jul. 19	July 20	Jul. 21	July 22	July 23
4 months.	Aug. 19	Aug. 20	Aug. 21	Aug. 22	Aug. 23
5 months.	Sep. 19	Sep. 20	Sep. 21	Sep. 22	Sep. 23
6 months.	Oct. 19	Oct. 20	Oct. 21	Oct. 22	Oct. 23
7 months.	Nov. 19	Nov. 20	Nov. 21	Nov. 22	Nov. 23
8 months.	Dec. 19	Dec. 20	Dec. 21	Dec. 22	Dec. 23
9 months.	Jan. 19	Jan. 20	Jan. 21	Jan. 22	Jan. 23
10 months.	Feb. 19	Feb. 20	Feb. 21	Feb. 22	Feb. 23
11 months.	Mar. 19	Mar. 20	Mar. 21	Mar. 22	Mar. 23
12 months.	Apr. 19	Apr. 20	Apr. 21	Apr. 22	Apr. 23

Time.	April 21.	April 22.	April 23.	April 24.	April 25.
5 days.	Apr. 29	Apr. 30	May 1	May 2	May 3
10 days.	May 4	May 5	May 6	May 7	May 8
15 days.	May 9	May 10	May 11	May 12	May 13
20 days.	May 14	May 15	May 16	May 17	May 18
25 days.	May 19	May 20	May 21	May 22	May 23
30. days.	May 24	May 25	May 26	May 27	May 28
35 days.	May 29	May 30	May 31	Jun. 1	June 2
40 days.	June 3	June 4	June 5	June 6	June 7
45 days.	June 8	June 9	June 10	June 11	June 12
50 days.	June 13	June 14	June 15	June 16	June 17
55 days.	June 18	June 19	June 20	June 21	June 22
60 days.	June 23	June 24	June 25	June 26	June 27
65 days.	June 28	June 29	June 30	July 1	July 2
70 days.	July 3	July 4	July 5	July 6	July 7
75 days.	July 8	July 9	July 10	July 11	July 12
80 days.	July 13	July 14	July 15	July 16	July 17
85 days.	July 18	July 19	July 20	July 21	July 22
90 days.	July 23	July 24	July 25	July 26	July 27
95 days.	July 28	July 29	July 30	July 31	Aug. 1
100 days.	Aug. 2	Aug. 3	Aug. 4	Aug. 5	Aug. 6
1 month.	May 24	May 25	May 26	May 27	May 28
2 months.	Jun. 24	June 25	Jun. 26	June 27	June 28
3 months.	Jul. 24	July 25	Jul. 26	July 27	July 28
4 months.	Aug. 24	Aug. 25	Aug. 26	Aug. 27	Aug. 28
5 months.	Sep. 24	Sep. 25	Sep. 26	Sep. 27	Sep. 28
6 months.	Oct. 24	Oct. 25	Oct. 26	Oct. 27	Oct. 28
7 months.	Nov. 24	Nov. 25	Nov. 26	Nov. 27	Nov. 28
8 months.	Dec. 24	Dec. 25	Dec. 26	Dec. 27	Dec. 28
9 months.	Jan. 24	Jan. 25	Jan. 26	Jan. 27	Jan. 28
10 months.	Feb. 24	Feb. 25	Feb. 26	Feb. 27	Feb. 28
11 months.	Mar. 24	Mar. 25	Mar. 26	Mar. 27	Mar. 28
12 months.	Apr. 24	Apr. 25	Apr. 26	Apr. 27	Apr. 28

Time.	April 26.	April 27.	April 28.	April 29.	April 30.
5 days.	May 4	May 5	May 6	May 7	May 8
10 days.	May 9	May 10	May 11	May 12	May 13
15 days.	May 14	May 15	May 16	May 17	May 18
20 days.	May 19	May 20	May 21	May 22	May 23
25 days.	May 24	May 25	May 26	May 27	May 28
30 days.	May 29	May 30	May 31	Jun. 1	June 2
35 days.	June 3	June 4	June 5	June 6	June 7
40 days.	June 8	June 9	June 10	June 11	June 12
45 days.	June 13	June 14	June 15	June 16	June 17
50 days.	June 18	June 19	June 20	June 21	June 22
55 days.	June 23	June 24	June 25	June 26	June 27
60 days.	June 28	June 29	June 30	July 1	July 2
65 days.	July 3	July 4	July 5	July 6	July 7
70 days.	July 8	July 9	July 10	July 11	July 12
75 days.	July 13	July 14	July 15	July 16	July 17
80 days.	July 18	July 19	July 20	July 21	July 22
85 days.	July 23	July 24	July 25	July 26	July 27
90 days.	July 28	July 29	July 30	July 31	Aug. 1
95 days.	Aug. 2	Aug. 3	Aug. 4	Aug. 5	Aug. 6
100 days.	Aug. 7	Aug. 8	Aug. 9	Aug. 10	Aug. 11
1 month.	May 29	May 30	May 31	June 1	June 2
2 months.	Jun. 29	June 30	July 1	July 2	July 3
3 months.	Jul. 29	July 30	Jul. 31	Aug. 1	Aug. 2
4 months.	Aug. 29	Aug. 30	Aug. 31	Sep. 1	Sep. 2
5 months.	Sep. 29	Sep. 30	Oct. 1	Oct. 2	Oct. 3
6 months.	Oct. 29	Oct. 30	Oct. 31	Nov. 1	Nov. 2
7 months.	Nov. 29	Nov. 30	Dec. 1	Dec. 2	Dec. 3
8 months.	Dec. 29	Dec. 30	Dec. 31	Jan. 1	Jan. 2
9 months.	Jan. 29	Jan. 30	Jan. 31	Feb. 1	Feb. 2
10 months.	Mar. 1	Mar. 2	Mar. 3	Mar. 3	Mar. 3
*10 mos,L.Y.	Feb. 29	Mar. 1	Mar. 2	Mar. 3	Mar. 3
11 months.	Mar. 29	Mar. 30	Mar. 31	Apr. 1	Apr. 2
12 months.	Apr. 29	Apr. 30	May 1	May 2	May 3

*Use this line for notes maturing in Leap-Year.

Time.	May 1.	May 2.	May 3.	May 4.	May 5.
5 days.	May 9	May 10	May 11	May 12	May 13
10 days.	May 14	May 15	May 16	May 17	May 18
15 days.	May 19	May 20	May 21	May 22	May 23
20 days.	May 24	May 25	May 26	May 27	May 28
25 days.	May 29	May 30	May 31	June 1	June 2
30 days.	June 3	June 4	June 5	June 6	June 7
35 days.	June 8	June 9	June 10	June 11	June 12
40 days.	June 13	June 14	June 15	June 16	June 17
45 days.	June 18	June 19	June 20	June 21	June 22
50 days.	June 23	June 24	June 25	June 26	June 27
55 days.	June 28	June 29	June 30	July 1	July 2
60 days.	July 3	July 4	July 5	July 6	July 7
65 days.	July 8	July 9	July 10	July 11	July 12
70 days.	July 13	July 14	July 15	July 16	July 17
75 days.	July 18	July 19	July 20	July 21	July 22
80 days.	July 23	July 24	July 25	July 26	July 27
85 days.	July 28	July 29	July 30	July 31	Aug. 1
90 days.	Aug. 2	Aug. 3	Aug. 4	Aug. 5	Aug. 6
95 days.	Aug. 7	Aug. 8	Aug. 9	Aug. 10	Aug. 11
100 days.	Aug. 12	Aug. 13	Aug. 14	Aug. 15	Aug. 16
1 month.	June 4	June 5	June 6	June 7	June 8
2 mouths.	July 4	July 5	July 6	July 7	July 8
3 months.	Aug. 4	Aug. 5	Aug. 6	Aug. 7	Aug. 8
4 months.	Sep. 4	Sep. 5	Sep. 6	Sep. 7	Sep. 8
5 months.	Oct. 4	Oct. 5	Oct. 6	Oct. 7	Oct. 8
6 months.	Nov. 4	Nov. 5	Nov. 6	Nov. 7	Nov. 8
7 months.	Dec. 4	Dec. 5	Dec. 6	Dec. 7	Dec. 8
8 months.	Jan. 4	Jan. 5	Jan. 6	Jan. 7	Jan. 8
9 months.	Feb. 4	Feb. 5	Feb. 6	Feb. 7	Feb. 8
10 months.	Mar. 4	Mar. 5	Mar. 6	Mar. 7	Mar. 8
11 months.	Apr. 4	Apr. 5	Apr. 6	Apr. 7	Apr. 8
12 mouths.	May 4	May 5	May 6	May 7	May 8

Time.	May 6.	May 7.	May 8.	May 9.	May 10.
5 days.	May 14	May 15	May 16	May 17	May 18
10 days.	May 19	May 20	May 21	May 22	May 23
15 days.	May 24	May 25	May 26	May 27	May 28
20 days.	May 29	May 30	May 31	June 1	June 2
25 days.	June 3	June 4	June 5	June 6	June 7
30 days.	June 8	June 9	June 10	June 11	June 12
35 days.	June 13	June 14	June 15	June 16	June 17
40 days.	June 18	June 19	June 20	June 21	June 22
45 days.	June 23	June 24	June 25	June 26	June 27
50 days.	June 28	June 29	June 30	July 1	July 2
55 days.	July 3	July 4	July 5	July 6	July 7
60 days.	July 8	July 9	July 10	July 11	July 12
65 days.	July 13	July 14	July 15	July 16	July 17
70 days.	July 18	July 19	July 20	July 21	July 22
75 days.	July 23	July 24	July 25	July 26	July 27
80 days.	July 28	July 29	July 30	July 31	Aug. 1
85 days.	Aug. 2	Aug. 3	Aug. 4	Aug. 5	Aug. 6
90 days.	Aug. 7	Aug. 8	Aug. 9	Aug. 10	Aug. 11
95 days.	Aug. 12	Aug. 13	Aug. 14	Aug. 15	Aug. 16
100 days:	Aug. 17	Aug. 18	Aug. 19	Aug. 20	Aug. 21
1 month.	June 9	June 10	June 11	June 12	June 13
2 mouths.	July 9	July 10	July 11	July 12	July 13
3 months.	Aug. 9	Aug. 10	Aug. 11	Aug. 12	Aug. 13
4 months.	Sep. 9	Sep. 10	Sep. 11	Sep. 12	Sep. 13
5 months.	Oct. 9	Oct. 10	Oct. 11	Oct. 12	Oct. 13
6 months.	Nov. 9	Nov. 10	Nov. 11	Nov. 12	Nov. 13
7 months.	Dec. 9	Dec. 10	Dec. 11	Dec. 12	Dec. 13
8 months.	Jan. 9	Jan. 10	Jan. 11	Jan. 12	Jan. 13
9 months.	Feb. 9	Feb. 10	Feb. 11	Feb. 12	Feb. 13
10 months.	Mar. 9	Mar. 10	Mar. 11	Mar. 12	Mar. 13
11 months.	Apr. 9	Apr. 10	Apr. 11	Apr. 12	Apr. 13
12 mouths.	May 9	May 10	May 11	May 12	May 13

Time.	May 11.	May 12.	May 13.	May 14.	May 15.
5 days.	May 19	May 20	May 21	May 22	May 23
10 days.	May 24	May 25	May 26	May 27	May 28
15 days.	May 29	May 30	May 31	June 1	June 2
20 days.	June 3	June 4	June 5	June 6	June 7
25 days.	June 8	June 9	June 10	June 11	June 12
30 days.	June 13	June 14	June 15	June 16	June 17
35 days.	June 18	June 19	June 20	June 21	June 22
40 days.	June 23	June 24	June 25	June 26	June 27
45 days.	June 28	June 29	June 30	July 1	July 2
50 days.	July 3	July 4	July 5	July 6	July 7
55 days.	July 8	July 9	July 10	July 11	July 12
60 days.	July 13	July 14	July 15	July 16	July 17
65 days.	July 18	July 19	July 20	July 21	July 22
70 days.	July 23	July 24	July 25	July 26	July 27
75 days.	July 28	July 29	July 30	July 31	Aug. 1
80 days.	Aug. 2	Aug. 3	Aug. 4	Aug. 5	Aug. 6
85 days.	Aug. 7	Aug. 8	Aug. 9	Aug. 10	Aug. 11
90 days.	Aug. 12	Aug. 13	Aug. 14	Aug. 15	Aug. 16
95 days.	Aug. 17	Aug. 18	Aug. 19	Aug. 20	Aug. 21
100 days.	Aug. 22	Aug. 23	Aug. 24	Aug. 25	Aug. 26
1 month.	June 14	June 15	June 16	June 17	June 18
2 months.	July 14	July 15	July 16	July 17	July 18
3 months.	Aug. 14	Aug. 15	Aug. 16	Aug. 17	Aug. 18
4 months.	Sep. 14	Sep. 15	Sep. 16	Sep. 17	Sep. 18
5 months.	Oct. 14	Oct. 15	Oct. 16	Oct. 17	Oct. 18
6 months.	Nov. 14	Nov. 15	Nov. 16	Nov. 17	Nov. 18
7 months.	Dec. 14	Dec. 15	Dec. 16	Dec. 17	Dec. 18
8 months.	Jan. 14	Jan. 15	Jan. 16	Jan. 17	Jan. 18
9 months.	Feb. 14	Feb. 15	Feb. 16	Feb. 17	Feb. 18
10 months.	Mar. 14	Mar. 15	Mar. 16	Mar. 17	Mar. 18
11 months.	Apr. 14	Apr. 15	Apr. 16	Apr. 17	Apr. 18
12 months.	May 14	May 15	May 16	May 17	May 18

Time.	May 16.	May 17.	May 18.	May 19.	May 20.
5 days.	May 24	May 25	May 26	May 27	May 28
10 days.	May 29	May 30	May 31	June 1	June 2
15 days.	June 3	June 4	June 5	June 6	June 7
20 days.	June 8	June 9	June 10	June 11	June 12
25 days.	June 13	June 14	June 15	June 16	June 17
30 days.	June 18	June 19	June 20	June 21	June 22
35 days.	June 23	June 24	June 25	June 26	June 27
40 days.	June 28	June 29	June 30	July 1	July 2
45 days.	July 3	July 4	July 5	July 6	July 7
50 days.	July 8	July 9	July 10	July 11	July 12
55 days.	July 13	July 14	July 15	July 16	July 17
60 days.	July 18	July 19	July 20	July 21	July 22
65 days.	July 23	July 24	July 25	July 26	July 27
70 days.	July 28	July 29	July 30	July 31	Aug. 1
75 days.	Aug. 2	Aug. 3	Aug. 4	Aug. 5	Aug. 6
80 days.	Aug. 7	Aug. 8	Aug. 9	Aug. 10	Aug. 11
85 days.	Aug. 12	Aug. 13	Aug. 14	Aug. 15	Aug. 16
90 days.	Aug. 17	Aug. 18	Aug. 19	Aug. 20	Aug. 21
95 days.	Aug. 22	Aug. 23	Aug. 24	Aug. 25	Aug. 26
100 days.	Aug. 27	Aug. 28	Aug. 29	Aug. 30	Aug. 31
1 month.	June 19	June 20	June 21	June 22	June 23
2 months.	July 19	July 20	July 21	July 22	July 23
3 months.	Aug. 19	Aug. 20	Aug. 21	Aug. 22	Aug. 23
4 months.	Sep. 19	Sep. 20	Sep. 21	Sep. 22	Sep. 23
5 months.	Oct. 19	Oct. 20	Oct. 21	Oct. 22	Oct. 23
6 months.	Nov. 19	Nov. 20	Nov. 21	Nov. 22	Nov. 23
7 months.	Dec. 19	Dec. 20	Dec. 21	Dec. 22	Dec. 23
8 months.	Jan. 19	Jan. 20	Jan. 21	Jan. 22	Jan. 23
9 months.	Feb. 19	Feb. 20	Feb. 21	Feb. 22	Feb. 23
10 months.	Mar. 19	Mar. 20	Mar. 21	Mar. 22	Mar. 23
11 months.	Apr. 19	Apr. 20	Apr. 21	Apr. 22	Apr. 23
12 months.	May 19	May 20	May 21	May 22	May 23

Time.	May 21.	May 22.	May 23.	May 24.	May 25.
5 days.	May 29	May 30	May 31	June 1	June 2
10 days.	June 3	June 4	June 5	June 6	June 7
15 days.	June 8	June 9	June 10	June 11	June 12
20 days.	June 13	June 14	June 15	June 16	June 17
25 days.	June 18	June 19	June 20	June 21	June 22
30 days.	June 23	June 24	June 25	June 26	June 27
35 days.	June 28	June 29	June 30	July 1	July 2
40 days.	July 3	July 4	July 5	July 6	July 7
45 days.	July 8	July 9	July 10	July 11	July 12
50 days.	July 13	July 14	July 15	July 16	July 17
55 days.	July 18	July 19	July 20	July 21	July 22
60 days.	July 23	July 24	July 25	July 26	July 27
65 days.	July 28	July 29	July 30	July 31	Aug. 1
70 days.	Aug. 2	Aug. 3	Aug. 4	Aug. 5	Aug. 6
75 days.	Aug. 7	Aug. 8	Aug. 9	Aug. 10	Aug. 11
80 days.	Aug. 12	Aug. 13	Aug. 14	Aug. 15	Aug. 16
85 days.	Aug. 17	Aug. 18	Aug. 19	Aug. 20	Aug. 21
90 days.	Aug. 22	Aug. 23	Aug. 24	Aug. 25	Aug. 26
95 days.	Aug. 27	Aug. 28	Aug. 29	Aug. 30	Aug. 31
100 days.	Sep. 1	Sep. 2	Sep. 3	Sep. 4	Sep. 5
1 month.	June 24	June 25	June 26	June 27	June 28
2 months.	July 24	July 25	July 26	July 27	July 28
3 months.	Aug. 24	Aug. 25	Aug. 26	Aug. 27	Aug. 28
4 months.	Sep. 24	Sep. 25	Sep. 26	Sep. 27	Sep. 28
5 months.	Oct. 24	Oct. 25	Oct. 26	Oct. 27	Oct. 28
6 months.	Nov. 24	Nov. 25	Nov. 26	Nov. 27	Nov. 28
7 months.	Dec. 24	Dec. 25	Dec. 26	Dec. 27	Dec. 28
8 months.	Jan. 24	Jan. 25	Jan. 26	Jan. 27	Jan. 28
9 months.	Feb. 24	Feb. 25	Feb. 26	Feb. 27	Feb. 28
10 months.	Mar. 24	Mar. 25	Mar. 26	Mar. 27	Mar. 28
11 months.	Apr. 24	Apr. 25	Apr. 26	Apr. 27	Apr. 28
12 months.	May 24	May 25	May 26	May 27	May 28

Time.	May 26.	May 27.	May 28.	May 29.	May 30.
5 days.	June 3	June 4	June 5	June 6	June 7
10 days.	June 8	June 9	June 10	June 11	June 12
15 days.	June 13	June 14	June 15	June 16	June 17
20 days.	June 18	June 19	June 20	June 21	June 22
25 days.	June 23	June 24	June 25	June 26	June 27
30 days.	June 28	June 29	June 30	July 1	July 2
35 days.	July 3	July 4	July 5	July 6	July 7
40 days.	July 8	July 9	July 10	July 11	July 12
45 days.	July 13	July 14	July 15	July 16	July 17
50 days.	July 18	July 19	July 20	July 21	July 22
55 days.	July 23	July 24	July 25	July 26	July 27
60 days.	July 28	July 29	July 30	July 31	Aug. 1
65 days.	Aug. 2	Aug. 3	Aug. 4	Aug. 5	Aug. 6
70 days.	Aug. 7	Aug. 8	Aug. 9	Aug. 10	Aug. 11
75 days.	Aug. 12	Aug. 13	Aug. 14	Aug. 15	Aug. 16
80 days.	Aug. 17	Aug. 18	Aug. 19	Aug. 20	Aug. 21
85 days.	Aug. 22	Aug. 23	Aug. 24	Aug. 25	Aug. 26
90 days.	Aug. 27	Aug. 28	Aug. 29	Aug. 30	Aug. 31
95 days.	Sep. 1	Sep. 2	Sep. 3	Sep. 4	Sep. 5
100 days.	Sep. 6	Sep. 7	Sep. 8	Sep. 9	Sep. 10
1 month.	June 29	June 30	July 1	July 2	July 3
2 months.	July 29	July 30	July 31	Aug. 1	Aug. 2
3 months.	Aug. 29	Aug. 30	Aug. 31	Sep. 1	Sep. 2
4 months.	Sep. 29	Sep. 30	Oct. 1	Oct. 2	Oct. 3
5 months.	Oct. 29	Oct. 30	Oct. 31	Nov. 1	Nov. 2
6 months.	Nov. 29	Nov. 30	Dec. 1	Dec. 2	Dec. 3
7 months.	Dec. 29	Dec. 30	Dec. 31	Jan. 1	Jan. 2
8 months.	Jan. 29	Jan. 30	Jan. 31	Feb. 1	Feb. 2
9 months.	Mar. 1	Mar. 2	Mar. 3	Mar. 3	Mar. 3
*9 mo's, L.Y.	Feb. 29	Mar. 1	Mar. 2	Mar. 3	Mar. 3
10 months.	Mar. 29	Mar. 30	Mar. 31	Apr. 1	Apr. 2
11 months.	Apr. 29	Apr. 30	May 1	May 2	May 3
12 months.	May 29	May 30	May 31	June 1	June 2

* Use this line for notes maturing in Leap Year.

Time.	May 31.	June 1.	June 2.	June 3.	June 4.
5 days.	June 8	June 9	June 10	June 11	June 12
10 days.	June 13	June 14	June 15	June 16	June 17
15 days.	June 18	June 19	June 20	June 21	June 22
20 days.	June 23	June 24	June 25	June 26	June 27
25 days.	June 28	June 29	June 30	July 1	July 2
30 days.	July 3	July 4	July 5	July 6	July 7
35 days.	July 8	July 9	July 10	July 11	July 12
40 days.	July 13	July 14	July 15	July 16	July 17
45 days.	July 18	July 19	July 20	July 21	July 22
50 days.	July 23	July 24	July 25	July 26	July 27
55 days.	July 28	July 29	July 30	July 31	Aug. 1
60 days.	Aug. 2	Aug. 3	Aug. 4	Aug. 5	Aug. 6
65 days.	Aug. 7	Aug. 8	Aug. 9	Aug. 10	Aug. 11
70 days.	Aug. 12	Aug. 13	Aug. 14	Aug. 15	Aug. 16
75 days.	Aug. 17	Aug. 18	Aug. 19	Aug. 20	Aug. 21
80 days.	Aug. 22	Aug. 23	Aug. 24	Aug. 25	Aug. 26
85 days.	Aug. 27	Aug. 28	Aug. 29	Aug. 30	Aug. 31
90 days.	Sep. 1	Sep. 2	Sep. 3	Sep. 4	Sep. 5
95 days.	Sep. 6	Sep. 7	Sep. 8	Sep. 9	Sep. 10
100 days.	Sep. 11	Sep. 12	Sep. 13	Sep. 14	Sep. 15
1 month.	July 3	July 4	July 5	July 6	July 7
2 months.	Aug. 3	Aug. 4	Aug. 5	Aug. 6	Aug. 7
3 months.	Sep. 3	Sep. 4	Sep. 5	Sep. 6	Sep. 7
4 months.	Oct. 3	Oct. 4	Oct. 5	Oct. 6	Oct. 7
5 months.	Nov. 3	Nov. 4	Nov. 5	Nov. 6	Nov. 7
6 months.	Dec. 3	Dec. 4	Dec. 5	Dec. 6	Dec. 7
7 months.	Jan. 3	Jan. 4	Jan. 5	Jan. 6	Jan. 7
8 months.	Feb. 3	Feb. 4	Feb. 5	Feb. 6	Feb. 7
9 months.	Mar. 3	Mar. 4	Mar. 5	Mar. 6	Mar. 7
10 months.	Apr. 3	Apr. 4	Apr. 5	Apr. 6	Apr. 7
11 months.	May 3	May 4	May 5	May 6	May 7
12 months.	June 3	June 4	June 5	June 6	June 7

Time.	June 5.	June 6.	June 7.	June 8.	June 9.
5 days.	June 13	June 14	June 15	June 16	June 17
10 days.	June 18	June 19	June 20	June 21	June 22
15 days.	June 23	June 24	June 25	June 26	June 27
20 days.	June 28	June 29	June 30	July 1	July 2
25 days.	July 3	July 4	July 5	July 6	July 7
30 days.	July 8	July 9	July 10	July 11	July 12
35 days.	July 13	July 14	July 15	July 16	July 17
40 days.	July 18	July 19	July 20	July 21	July 22
45 days.	July 23	July 24	July 25	July 26	July 27
50 days.	July 28	July 29	July 30	July 31	Aug. 1
55 days.	Aug. 2	Aug. 3	Aug. 4	Aug. 5	Aug. 6
60 days.	Aug. 7	Aug. 8	Aug. 9	Aug. 10	Aug. 11
65 days.	Aug. 12	Aug. 13	Aug. 14	Aug. 15	Aug. 16
70 days.	Aug. 17	Aug. 18	Aug. 19	Aug. 20	Aug. 21
75 days.	Aug. 22	Aug. 23	Aug. 24	Aug. 25	Aug. 26
80 days.	Aug. 27	Aug. 28	Aug. 29	Aug. 30	Aug. 31
85 days.	Sep. 1	Sep. 2	Sep. 3	Sep. 4	Sep. 5
90 days.	Sep. 6	Sep. 7	Sep. 8	Sep. 9	Sep. 10
95 days.	Sep. 11	Sep. 12	Sep. 13	Sep. 14	Sep. 15
100 days.	Sep. 16	Sep. 17	Sep. 18	Sep. 19	Sep. 20
1 month.	July 8	July 9	July 10	July 11	July 12
2 months.	Aug. 8	Aug. 9	Aug. 10	Aug. 11	Aug. 12
3 months.	Sep. 8	Sep. 9	Sep. 10	Sep. 11	Sep. 12
4 months.	Oct. 8	Oct. 9	Oct. 10	Oct. 11	Oct. 12
5 months.	Nov. 8	Nov. 9	Nov. 10	Nov. 11	Nov. 12
6 months.	Dec. 8	Dec. 9	Dec. 10	Dec. 11	Dec. 12
7 months.	Jan. 8	Jan. 9	Jan. 10	Jan. 11	Jan. 12
8 months.	Feb. 8	Feb. 9	Feb. 10	Feb. 11	Feb. 12
9 months.	Mar. 8	Mar. 9	Mar. 10	Mar. 11	Mar. 12
10 months.	Apr. 8	Apr. 9	Apr. 10	Apr. 11	Apr. 12
11 months.	May 8	May 9	May 10	May 11	May 12
12 months.	June 8	June 9	June 10	June 11	June 12

Time.	June 10.	June 11.	June 12.	June 13.	June 14.
5 days.	June 18	June 19	June 20	June 21	June 22
10 days.	June 23	June 24	June 25	June 26	June 27
15 days.	June 28	June 29	June 30	July 1	July 2
20 days.	July 3	July 4	July 5	July 6	July 7
25 days.	July 8	July 9	July 10	July 11	July 12
30 days.	July 13	July 14	July 15	July 16	July 17
35 days.	July 18	July 19	July 20	July 21	July 22
40 days.	July 23	July 24	July 25	July 26	July 27
45 days.	July 28	July 29	July 30	July 31	Aug. 1
50 days.	Aug. 2	Aug. 3	Aug. 4	Aug. 5	Aug. 6
55 days.	Aug. 7	Aug. 8	Aug. 9	Aug. 10	Aug. 11
60 days.	Aug. 12	Aug. 13	Aug. 14	Aug. 15	Aug. 16
65 days.	Aug. 17	Aug. 18	Aug. 19	Aug. 20	Aug. 21
70 days.	Aug. 22	Aug. 23	Aug. 24	Aug. 25	Aug. 26
75 days.	Aug. 27	Aug. 28	Aug. 29	Aug. 30	Aug. 31
80 days.	Sep. 1	Sep. 2	Sep. 3	Sep. 4	Sep. 5
85 days.	Sep. 6	Sep. 7	Sep. 8	Sep. 9	Sep. 10
90 days.	Sep. 11	Sep. 12	Sep. 13	Sep. 14	Sep. 15
95 days.	Sep. 16	Sep. 17	Sep. 18	Sep. 19	Sep. 20
100 days.	Sep. 21	Sep. 22	Sep. 23	Sep. 24	Sep. 25
1 month.	July 13	July 14	July 15	July 16	July 17
2 months.	Aug. 13	Aug. 14	Aug. 15	Aug. 16	Aug. 17
3 months.	Sep. 13	Sep. 14	Sep. 15	Sep. 16	Sep. 17
4 months.	Oct. 13	Oct. 14	Oct. 15	Oct. 16	Oct. 17
5 months.	Nov. 13	Nov. 14	Nov. 15	Nov. 16	Nov. 17
6 months.	Dec. 13	Dec. 14	Dec. 15	Dec. 16	Dec. 17
7 months.	Jan. 13	Jan. 14	Jan. 15	Jan. 16	Jan. 17
8 months.	Feb. 13	Feb. 14	Feb. 15	Feb. 16	Feb. 17
9 months.	Mar. 13	Mar. 14	Mar. 15	Mar. 16	Mar. 17
10 months.	Apr. 13	Apr. 14	Apr. 15	Apr. 16	Apr. 17
11 months.	May 13	May 14	May 15	May 16	May 17
12 months.	June 13	June 14	June 15	June 16	June 17

Time.	June 15.	June 16.	June 17.	June 18.	June 19.
5 days.	June 23	June 24	June 25	June 26	June 27
10 days.	June 28	June 29	June 30	July 1	July 2
15 days.	July 3	July 4	July 5	July 6	July 7
20 days.	July 8	July 9	July 10	July 11	July 12
25 days.	July 13	July 14	July 15	July 16	July 17
30 days.	July 18	July 19	July 20	July 21	July 22
35 days.	July 23	July 24	July 25	July 26	July 27
40 days.	July 28	July 29	July 30	July 31	Aug. 1
45 days.	Aug. 2	Aug. 3	Aug. 4	Aug. 5	Aug. 6
50 days.	Aug. 7	Aug. 8	Aug. 9	Aug. 10	Aug. 11
55 days.	Aug. 12	Aug. 13	Aug. 14	Aug. 15	Aug. 16
60 days.	Aug. 17	Aug. 18	Aug. 19	Aug. 20	Aug. 21
65 days.	Aug. 22	Aug. 23	Aug. 24	Aug. 25	Aug. 26
70 days.	Aug. 27	Aug. 28	Aug. 29	Aug. 30	Aug. 31
75 days.	Sep. 1	Sep. 2	Sep. 3	Sep. 4	Sep. 5
80 days.	Sep. 6	Sep. 7	Sep. 8	Sep. 9	Sep. 10
85 days.	Sep. 11	Sep. 12	Sep. 13	Sep. 14	Sep. 15
90 days.	Sep. 16	Sep. 17	Sep. 18	Sep. 19	Sep. 20
95 days.	Sep. 21	Sep. 22	Sep. 23	Sep. 24	Sep. 25
100 days.	Sep. 26	Sep. 27	Sep. 28	Sep. 29	Sep. 30
1 month.	July 18	July 19	July 20	July 21	July 22
2 months.	Aug. 18	Aug. 19	Aug. 20	Aug. 21	Aug. 22
3 months.	Sep. 18	Sep. 19	Sep. 20	Sep. 21	Sep. 22
4 months.	Oct. 18	Oct. 19	Oct. 20	Oct. 21	Oct. 22
5 months.	Nov. 18	Nov. 19	Nov. 20	Nov. 21	Nov. 22
6 months.	Dec. 18	Dec. 19	Dec. 20	Dec. 21	Dec. 22
7 months.	Jan. 18	Jan. 19	Jan. 20	Jan. 21	Jan. 22
8 months.	Feb. 18	Feb. 19	Feb. 20	Feb. 21	Feb. 22
9 months.	Mar. 18	Mar. 19	Mar. 20	Mar. 21	Mar. 22
10 months.	Apr. 18	Apr. 19	Apr. 20	Apr. 21	Apr. 22
11 months.	May 18	May 19	May 20	May 21	May 22
12 months.	June 18	June 19	June 20	June 21	June 22

Time.	June 20.	June 21.	June 22.	June 23.	June 24.
5 days.	June 28	June 29	June 30	July 1	July 2
10 days.	July 3	July 4	July 5	July 6	July 7
15 days.	July 8	July 9	July 10	July 11	July 12
20 days.	July 13	July 14	July 15	July 16	July 17
25 days.	July 18	July 19	July 20	July 21	July 22
30 days.	July 23	July 24	July 25	July 26	July 27
35 days.	July 28	July 29	July 30	July 31	Aug. 1
40 days.	Aug. 2	Aug. 3	Aug. 4	Aug. 5	Aug. 6
45 days.	Aug. 7	Aug. 8	Aug. 9	Aug. 10	Aug. 11
50 days.	Aug. 12	Aug. 13	Aug. 14	Aug. 15	Aug. 16
55 days.	Aug. 17	Aug. 18	Aug. 19	Aug. 20	Aug. 21
60 days.	Aug. 22	Aug. 23	Aug. 24	Aug. 25	Aug. 26
65 days.	Aug. 27	Aug. 28	Aug. 29	Aug. 30	Aug. 31
70 days.	Sep. 1	Sep. 2	Sep. 3	Sep. 4	Sep. 5
75 days.	Sep. 6	Sep. 7	Sep. 8	Sep. 9	Sep. 10
80 days.	Sep. 11	Sep. 12	Sep. 13	Sep. 14	Sep. 15
85 days.	Sep. 16	Sep. 17	Sep. 18	Sep. 19	Sep. 20
90 days.	Sep. 21	Sep. 22	Sep. 23	Sep. 24	Sep. 25
95 days.	Sep. 26	Sep. 27	Sep. 28	Sep. 29	Sep. 30
100 days.	Oct. 1	Oct. 2	Oct. 3	Oct. 4	Oct. 5
1 month.	July 23	July 24	July 25	July 26	July 27
2 months.	Aug. 23	Aug. 24	Aug. 25	Aug. 26	Aug. 27
3 months.	Sep. 23	Sep. 24	Sep. 25	Sep. 26	Sep. 27
4 months.	Oct. 23	Oct. 24	Oct. 25	Oct. 26	Oct. 27
5 months.	Nov. 23	Nov. 24	Nov. 25	Nov. 26	Nov. 27
6 months.	Dec. 23	Dec. 24	Dec. 25	Dec. 26	Dec. 27
7 months.	Jan. 23	Jan. 24	Jan. 25	Jan. 26	Jan. 27
8 months.	Feb. 23	Feb. 24	Feb. 25	Feb. 26	Feb. 27
9 months.	Mar. 23	Mar. 24	Mar. 25	Mar. 26	Mar. 27
10 months.	Apr. 23	Apr. 24	Apr. 25	Apr. 26	Apr. 27
11 months.	May 23	May 24	May 25	May 26	May 27
12 months.	June 23	June 24	June 25	June 26	June 27

Time.	June 25.	June 26.	June 27.	June 28.	June 29.
5 days.	July 3	July 4	July 5	July 6	July 7
10 days.	July 8	July 9	July 10	July 11	July 12
15 days.	July 13	July 14	July 15	July 16	July 17
20 days.	July 18	July 19	July 20	July 21	July 22
25 days.	July 23	July 24	July 25	July 26	July 27
30 days.	July 28	July 29	July 30	July 31	Aug. 1
35 days.	Aug. 2	Aug. 3	Aug. 4	Aug. 5	Aug. 6
40 days.	Aug. 7	Aug. 8	Aug. 9	Aug. 10	Aug. 11
45 days.	Aug. 12	Aug. 13	Aug. 14	Aug. 15	Aug. 16
50 days.	Aug. 17	Aug. 18	Aug. 19	Aug. 20	Aug. 21
55 days.	Aug. 22	Aug. 23	Aug. 24	Aug. 25	Aug. 26
60 days.	Aug. 27	Aug. 28	Aug. 29	Aug. 30	Aug. 31
65 days.	Sep. 1	Sep. 2	Sep. 3	Sep. 4	Sep. 5
70 days.	Sep. 6	Sep. 7	Sep. 8	Sep. 9	Sep. 10
75 days.	Sep. 11	Sep. 12	Sep. 13	Sep. 14	Sep. 15
80 days.	Sep. 16	Sep. 17	Sep. 18	Sep. 19	Sep. 20
85 days.	Sep. 21	Sep. 22	Sep. 23	Sep. 24	Sep. 25
90 days.	Sep. 26	Sep. 27	Sep. 28	Sep. 29	Sep. 30
95 days.	Oct. 1	Oct. 2	Oct. 3	Oct. 4	Oct. 5
100 days.	Oct. 6	Oct. 7	Oct. 8	Oct. 9	Oct. 10
1 month.	July 28	July 29	July 30	July 31	Aug. 1
2 months.	Aug. 28	Aug. 29	Aug. 30	Aug. 31	Sep. 1
3 months.	Sep. 28	Sep. 29	Sep. 30	Oct. 1	Oct. 2
4 months.	Oct. 28	Oct. 29	Oct. 30	Oct. 31	Nov. 1
5 months.	Nov. 28	Nov. 29	Nov. 30	Dec. 1	Dec. 2
6 months.	Dec. 28	Dec. 29	Dec. 30	Dec. 31	Jan 1
7 months.	Jan. 28	Jan. 29	Jan. 30	Jan. 31	Feb. 1
8 months.	Feb. 28	Mar. 1	Mar. 2	Mar. 3	Mar. 3
*8 mo's, L.Y.	Feb. 28	Feb. 29	Mar. 1	Mar. 2	Mar. 3
9 months.	Mar. 28	Mar. 29	Mar. 30	Mar. 31	Apr. 1
10 months.	Apr. 28	Apr. 29	Apr. 30	May 1	May 2
11 months.	May 28	May 29	May 30	May 31	June 1
12 months.	June 28	June 29	June 30	July 1	July 2

*Use this line for notes maturing in Leap Year.

Time.	June 30.	July 1.	July 2.	July 3.	July 4.
5 days.	July 8	July 9	July 10	July 11	July 12
10 days.	July 13	July 14	July 15	July 16	July 17
15 days.	July 18	July 19	July 20	July 21	July 22
20 days.	July 23	July 24	July 25	July 26	July 27
25 days.	July 28	July 29	July 30	July 31	Aug. 1
30 days.	Aug. 2	Aug. 3	Aug. 4	Aug. 5	Aug. 6
35 days.	Aug. 7	Aug. 8	Aug. 9	Aug. 10	Aug. 11
40 days.	Aug. 12	Aug. 13	Aug. 14	Aug. 15	Aug. 16
45 days.	Aug. 17	Aug. 18	Aug. 19	Aug. 20	Aug. 21
50 days.	Aug. 22	Aug. 23	Aug. 24	Aug. 25	Aug. 26
55 days.	Aug. 27	Aug. 28	Aug. 29	Aug. 30	Aug. 31
60 days.	Sep. 1	Sep. 2	Sep. 3	Sep. 4	Sep. 5
65 days.	Sep. 6	Sep. 7	Sep. 8	Sep. 9	Sep. 10
70 days.	Sep. 11	Sep. 12	Sep. 13	Sep. 14	Sep. 15
75 days.	Sep. 16	Sep. 17	Sep. 18	Sep. 19	Sep. 20
80 days.	Sep. 21	Sep. 22	Sep. 23	Sep. 24	Sep. 25
85 days.	Sep. 26	Sep. 27	Sep. 28	Sep. 29	Sep. 30
90 days.	Oct. 1	Oct. 2	Oct. 3	Oct. 4	Oct. 5
95 days.	Oct. 6	Oct. 7	Oct. 8	Oct. 9	Oct. 10
100 days.	Oct. 11	Oct. 12	Oct. 13	Oct. 14	Oct. 15
1 month.	Aug. 2	Aug. 4	Aug. 5	Aug. 6	Aug. 7
2 months.	Sep. 2	Sep. 4	Sep. 5	Sep. 6	Sep. 7
3 months.	Oct. 3	Oct. 4	Oct. 5	Oct. 6	Oct. 7
4 months.	Nov. 2	Nov. 4	Nov. 5	Nov. 6	Nov. 7
5 months.	Dec. 3	Dec. 4	Dec. 5	Dec. 6	Dec. 7
6 months.	Jan. 2	Jan. 4	Jan. 5	Jan. 6	Jan 7
7 months.	Feb. 2	Feb. 4	Feb. 5	Feb. 6	Feb. 7
8 months.	Mar. 3	Mar. 4	Mar. 5	Mar. 6	Mar. 7
9 months.	Apr. 2	Apr. 4	Apr. 5	Apr. 6	Apr. 7
10 months.	May 3	May 4	May 5	May 6	May 7
11 months.	June 2	June 4	June 5	June 6	June 7
12 months.	July 3	July 4	July 5	July 6	July 7

Time.	July 5.	July 6.	July 7.	July 8.	July 9.
5 days.	July 13	July 14	July 15	July 16	July 17
10 days.	July 18	July 19	July 20	July 21	July 22
15 days.	July 23	July 24	July 25	July 26	July 27
20 days.	July 28	July 29	July 30	July 31	Aug. 1
25 days.	Aug. 2	Aug. 3	Aug. 4	Aug. 5	Aug. 6
30 days.	Aug. 7	Aug. 8	Aug. 9	Aug. 10	Aug. 11
35 days.	Aug. 12	Aug. 13	Aug. 14	Aug. 15	Aug. 16
40 days.	Aug. 17	Aug. 18	Aug. 19	Aug. 20	Aug. 21
45 days.	Aug. 22	Aug. 23	Aug. 24	Aug. 25	Aug. 26
50 days.	Aug. 27	Aug. 28	Aug. 29	Aug. 30	Aug. 31
55 days.	Sep. 1	Sep. 2	Sep. 3	Sep. 4	Sep. 5
60 days.	Sep. 6	Sep. 7	Sep. 8	Sep. 9	Sep. 10
65 days.	Sep. 11	Sep. 12	Sep. 13	Sep. 14	Sep. 15
70 days.	Sep. 16	Sep. 17	Sep. 18	Sep. 19	Sep. 20
75 days.	Sep. 21	Sep. 22	Sep. 23	Sep. 24	Sep. 25
80 days.	Sep. 26	Sep. 27	Sep. 28	Sep. 29	Sep. 30
85 days.	Oct. 1	Oct. 2	Oct. 3	Oct. 4	Oct. 5
90 days.	Oct. 6	Oct. 7	Oct. 8	Oct. 9	Oct. 10
95 days.	Oct. 11	Oct. 12	Oct. 13	Oct. 14	Oct. 15
100 days.	Oct. 16	Oct. 17	Oct. 18	Oct. 19	Oct. 20
1 month.	Aug. 8	Aug. 9	Aug. 10	Aug. 11	Aug. 12
2 months.	Sep. 8	Sep. 9	Sep. 10	Sep. 11	Sep. 12
3 months.	Oct. 8	Oct. 9	Oct. 10	Oct. 11	Oct. 12
4 months.	Nov. 8	Nov. 9	Nov. 10	Nov. 11	Nov. 12
5 months.	Dec. 8	Dec. 9	Dec. 10	Dec. 11	Dec. 12
6 months.	Jan. 8	Jan. 9	Jan. 10	Jan. 11	Jan. 12
7 months.	Feb. 8	Feb. 9	Feb. 10	Feb. 11	Feb. 12
8 months.	Mar. 8	Mar. 9	Mar. 10	Mar. 11	Mar. 12
9 months.	Apr. 8	Apr. 9	Apr. 10	Apr. 11	Apr. 12
10 months.	May 8	May 9	May 10	May 11	May 12
11 months.	June 8	June 9	June 10	June 11	June 12
12 months.	July 8	July 9	July 10	July 11	July 12

Time.	July 10.	July 11.	July 12.	July 13.	July 14.
5 days.	July 18	July 19	July 20	July 21	July 22
10 days.	July 23	July 24	July 25	July 26	July 27
15 days.	July 28	July 29	July 30	July 31	Aug. 1
20 days.	Aug. 2	Aug. 3	Aug. 4	Aug. 5	Aug. 6
25 days.	Aug. 7	Aug. 8	Aug. 9	Aug. 10	Aug. 11
30 days.	Aug. 12	Aug. 13	Aug. 14	Aug. 15	Aug. 16
35 days.	Aug. 17	Aug. 18	Aug. 19	Aug. 20	Aug. 21
40 days.	Aug. 22	Aug. 23	Aug. 24	Aug. 25	Aug. 26
45 days.	Aug. 27	Aug. 28	Aug. 29	Aug. 30	Aug. 31
50 days.	Sep. 1	Sep. 2	Sep. 3	Sep. 4	Sep. 5
55 days.	Sep. 6	Sep. 7	Sep. 8	Sep. 9	Sep. 10
60 days.	Sep. 11	Sep. 12	Sep. 13	Sep. 14	Sep. 15
65 days.	Sep. 16	Sep. 17	Sep. 18	Sep. 19	Sep. 20
70 days.	Sep. 21	Sep. 22	Sep. 23	Sep. 24	Sep. 25
75 days.	Sep. 26	Sep. 27	Sep. 28	Sep. 29	Sep. 30
80 days.	Oct. 1	Oct. 2	Oct. 3	Oct. 4	Oct. 5
85 days.	Oct. 6	Oct. 7	Oct. 8	Oct. 9	Oct. 10
90 days.	Oct. 11	Oct. 12	Oct. 13	Oct. 14	Oct. 15
95 days.	Oct. 16	Oct. 17	Oct. 18	Oct. 19	Oct. 20
100 days.	Oct. 21	Oct. 22	Oct. 23	Oct. 24	Oct. 25
1 month.	Aug. 13	Aug. 14	Aug. 15	Aug. 16	Aug. 17
2 months.	Sep. 13	Sep. 14	Sep. 15	Sep. 16	Sep. 17
3 months.	Oct. 13	Oct. 14	Oct. 15	Oct. 16	Oct. 17
4 months.	Nov. 13	Nov. 14	Nov. 15	Nov. 16	Nov. 17
5 months.	Dec. 13	Dec. 14	Dec. 15	Dec. 16	Dec. 17
6 months.	Jan. 13	Jan. 14	Jan. 15	Jan. 16	Jan 17
7 months.	Feb. 13	Feb. 14	Feb. 15	Feb. 16	Feb. 17
8 months.	Mar. 13	Mar. 14	Mar. 15	Mar. 16	Mar. 17
9 months.	Apr. 13	Apr. 14	Apr. 15	Apr. 16	Apr. 17
10 months.	May 13	May 14	May 15	May 16	May 17
11 months.	June 13	June 14	June 15	June 16	June 17
12 months.	July 13	July 14	July 15	July 16	July 17

Time.	July 15.	July 16.	July 17.	July 18.	July 19.
5 days.	July 23	July 24	July 25	July 26	July 27
10 days.	July 28	July 29	July 30	July 31	Aug. 1
15 days.	Aug. 2	Aug. 3	Aug. 4	Aug. 5	Aug. 6
20 days.	Aug. 7	Aug. 8	Aug. 9	Aug. 10	Aug. 11
25 days.	Aug. 12	Aug. 13	Aug. 14	Aug. 15	Aug. 16
30 days.	Aug. 17	Aug. 18	Aug. 19	Aug. 20	Aug. 21
35 days.	Aug. 22	Aug. 23	Aug. 24	Aug. 25	Aug. 26
40 days.	Aug. 27	Aug. 28	Aug. 29	Aug. 30	Aug. 31
45 days.	Sep. 1	Sep. 2	Sep. 3	Sep. 4	Sep. 5
50 days.	Sep. 6	Sep. 7	Sep. 8	Sep. 9	Sep. 10
55 days.	Sep. 11	Sep. 12	Sep. 13	Sep. 14	Sep. 15
60 days.	Sep. 16	Sep. 17	Sep. 18	Sep. 19	Sep. 20
65 days.	Sep. 21	Sep. 22	Sep. 23	Sep. 24	Sep. 25
70 days.	Sep. 26	Sep. 27	Sep. 28	Sep. 29	Sep. 30
75 days.	Oct. 1	Oct. 2	Oct. 3	Oct. 4	Oct. 5
80 days.	Oct. 6	Oct. 7	Oct. 8	Oct. 9	Oct. 10
85 days.	Oct. 11	Oct. 12	Oct. 13	Oct. 14	Oct. 15
90 days.	Oct. 16	Oct. 17	Oct. 18	Oct. 19	Oct. 20
95 days.	Oct. 21	Oct. 22	Oct. 23	Oct. 24	Oct. 25
100 days.	Oct. 26	Oct. 27	Oct. 28	Oct. 29	Oct. 30
1 month.	Aug. 18	Aug. 19	Aug. 20	Aug. 21	Aug. 22
2 months.	Sep. 18	Sep. 19	Sep. 20	Sep. 21	Sep. 22
3 months.	Oct. 18	Oct. 19	Oct. 20	Oct. 21	Oct. 22
4 months.	Nov. 18	Nov. 19	Nov. 20	Nov. 21	Nov. 22
5 months.	Dec. 18	Dec. 19	Dec. 20	Dec. 21	Dec. 22
6 months.	Jan. 18	Jan. 19	Jan. 20	Jan. 21	Jan 22
7 months.	Feb. 18	Feb. 19	Feb. 20	Feb. 21	Feb. 22
8 months.	Mar. 18	Mar. 19	Mar. 20	Mar. 21	Mar. 22
9 months.	Apr. 18	Apr. 19	Apr. 20	Apr. 21	Apr. 22
10 months.	May 18	May 19	May 20	May 21	May 22
11 months.	June 18	June 19	June 20	June 21	June 22
12 months.	July 18	July 19	July 20	July 21	July 22

Time.	July 20.	July 21.	July 22.	July 23.	July 24.
5 days.	July 28	July 29	July 30	July 31	Aug. 1
10 days.	Aug. 2	Aug. 3	Aug. 4	Aug. 5	Aug. 6
15 days.	Aug. 7	Aug. 8	Aug. 9	Aug. 10	Aug. 11
20 days.	Aug. 12	Aug. 13	Aug. 14	Aug. 15	Aug. 16
25 days.	Aug. 17	Aug. 18	Aug. 19	Aug. 20	Aug. 21
30 days.	Aug. 22	Aug. 23	Aug. 24	Aug. 25	Aug. 26
35 days.	Aug. 27	Aug. 28	Aug. 29	Aug. 30	Aug. 31
40 days.	Sep. 1	Sep. 2	Sep. 3	Sep. 4	Sep. 5
45 days.	Sep. 6	Sep. 7	Sep. 8	Sep. 9	Sep. 10
50 days.	Sep. 11	Sep. 12	Sep. 13	Sep. 14	Sep. 15
55 days.	Sep. 16	Sep. 17	Sep. 18	Sep. 19	Sep. 20
60 days.	Sep. 21	Sep. 22	Sep. 23	Sep. 24	Sep. 25
65 days.	Sep. 26	Sep. 27	Sep. 28	Sep. 29	Sep. 30
70 days.	Oct. 1	Oct. 2	Oct. 3	Oct. 4	Oct. 5
75 days.	Oct. 6	Oct. 7	Oct. 8	Oct. 9	Oct. 10
80 days.	Oct. 11	Oct. 12	Oct. 13	Oct. 14	Oct. 15
85 days.	Oct. 16	Oct. 17	Oct. 18	Oct. 19	Oct. 20
90 days.	Oct. 21	Oct. 22	Oct. 23	Oct. 24	Oct. 25
95 days.	Oct. 26	Oct. 27	Oct. 28	Oct. 29	Oct. 30
100 days.	Oct. 31	Nov. 1	Nov. 2	Nov. 3	Nov. 4
1 month.	Aug. 23	Aug. 24	Aug. 25	Aug. 26	Aug. 27
2 months.	Sep. 23	Sep. 24	Sep. 25	Sep. 26	Sep. 27
3 months.	Oct. 23	Oct. 24	Oct. 25	Oct. 26	Oct. 27
4 months.	Nov. 23	Nov. 24	Nov. 25	Nov. 26	Nov. 27
5 months.	Dec. 23	Dec. 24	Dec. 25	Dec. 26	Dec. 27
6 months.	Jan. 23	Jan. 24	Jan. 25	Jan. 26	Jan 27
7 months.	Feb. 23	Feb. 24	Feb. 25	Feb. 26	Feb. 27
8 months.	Mar. 23	Mar. 24	Mar. 25	Mar. 26	Mar. 27
9 months.	Apr. 23	Apr. 24	Apr. 25	Apr. 26	Apr. 27
10 months.	May 23	May 24	May 25	May 26	May 27
11 months.	June 23	June 24	June 25	June 26	June 27
12 months.	July 23	July 24	July 25	July 26	July 27

Time.	July 25.	July 26.	July 27.	July 28.	July 29.
5 days.	Aug. 2	Aug. 3	Aug. 4	Aug. 5	Aug. 6
10 days.	Aug. 7	Aug. 8	Aug. 9	Aug. 10	Aug. 11
15 days.	Aug. 12	Aug. 13	Aug. 14	Aug. 15	Aug. 16
20 days.	Aug. 17	Aug. 18	Aug. 19	Aug. 20	Aug. 21
25 days.	Aug. 22	Aug. 23	Aug. 24	Aug. 25	Aug. 26
30 days.	Aug. 27	Aug. 28	Aug. 29	Aug. 30	Aug. 31
35 days.	Sep. 1	Sep. 2	Sep. 3	Sep. 4	Sep. 5
40 days.	Sep. 6	Sep. 7	Sep. 8	Sep. 9	Sep. 10
45 days.	Sep. 11	Sep. 12	Sep. 13	Sep. 14	Sep. 15
50 days.	Sep. 16	Sep. 17	Sep. 18	Sep. 19	Sep. 20
55 days.	Sep. 21	Sep. 22	Sep. 23	Sep. 24	Sep. 25
60 days.	Sep. 26	Sep. 27	Sep. 28	Sep. 29	Sep. 30
65 days.	Oct. 1	Oct. 2	Oct. 3	Oct. 4	Oct. 5
70 days.	Oct. 6	Oct. 7	Oct. 8	Oct. 9	Oct. 10
75 days.	Oct. 11	Oct. 12	Oct. 13	Oct. 14	Oct. 15
80 days.	Oct. 16	Oct. 17	Oct. 18	Oct. 19	Oct. 20
85 days.	Oct. 21	Oct. 22	Oct. 23	Oct. 24	Oct. 25
90 days.	Oct. 26	Oct. 27	Oct. 28	Oct. 29	Oct. 30
95 days.	Oct. 31	Nov. 1	Nov. 2	Nov. 3	Nov. 4
100 days.	Nov. 5	Nov. 6	Nov. 7	Nov. 8	Nov. 9
1 month.	Aug. 28	Aug. 29	Aug. 30	Aug. 31	Sep. 1
2 months.	Sep. 28	Sep. 29	Sep. 30	Oct. 1	Oct. 2
3 months.	Oct. 28	Oct. 29	Oct. 30	Oct. 31	Nov. 1
4 months.	Nov. 28	Nov. 29	Nov. 30	Dec. 1	Dec. 2
5 months.	Dec. 28	Dec. 29	Dec. 30	Dec. 31	Jan 1
6 months.	Jan. 28	Jan. 29	Jan. 30	Jan. 31	Feb. 1
7 months.	Feb. 28	Mar. 1	Mar. 2	Mar. 3	Mar. 3
*7 mo's, L.Y.	Feb. 28	Feb. 29	Mar. 1	Mar. 2	Mar. 3
8 months.	Mar. 28	Mar. 29	Mar. 30	Mar. 31	Apr. 1
9 months.	Apr. 28	Apr. 29	Apr. 30	May 1	May 2
10 months.	May 28	May 29	May 30	May 31	June 1
11 months.	June 28	June 29	June 30	July 1	July 2
12 months.	July 28	July 29	July 30	July 31	Aug. 1

*Use this line for notes maturing in Leap Year.

Time.	July 30.	July 31.	August 1.	August 2.	August 3.
5 days.	Aug. 7	Aug. 8	Aug. 9	Aug. 10	Aug. 11
10 days.	Aug. 12	Aug. 13	Aug. 14	Aug. 15	Aug. 16
15 days.	Aug. 17	Aug. 18	Aug. 19	Aug. 20	Aug. 21
20 days.	Aug. 22	Aug. 23	Aug. 24	Aug. 25	Aug. 26
25 days.	Aug. 27	Aug. 28	Aug. 29	Aug. 30	Aug. 31
30 days.	Sep. 1	Sep. 2	Sep. 3	Sep. 4	Sep. 5
35 days.	Sep. 6	Sep. 7	Sep. 8	Sep. 9	Sep. 10
40 days.	Sep. 11	Sep. 12	Sep. 13	Sep. 14	Sep. 15
45 days.	Sep. 16	Sep. 17	Sep. 18	Sep. 19	Sep. 20
50 days.	Sep. 21	Sep. 22	Sep. 23	Sep. 24	Sep. 25
55 days.	Sep. 26	Sep. 27	Sep. 28	Sep. 29	Sep. 30
60 days.	Oct. 1	Oct. 2	Oct. 3	Oct. 4	Oct. 5
65 days.	Oct. 6	Oct. 7	Oct. 8	Oct. 9	Oct. 10
70 days.	Oct. 11	Oct. 12	Oct. 13	Oct. 14	Oct. 15
75 days.	Oct. 16	Oct. 17	Oct. 18	Oct. 19	Oct. 20
80 days.	Oct. 21	Oct. 22	Oct. 23	Oct. 24	Oct. 25
85 days.	Oct. 26	Oct. 27	Oct. 28	Oct. 29	Oct. 30
90 days.	Oct. 31	Nov. 1	Nov. 2	Nov. 3	Nov. 4
95 days.	Nov. 5	Nov. 6	Nov. 7	Nov. 8	Nov. 9
100 days.	Nov. 10	Nov. 11	Nov. 12	Nov. 13	Nov. 14
1 month.	Sep. 2	Sep. 3	Sep. 4	Sep. 5	Sep. 6
2 months.	Oct. 3	Oct. 3	Oct. 4	Oct. 5	Oct. 6
3 months.	Nov. 2	Nov. 3	Nov. 4	Nov. 5	Nov. 6
4 months.	Dec. 3	Dec. 3	Dec. 4	Dec. 5	Dec. 6
5 months.	Jan. 2	Jan. 3	Jan. 4	Jan. 5	Jan 6
6 months.	Feb. 2	Feb. 3	Feb. 4	Feb. 5	Feb. 6
7 months.	Mar. 3	Mar. 3	Mar. 4	Mar. 5	Mar. 6
8 months.	Apr. 2	Apr. 3	Apr. 4	Apr. 5	Apr. 6
9 months.	May 3	May 3	May 4	May 5	May 6
10 months.	June 2	June 3	June 4	June 5	June 6
11 months.	July 3	July 3	July 4	July 5	July 6
12 months.	Aug. 2	Aug. 3	Aug. 4	Aug. 5	Aug. 6

Time.	August 4.	August 5.	August 6.	August 7.	August 8.
5 days.	Aug. 12	Aug. 13	Aug. 14	Aug. 15	Aug. 16
10 days.	Aug. 17	Aug. 18	Aug. 19	Aug. 20	Aug. 21
15 days.	Aug. 22	Aug. 23	Aug. 24	Aug. 25	Aug. 26
20 days.	Aug. 27	Aug. 28	Aug. 29	Aug. 30	Aug. 31
25 days.	Sep. 1	Sep. 2	Sep. 3	Sep. 4	Sep. 5
30 days.	Sep. 6	Sep. 7	Sep. 8	Sep. 9	Sep. 10
35 days.	Sep. 11	Sep. 12	Sep. 13	Sep. 14	Sep. 15
40 days.	Sep. 16	Sep. 17	Sep. 18	Sep. 19	Sep. 20
45 days.	Sep. 21	Sep. 22	Sep. 23	Sep. 24	Sep. 25
50 days.	Sep. 26	Sep. 27	Sep. 28	Sep. 29	Sep. 30
55 days.	Oct. 1	Oct. 2	Oct. 3	Oct. 4	Oct. 5
60 days.	Oct. 6	Oct. 7	Oct. 8	Oct. 9	Oct. 10
65 days.	Oct. 11	Oct. 12	Oct. 13	Oct. 14	Oct. 15
70 days.	Oct. 16	Oct. 17	Oct. 18	Oct. 19	Oct. 20
75 days.	Oct. 21	Oct. 22	Oct. 23	Oct. 24	Oct. 25
80 days.	Oct. 26	Oct. 27	Oct. 28	Oct. 29	Oct. 30
85 days.	Oct. 31	Nov. 1	Nov. 2	Nov. 3	Nov. 4
90 days.	Nov. 5	Nov. 6	Nov. 7	Nov. 8	Nov. 9
95 days.	Nov. 10	Nov. 11	Nov. 12	Nov. 13	Nov. 14
100 days.	Nov. 15	Nov. 16	Nov. 17	Nov. 18	Nov. 19
1 month.	Sep. 7	Sep. 8	Sep. 9	Sep. 10	Sep. 11
2 months.	Oct. 7	Oct. 8	Oct. 9	Oct. 10	Oct. 11
3 months.	Nov. 7	Nov. 8	Nov. 9	Nov. 10	Nov. 11
4 months.	Dec. 7	Dec. 8	Dec. 9	Dec. 10	Dec. 11
5 months.	Jan. 7	Jan. 8	Jan. 9	Jan. 10	Jan 11
6 months.	Feb. 7	Feb. 8	Feb. 9	Feb. 10	Feb. 11
7 months.	Mar. 7	Mar. 8	Mar. 9	Mar. 10	Mar. 11
8 months.	Apr. 7	Apr. 8	Apr. 9	Apr. 10	Apr. 11
9 months.	May 7	May 8	May 9	May 10	May 11
10 months.	June 7	June 8	June 9	June 10	June 11
11 months.	July 7	July 8	July 9	July 10	July 11
12 months.	Aug. 7	Aug. 8	Aug. 9	Aug. 10	Aug. 11

Time.	August 9.	August 10.	August 11.	August 12.	August 13.
5 days.	Aug. 17	Aug. 18	Aug. 19	Aug. 20	Aug. 21
10 days.	Aug. 22	Aug. 23	Aug. 24	Aug. 25	Aug. 26
15 days.	Aug. 27	Aug. 28	Aug. 29	Aug. 30	Aug. 31
20 days.	Sep. 1	Sep. 2	Sep. 3	Sep. 4	Sep. 5
25 days.	Sep. 6	Sep. 7	Sep. 8	Sep. 9	Sep. 10
30 days.	Sep. 11	Sep. 12	Sep. 13	Sep. 14	Sep. 15
35 days.	Sep. 16	Sep. 17	Sep. 18	Sep. 19	Sep. 20
40 days.	Sep. 21	Sep. 22	Sep. 23	Sep. 24	Sep. 25
45 days.	Sep. 26	Sep. 27	Sep. 28	Sep. 29	Sep. 30
50 days.	Oct. 1	Oct. 2	Oct. 3	Oct. 4	Oct. 5
55 days.	Oct. 6	Oct. 7	Oct. 8	Oct. 9	Oct. 10
60 days.	Oct. 11	Oct. 12	Oct. 13	Oct. 14	Oct. 15
65 days.	Oct. 16	Oct. 17	Oct. 18	Oct. 19	Oct. 20
70 days.	Oct. 21	Oct. 22	Oct. 23	Oct. 24	Oct. 25
75 days.	Oct. 26	Oct. 27	Oct. 28	Oct. 29	Oct. 30
80 days.	Oct. 31	Nov. 1	Nov. 2	Nov. 3	Nov. 4
85 days.	Nov. 5	Nov. 6	Nov. 7	Nov. 8	Nov. 9
90 days.	Nov. 10	Nov. 11	Nov. 12	Nov. 13	Nov. 14
95 days.	Nov. 15	Nov. 16	Nov. 17	Nov. 18	Nov. 19
100 days.	Nov. 20	Nov. 21	Nov. 22	Nov. 23	Nov. 24
1 month.	Sep. 12	Sep. 13	Sep. 14	Sep. 15	Sep. 16
2 months.	Oct. 12	Oct. 13	Oct. 14	Oct. 15	Oct. 16
3 months.	Nov. 12	Nov. 13	Nov. 14	Nov. 15	Nov. 16
4 months.	Dec. 12	Dec. 13	Dec. 14	Dec. 15	Dec. 16
5 months.	Jan. 12	Jan. 13	Jan. 14	Jan. 15	Jan 16
6 months.	Feb. 12	Feb. 13	Feb. 14	Feb. 15	Feb. 16
7 months.	Mar. 12	Mar. 13	Mar. 14	Mar. 15	Mar. 16
8 months.	Apr. 12	Apr. 13	Apr. 14	Apr. 15	Apr. 16
9 months.	May 12	May 13	May 14	May 15	May 16
10 months.	June 12	June 13	June 14	June 15	June 16
11 months.	July 12	July 13	July 14	July 15	July 16
12 months.	Aug. 12	Aug. 13	Aug. 14	Aug. 15	Aug. 16

Time.	August 14.	August 15.	August 16.	August 17.	August 18.
5 days.	Aug. 22	Aug. 23	Aug. 24	Aug. 25	Aug. 26
10 days.	Aug. 27	Aug. 28	Aug. 29	Aug. 30	Aug. 31
15 days.	Sep. 1	Sep. 2	Sep. 3	Sep. 4	Sep. 5
20 days.	Sep. 6	Sep. 7	Sep. 8	Sep. 9	Sep. 10
25 days.	Sep. 11	Sep. 12	Sep. 13	Sep. 14	Sep. 15
30 days.	Sep. 16	Sep. 17	Sep. 18	Sep. 19	Sep. 20
35 days.	Sep. 21	Sep. 22	Sep. 23	Sep. 24	Sep. 25
40 days.	Sep. 26	Sep. 27	Sep. 28	Sep. 29	Sep. 30
45 days.	Oct. 1	Oct. 2	Oct. 3	Oct. 4	Oct. 5
50 days.	Oct. 6	Oct. 7	Oct. 8	Oct. 9	Oct. 10
55 days.	Oct. 11	Oct. 12	Oct. 13	Oct. 14	Oct. 15
60 days.	Oct. 16	Oct. 17	Oct. 18	Oct. 19	Oct. 20
65 days.	Oct. 21	Oct. 22	Oct. 23	Oct. 24	Oct. 25
70 days.	Oct. 26	Oct. 27	Oct. 28	Oct. 29	Oct. 30
75 days.	Oct. 31	Nov. 1	Nov. 2	Nov. 3	Nov. 4
80 days.	Nov. 5	Nov. 6	Nov. 7	Nov. 8	Nov. 9
85 days.	Nov. 10	Nov. 11	Nov. 12	Nov. 13	Nov. 14
90 days.	Nov. 15	Nov. 16	Nov. 17	Nov. 18	Nov. 19
95 days.	Nov. 20	Nov. 21	Nov. 22	Nov. 23	Nov. 24
100 days.	Nov. 25	Nov. 26	Nov. 27	Nov. 28	Nov. 29
1 month.	Sep. 17	Sep. 18	Sep. 19	Sep. 20	Sep. 21
2 months.	Oct. 17	Oct. 18	Oct. 19	Oct. 20	Oct. 21
3 months.	Nov. 17	Nov. 18	Nov. 19	Nov. 20	Nov. 21
4 months.	Dec. 17	Dec. 18	Dec. 19	Dec. 20	Dec. 21
5 months.	Jan. 17	Jan. 18	Jan. 19	Jan. 20	Jan 21
6 months.	Feb. 17	Feb. 18	Feb. 19	Feb. 20	Feb. 21
7 months.	Mar. 17	Mar. 18	Mar. 19	Mar. 20	Mar. 21
8 months.	Apr. 17	Apr. 18	Apr. 19	Apr. 20	Apr. 21
9 months.	May 17	May 18	May 19	May 20	May 21
10 months.	June 17	June 18	June 19	June 20	June 21
11 months.	July 17	July 18	July 19	July 20	July 21
12 months.	Aug. 17	Aug. 18	Aug. 19	Aug 20	Aug. 21

Time.	August 19.	August 20.	August 21.	August 22.	August 23.
5 days.	Aug. 27	Aug. 28	Aug. 29	Aug. 30	Aug. 31
10 days.	Sep. 1	Sep. 2	Sep. 3	Sep. 4	Sep. 5
15 days.	Sep. 6	Sep. 7	Sep. 8	Sep. 9	Sep. 10
20 days.	Sep. 11	Sep. 12	Sep. 13	Sep. 14	Sep. 15
25 days.	Sep. 16	Sep. 17	Sep. 18	Sep. 19	Sep. 20
30 days.	Sep. 21	Sep. 22	Sep. 23	Sep. 24	Sep. 25
35 days.	Sep. 26	Sep. 27	Sep. 28	Sep. 29	Sep. 30
40 days.	Oct. 1	Oct. 2	Oct. 3	Oct. 4	Oct. 5
45 days.	Oct. 6	Oct. 7	Oct. 8	Oct. 9	Oct. 10
50 days.	Oct. 11	Oct. 12	Oct. 13	Oct. 14	Oct. 15
55 days.	Oct. 16	Oct. 17	Oct. 18	Oct. 19	Oct. 20
60 days.	Oct. 21	Oct. 22	Oct. 23	Oct. 24	Oct. 25
65 days.	Oct. 26	Oct. 27	Oct. 28	Oct. 29	Oct. 30
70 days.	Oct. 31	Nov. 1	Nov. 2	Nov. 3	Nov. 4
75 days.	Nov. 5	Nov. 6	Nov. 7	Nov. 8	Nov. 9
80 days.	Nov. 10	Nov. 11	Nov. 12	Nov. 13	Nov. 14
85 days.	Nov. 15	Nov. 16	Nov. 17	Nov. 18	Nov. 19
90 days.	Nov. 20	Nov. 21	Nov. 22	Nov. 23	Nov. 24
95 days.	Nov. 25	Nov. 26	Nov. 27	Nov. 28	Nov. 29
100 days.	Nov. 30	Dec. 1	Dec. 2	Dec. 3	Dec. 4
1 month.	Sep. 22	Sep. 23	Sep. 24	Sep. 25	Sep. 26
2 months.	Oct. 22	Oct. 23	Oct. 24	Oct. 25	Oct. 26
3 months.	Nov. 22	Nov. 23	Nov. 24	Nov. 25	Nov. 26
4 months.	Dec. 22	Dec. 23	Dec. 24	Dec. 25	Dec. 26
5 months.	Jan. 22	Jan. 23	Jan. 24	Jan. 25	Jan. 26
6 months.	Feb. 22	Feb. 23	Feb. 24	Feb. 25	Feb. 26
7 months.	Mar. 22	Mar. 23	Mar. 24	Mar. 25	Mar. 26
8 months.	Apr. 22	Apr. 23	Apr. 24	Apr. 25	Apr. 26
9 months.	May 22	May 23	May 24	May 25	May 26
10 months.	June 22	June 23	June 24	June 25	June 26
11 months.	July 22	July 23	July 24	July 25	July 26
12 months.	Aug. 22	Aug. 23	Aug. 24	Aug. 25	Aug. 26

Time.	August 24.	August 25.	August 26.	August 27.	August 28.
5 days.	Sep. 1	Sep. 2	Sep. 3	Sep. 4	Sep. 5
10 days.	Sep. 6	Sep. 7	Sep. 8	Sep. 9	Sep. 10
15 days.	Sep. 11	Sep. 12	Sep. 13	Sep. 14	Sep. 15
20 days.	Sep. 16	Sep. 17	Sep. 18	Sep. 19	Sep. 20
25 days.	Sep. 21	Sep. 22	Sep. 23	Sep. 24	Sep. 25
30 days.	Sep. 26	Sep. 27	Sep. 28	Sep. 29	Sep. 30
35 days.	Oct. 1	Oct. 2	Oct. 3	Oct. 4	Oct. 5
40 days.	Oct. 6	Oct. 7	Oct. 8	Oct. 9	Oct. 10
45 days.	Oct. 11	Oct. 12	Oct. 13	Oct. 14	Oct. 15
50 days.	Oct. 16	Oct. 17	Oct. 18	Oct. 19	Oct. 20
55 days.	Oct. 21	Oct. 22	Oct. 23	Oct. 24	Oct. 25
60 days.	Oct. 26	Oct. 27	Oct. 28	Oct. 29	Oct. 30
65 days.	Oct. 31	Nov. 1	Nov. 2	Nov. 3	Nov. 4
70 days.	Nov. 5	Nov. 6	Nov. 7	Nov. 8	Nov. 9
75 days.	Nov. 10	Nov. 11	Nov. 12	Nov. 13	Nov. 14
80 days.	Nov. 15	Nov. 16	Nov. 17	Nov. 18	Nov. 19
85 days.	Nov. 20	Nov. 21	Nov. 22	Nov. 23	Nov. 24
90 days.	Nov. 25	Nov. 26	Nov. 27	Nov. 28	Nov. 29
95 days.	Nov. 30	Dec. 1	Dec. 2	Dec. 3	Dec. 4
100 days.	Dec. 5	Dec. 6	Dec. 7	Dec. 8	Dec. 9
1 month.	Sep. 27	Sep. 28	Sep. 29	Sep. 30	Oct. 1
2 months.	Oct. 27	Oct. 28	Oct. 29	Oct. 30	Oct. 31
3 months.	Nov. 27	Nov. 28	Nov. 29	Nov. 30	Dec. 1
4 months.	Dec. 27	Dec. 28	Dec. 29	Dec. 30	Dec. 31
5 months.	Jan. 27	Jan. 28	Jan. 29	Jan. 30	Jan 31
6 months.	Feb. 27	Feb. 28	Mar. 1	Mar. 2	Ma 3
*6 mo's, L.Y.	Feb. 27	Feb. 28	Feb. 29	Mar. 1	Mar. 2
7 months.	Mar. 27	Mar. 28	Mar. 29	Mar. 30	Mar. 31
8 months.	Apr. 27	Apr. 28	Apr. 29	Apr. 30	May 1
9 months.	May 27	May 28	May 29	May 30	May 31
10 months.	June 27	June 28	June 29	June 30	July 1
11 months.	July 27	July 28	July 29	July 30	July 31
12 months.	Aug. 27	Aug. 28	Aug. 29	Aug. 30	Aug. 31

* Use this line for notes maturing in Leap-Year.

Time.	August 29.	August 30.	August 31.	Sept'r 1.	Sept'r 2.
5 days.	Sep. 6	Sep. 7	Sep. 8	Sep. 9	Sep. 10
10 days.	Sep. 11	Sep. 12	Sep. 13	Sep. 14	Sep. 15
15 days.	Sep. 16	Sep. 17	Sep. 18	Sep. 19	Sep. 20
20 days.	Sep. 21	Sep. 22	Sep. 23	Sep. 24	Sep. 25
25 days.	Sep. 26	Sep. 27	Sep. 28	Sep. 29	Sep. 30
30 days.	Oct. 1	Oct. 2	Oct. 3	Oct. 4	Oct. 5
35 days.	Oct. 6	Oct. 7	Oct. 8	Oct. 9	Oct. 10
40 days.	Oct. 11	Oct. 12	Oct. 13	Oct. 14	Oct. 15
45 days.	Oct. 16	Oct. 17	Oct. 18	Oct. 19	Oct. 20
50 days.	Oct. 21	Oct. 22	Oct. 23	Oct. 24	Oct. 25
55 days.	Oct. 26	Oct. 27	Oct. 28	Oct. 29	Oct. 30
60 days.	Oct. 31	Nov. 1	Nov. 2	Nov. 3	Nov. 4
65 days.	Nov. 5	Nov. 6	Nov. 7	Nov. 8	Nov. 9
70 days.	Nov. 10	Nov. 11	Nov. 12	Nov. 13	Nov. 14
75 days.	Nov. 15	Nov. 16	Nov. 17	Nov. 18	Nov. 19
80 days.	Nov. 20	Nov. 21	Nov. 22	Nov. 23	Nov. 24
85 days.	Nov. 25	Nov. 26	Nov. 27	Nov. 28	Nov. 29
90 days.	Nov. 30	Dec. 1	Dec. 2	Dec. 3	Dec. 4
95 days.	Dec. 5	Dec. 6	Dec. 7	Dec. 8	Dec. 9
100 days.	Dec. 10	Dec. 11	Dec. 12	Dec. 13	Dec. 14
1 month.	Oct. 2	Oct. 3	Oct. 3	Oct. 4	Oct. 5
2 months.	Nov. 1	Nov. 2	Nov. 3	Nov. 4	Nov. 5
3 months.	Dec. 2	Dec. 3	Dec. 3	Dec. 4	Dec. 5
4 months.	Jan. 1	Jan. 2	Jan. 3	Jan. 4	Jan. 5
5 months.	Feb. 1	Feb. 2	Feb. 3	Feb. 4	Feb. 5
6 months.	Mar. 3	Mar. 3	Mar. 3	Mar. 4	Mar. 5
7 months.	Apr. 1	Apr. 2	Apr. 3	Apr. 4	Apr. 5
8 months.	May 2	May 3	May 3	May 4	May 5
9 months.	Jun. 1	Jun. 2	Jun. 3	Jun. 4	Jun. 5
10 months.	Jul. 2	Jul. 3	Jul. 3	Jul. 4	Jul. 5
11 months.	Aug. 1	Aug. 2	Aug. 3	Aug 4	Aug. 5
12 months.	Sep. 1	Sep. 2	Sep. 3	Sep. 4	Sep. 5

Time.	Sept'r 3.	Sept'r 4.	Sept'r 5.	Sept'r 6.	Sept'r 7.
5 days.	Sep. 11	Sep. 12	Sep. 13	Sep. 14	Sep. 15
10 days.	Sep. 16	Sep. 17	Sep. 18	Sep. 19	Sep. 20
15 days.	Sep. 21	Sep. 22	Sep. 23	Sep. 24	Sep. 25
20 days.	Sep. 26	Sep. 27	Sep. 28	Sep. 29	Sep. 30
25 days.	Oct. 1	Oct. 2	Oct. 3	Oct. 4	Oct. 5
30 days.	Oct. 6	Oct. 7	Oct. 8	Oct. 9	Oct. 10
35 days.	Oct. 11	Oct. 12	Oct. 13	Oct. 14	Oct. 15
40 days.	Oct. 16	Oct. 17	Oct. 18	Oct. 19	Oct. 20
45 days.	Oct. 21	Oct. 22	Oct. 23	Oct. 24	Oct. 25
50 days.	Oct. 26	Oct. 27	Oct. 28	Oct. 29	Oct. 30
55 days.	Oct. 31	Nov. 1	Nov. 2	Nov. 3	Nov. 4
60 days.	Nov. 5	Nov. 6	Nov. 7	Nov. 8	Nov. 9
65 days.	Nov. 10	Nov. 11	Nov. 12	Nov. 13	Nov. 14
70 days.	Nov. 15	Nov. 16	Nov. 17	Nov. 18	Nov. 19
75 days.	Nov. 20	Nov. 21	Nov. 22	Nov. 23	Nov. 24
80 days.	Nov. 25	Nov. 26	Nov. 27	Nov. 28	Nov. 29
85 days.	Nov. 30	Dec. 1	Dec. 2	Dec. 3	Dec. 4
90 days.	Dec. 5	Dec. 6	Dec. 7	Dec. 8	Dec. 9
95 days.	Dec. 10	Dec. 11	Dec. 12	Dec. 13	Dec. 14
100 days.	Dec. 15	Dec. 16	Dec. 17	Dec. 18	Dec. 19
1 month.	Oct. 6	Oct. 7	Oct. 8	Oct. 9	Oct. 10
2 months.	Nov. 6	Nov. 7	Nov. 8	Nov. 9	Nov. 10
3 months.	Dec. 6	Dec. 7	Dec. 8	Dec. 9	Dec. 10
4 months.	Jan. 6	Jan. 7	Jan. 8	Jan. 9	Jan. 10
5 months.	Feb. 6	Feb. 7	Feb. 8	Feb. 9	Feb. 10
6 months.	Mar. 6	Mar. 7	Mar. 8	Mar. 9	Mar. 10
7 months.	Apr. 6	Apr. 7	Apr. 8	Apr. 9	Apr. 10
8 months.	May 6	May 7	May 8	May 9	May 10
9 months.	Jun 6	Jun. 7	Jun. 8	Jun. 9	Jun. 10
10 months.	Jul. 6	Jul. 7	Jul. 8	Jul. 9	Jul. 10
11 months.	Aug. 6	Aug. 7	Aug. 8	Aug. 9	Aug. 10
12 months.	Sep. 6	Sep. 7	Sep. 8	Sep. 9	Sep. 10

Time.	Sept'r 8.	Sept'r 9.	Sept'r 10.	Sept'r 11.	Sept'r 12.
5 days.	Sep. 16	Sep. 17	Sep. 18	Sep. 19	Sep. 20
10 days.	Sep. 21	Sep. 22	Sep. 23	Sep. 24	Sep. 25
15 days.	Sep. 26	Sep. 27	Sep. 28	Sep. 29	Sep. 30
20 days.	Oct. 1	Oct. 2	Oct. 3	Oct. 4	Oct. 5
25 days.	Oct. 6	Oct. 7	Oct. 8	Oct. 9	Oct. 10
30 days.	Oct. 11	Oct. 12	Oct. 13	Oct. 14	Oct. 15
35 days.	Oct. 16	Oct. 17	Oct. 18	Oct. 19	Oct. 20
40 days.	Oct. 21	Oct. 22	Oct. 23	Oct. 24	Oct. 25
45 days.	Oct. 26	Oct. 27	Oct. 28	Oct. 29	Oct. 30
50 days.	Oct. 31	Nov. 1	Nov. 2	Nov. 3	Nov. 4
55 days.	Nov. 5	Nov. 6	Nov. 7	Nov. 8	Nov. 9
60 days.	Nov. 10	Nov. 11	Nov. 12	Nov. 13	Nov. 14
65 days.	Nov. 15	Nov. 16	Nov. 17	Nov. 18	Nov. 19
70 days.	Nov. 20	Nov. 21	Nov. 22	Nov. 23	Nov. 24
75 days.	Nov. 25	Nov. 26	Nov. 27	Nov. 28	Nov. 29
80 days.	Nov. 30	Dec. 1	Dec. 2	Dec. 3	Dec. 4
85 days.	Dec. 5	Dec. 6	Dec. 7	Dec. 8	Dec. 9
90 days.	Dec. 10	Dec. 11	Dec. 12	Dec. 13	Dec. 14
95 days.	Dec. 15	Dec. 16	Dec. 17	Dec. 18	Dec. 19
100 days.	Dec. 20	Dec. 21	Dec. 22	Dec. 23	Dec. 24
1 month.	Oct. 11	Oct. 12	Oct. 13	Oct. 14	Oct. 15
2 months.	Nov. 11	Nov. 12	Nov. 13	Nov. 14	Nov. 15
3 months.	Dec. 11	Dec. 12	Dec. 13	Dec. 14	Dec. 15
4 months.	Jan. 11	Jan. 12	Jan. 13	Jan. 14	Jan. 15
5 months.	Feb. 11	Feb. 12	Feb. 13	Feb. 14	Feb. 15
6 months.	Mar. 11	Mar. 12	Mar. 13	Mar. 14	Mar. 15
7 months.	Apr. 11	Apr. 12	Apr. 13	Apr. 14	Apr. 15
8 months.	May 11	May 12	May 13	May 14	May 15
9 months.	Jun. 11	Jun. 12	Jun. 13	Jun. 14	Jun. 15
10 months.	Jul. 11	Jul. 12	Jul. 13	Jul. 14	Jul. 15
11 months.	Aug. 11	Aug. 12	Aug. 13	Aug. 14	Aug. 15
12 months.	Sep. 11	Sep. 12	Sep. 13	Sep. 14	Sep. 15

Time.	Sept'r 13.	Sept'r 14.	Sept'r 15.	Sept'r 16.	Sept'r 17.
5 days.	Sep. 21	Sep. 22	Sep. 23	Sep. 24	Sep. 25
10 days.	Sep. 26	Sep. 27	Sep. 28	Sep. 29	Sep. 30
15 days.	Oct. 1	Oct. 2	Oct. 3	Oct. 4	Oct. 5
20 days.	Oct. 6	Oct. 7	Oct. 8	Oct. 9	Oct. 10
25 days.	Oct. 11	Oct. 12	Oct. 13	Oct. 14	Oct. 15
30 days.	Oct. 16	Oct. 17	Oct. 18	Oct. 19	Oct. 20
35 days.	Oct. 21	Oct. 22	Oct. 23	Oct. 24	Oct. 25
40 days.	Oct. 26	Oct. 27	Oct. 28	Oct. 29	Oct. 30
45 days.	Oct. 31	Nov. 1	Nov. 2	Nov. 3	Nov. 4
50 days.	Nov. 5	Nov. 6	Nov. 7	Nov. 8	Nov. 9
55 days.	Nov. 10	Nov. 11	Nov. 12	Nov. 13	Nov. 14
60 days.	Nov. 15	Nov. 16	Nov. 17	Nov. 18	Nov. 19
65 days.	Nov. 20	Nov. 21	Nov. 22	Nov. 23	Nov. 24
70 days.	Nov. 25	Nov. 26	Nov. 27	Nov. 28	Nov. 29
75 days.	Nov. 30	Dec. 1	Dec. 2	Dec. 3	Dec. 4
80 days.	Dec. 5	Dec. 6	Dec. 7	Dec. 8	Dec. 9
85 days.	Dec. 10	Dec. 11	Dec. 12	Dec. 13	Dec. 14
90 days.	Dec. 15	Dec. 16	Dec. 17	Dec. 18	Dec. 19
95 days.	Dec. 20	Dec. 21	Dec. 22	Dec. 23	Dec. 24
100 days.	Dec. 25	Dec. 26	Dec. 27	Dec. 28	Dec. 29
1 month.	Oct. 16	Oct. 17	Oct. 18	Oct. 19	Oct. 20
2 months.	Nov. 16	Nov. 17	Nov. 18	Nov. 19	Nov. 20
3 months.	Dec. 16	Dec. 17	Dec. 18	Dec. 19	Dec. 20
4 months.	Jan. 16	Jan. 17	Jan. 18	Jan. 19	Jan. 20
5 months.	Feb. 16	Feb. 17	Feb. 18	Feb. 19	Feb. 20
6 months.	Mar. 16	Mar. 17	Mar. 18	Mar. 19	Mar. 20
7 months.	Apr. 16	Apr. 17	Apr. 18	Apr. 19	Apr. 20
8 months.	May 16	May 17	May 18	May 19	May 20
9 months.	Jun. 16	Jun. 17	Jun. 18	Jun. 19	Jun. 20
10 months.	Jul. 16	Jul. 17	Jul. 18	Jul. 19	Jul. 20
11 months.	Aug. 16	Aug. 17	Aug. 18	Aug. 19	Aug. 20
12 months.	Sep. 16	Sep. 17	Sep. 18	Sep. 19	Sep. 20

Time.	Sept'r 18.	Sept'r 19.	Sept'r 20.	Sept'r 21.	Sept'r 22.
5 days.	Sep. 26	Sep. 27	Sep. 28	Sep. 29	Sep. 30
10 days.	Oct. 1	Oct. 2	Oct. 3	Oct. 4	Oct. 5
15 days.	Oct. 6	Oct. 7	Oct. 8	Oct. 9	Oct. 10
20 days.	Oct. 11	Oct. 12	Oct. 13	Oct. 14	Oct. 15
25 days.	Oct. 16	Oct. 17	Oct. 18	Oct. 19	Oct. 20
30 days.	Oct. 21	Oct. 22	Oct. 23	Oct. 24	Oct. 25
35 days.	Oct. 26	Oct. 27	Oct. 28	Oct. 29	Oct. 30
40 days.	Oct. 31	Nov. 1	Nov. 2	Nov. 3	Nov. 4
45 days.	Nov. 5	Nov. 6	Nov. 7	Nov. 8	Nov. 9
50 days.	Nov. 10	Nov. 11	Nov. 12	Nov. 13	Nov. 14
55 days.	Nov. 15	Nov. 16	Nov. 17	Nov. 18	Nov. 19
60 days.	Nov. 20	Nov. 21	Nov. 22	Nov. 23	Nov. 24
65 days.	Nov. 25	Nov. 26	Nov. 27	Nov. 28	Nov. 29
70 days.	Nov. 30	Dec. 1	Dec. 2	Dec. 3	Dec. 4
75 days.	Dec. 5	Dec. 6	Dec. 7	Dec. 8	Dec. 9
80 days.	Dec. 10	Dec. 11	Dec. 12	Dec. 13	Dec. 14
85 days.	Dec. 15	Dec. 16	Dec. 17	Dec. 18	Dec. 19
90 days.	Dec. 20	Dec. 21	Dec. 22	Dec. 23	Dec. 24
95 days.	Dec. 25	Dec. 26	Dec. 27	Dec. 28	Dec. 29
100 days.	Dec. 30	Dec. 31	Jan. 1	Jan. 2	Jan. 3
1 month.	Oct. 21	Oct. 22	Oct. 23	Oct. 24	Oct. 25
2 months.	Nov. 21	Nov. 22	Nov. 23	Nov. 24	Nov. 25
3 months.	Dec. 21	Dec. 22	Dec. 23	Dec. 24	Dec. 25
4 months.	Jan. 21	Jan. 22	Jan. 23	Jan. 24	Jan. 25
5 months.	Feb. 21	Feb. 22	Feb. 23	Feb. 24	Feb. 25
6 months.	Mar. 21	Mar. 22	Mar. 23	Mar. 24	Mar. 25
7 months.	Apr. 21	Apr. 22	Apr. 23	Apr. 24	Apr. 25
8 months.	May 21	May 22	May 23	May 24	May 25
9 months.	Jun. 21	Jun. 22	Jun. 23	Jun. 24	Jun. 25
10 months.	Jul. 21	Jul. 22	Jul. 23	Jul. 24	Jul. 25
11 months.	Aug. 21	Aug. 22	Aug. 23	Aug. 24	Aug. 25
12 months.	Sep. 21	Sep. 22	Sep. 23	Sep. 24	Sep. 25

Time.	Sept'r 23.	Sept'r 24.	Sept'r 25.	Sept'r 26.	Sept'r 27.
5 days.	Oct. 1	Oct. 2	Oct. 3	Oct. 4	Oct. 5
10 days.	Oct. 6	Oct. 7	Oct. 8	Oct. 9	Oct. 10
15 days.	Oct. 11	Oct. 12	Oct. 13	Oct. 14	Oct. 15
20 days.	Oct. 16	Oct. 17	Oct. 18	Oct. 19	Oct. 20
25 days.	Oct. 21	Oct. 22	Oct. 23	Oct. 24	Oct. 25
30 days.	Oct. 26	Oct. 27	Oct. 28	Oct. 29	Oct. 30
35 days.	Oct. 31	Nov. 1	Nov. 2	Nov. 3	Nov. 4
40 days.	Nov. 5	Nov. 6	Nov. 7	Nov. 8	Nov. 9
45 days.	Nov. 10	Nov. 11	Nov. 12	Nov. 13	Nov. 14
50 days.	Nov. 15	Nov. 16	Nov. 17	Nov. 18	Nov. 19
55 days.	Nov. 20	Nov. 21	Nov. 22	Nov. 23	Nov. 24
60 days.	Nov. 25	Nov. 26	Nov. 27	Nov. 28	Nov. 29
65 days.	Nov. 30	Dec. 1	Dec. 2	Dec. 3	Dec. 4
70 days.	Dec. 5	Dec. 6	Dec. 7	Dec. 8	Dec. 9
75 days.	Dec. 10	Dec. 11	Dec. 12	Dec. 13	Dec. 14
80 days.	Dec. 15	Dec. 16	Dec. 17	Dec. 18	Dec. 19
85 days.	Dec. 20	Dec. 21	Dec. 22	Dec. 23	Dec. 24
90 days.	Dec. 25	Dec. 26	Dec. 27	Dec. 28	Dec. 29
95 days.	Dec. 30	Dec. 31	Jan. 1	Jan. 2	Jan. 3
100 days.	Jan. 4	Jan. 5	Jan. 6	Jan. 7	Jan. 8
1 month.	Oct. 26	Oct. 27	Oct. 28	Oct. 29	Oct. 30
2 months.	Nov. 26	Nov. 27	Nov. 28	Nov. 29	Nov. 30
3 months.	Dec. 26	Dec. 27	Dec. 28	Dec. 29	Dec. 30
4 months.	Jan. 26	Jan. 27	Jan. 28	Jan. 29	Jan. 30
5 months.	Feb. 26	Feb. 27	Feb. 28	Mar. 1	Mar. 2
*5 mo's, L.Y.	Feb. 26	Feb. 27	Feb. 28	Feb. 29	Mar. 1
6 months.	Mar. 26	Mar. 27	Mar. 28	Mar. 29	Mar. 30
7 months.	Apr. 26	Apr. 27	Apr. 28	Apr. 29	Apr. 30
8 months.	May 26	May 27	May 28	May 29	May 30
9 months.	Jun. 26	Jun. 27	Jun. 28	Jun. 29	Jun. 30
10 months.	Jul. 26	Jul. 27	Jul. 28	Jul. 29	Jul. 30
11 months.	Aug. 26	Aug. 27	Aug. 28	Aug. 29	Aug. 30
12 months.	Sep. 26	Sep. 27	Sep. 28	Sep. 29	Sep. 30

* Use this line for notes maturing in Leap Year.

Time.	Sept'r 28.	Sept'r 29.	Sept'r 30.	Oct'r 1.	Oct'r 2.
5 days.	Oct. 6	Oct. 7	Oct. 8	Oct. 9	Oct. 10
10 days.	Oct. 11	Oct. 12	Oct. 13	Oct. 14	Oct. 15
15 days.	Oct. 16	Oct. 17	Oct. 18	Oct. 19	Oct. 20
20 days.	Oct. 21	Oct. 22	Oct. 23	Oct. 24	Oct. 25
25 days.	Oct. 26	Oct. 27	Oct. 28	Oct. 29	Oct. 30
30 days.	Oct. 31	Nov. 1	Nov. 2	Nov. 3	Nov. 4
35 days.	Nov. 5	Nov. 6	Nov. 7	Nov. 8	Nov. 9
40 days.	Nov. 10	Nov. 11	Nov. 12	Nov. 13	Nov. 14
45 days.	Nov. 15	Nov. 16	Nov. 17	Nov. 18	Nov. 19
50 days.	Nov. 20	Nov. 21	Nov. 22	Nov. 23	Nov. 24
55 days.	Nov. 25	Nov. 26	Nov. 27	Nov. 28	Nov. 29
60 days.	Nov. 30	Dec. 1	Dec. 2	Dec. 3	Dec. 4
65 days.	Dec. 5	Dec. 6	Dec. 7	Dec. 8	Dec. 9
70 days.	Dec. 10	Dec. 11	Dec. 12	Dec. 13	Dec. 14
75 days.	Dec. 15	Dec. 16	Dec. 17	Dec. 18	Dec. 19
80 days.	Dec. 20	Dec. 21	Dec. 22	Dec. 23	Dec. 24
85 days.	Dec. 25	Dec. 26	Dec. 27	Dec. 28	Dec. 29
90 days.	Dec. 30	Dec. 31	Jan. 1	Jan. 2	Jan. 3
95 days.	Jan. 4	Jan. 5	Jan. 6	Jan. 7	Jan. 8
100 days.	Jan. 9	Jan. 10	Jan. 11	Jan. 12	Jan. 13
1 month.	Oct. 31	Nov. 1	Nov. 2	Nov. 4	Nov. 5
2 months.	Dec. 1	Dec. 2	Dec. 3	Dec. 4	Dec. 5
3 months.	Dec. 31	Jan. 1	Jan. 2	Jan. 4	Jan. 5
4 months.	Jan. 31	Feb. 1	Feb. 2	Feb. 4	Feb. 5
5 months.	Mar. 3	Mar. 3	Mar. 3	Mar. 4	Mar. 5
*5 mo's, L.Y.	Mar. 2				
6 months.	Mar. 31	Apr. 1	Apr. 2	Apr. 4	Apr. 5
7 months.	May 1	May 2	May 3	May 4	May 5
8 months.	May 31	Jun. 1	Jun. 2	Jun. 4	Jun. 5
9 months.	July 1	Jul. 2	Jul. 3	Jul. 4	Jul. 5
10 months.	Jul. 31	Aug. 1	Aug. 2	Aug. 4	Aug. 5
11 months.	Aug. 31	Sep. 1	Sep. 2	Sep. 4	Sep. 5
12 months.	Oct. 1	Oct. 2	Oct. 3	Oct. 4	Oct. 5

* Use this line for notes maturing in Leap Year.

Time.	Oct'r 3.	Oct'r 4.	Oct'r 5.	Oct'r 6.	Oct'r 7.
5 days.	Oct. 11	Oct. 12	Oct. 13	Oct. 14	Oct. 15
10 days.	Oct. 16	Oct. 17	Oct. 18	Oct. 19	Oct. 20
15 days.	Oct. 21	Oct. 22	Oct. 23	Oct. 24	Oct. 25
20 days.	Oct. 26	Oct. 27	Oct. 28	Oct. 29	Oct. 30
25 days.	Oct. 31	Nov. 1	Nov. 2	Nov. 3	Nov. 4
30 days.	Nov. 5	Nov. 6	Nov. 7	Nov. 8	Nov. 9
35 days.	Nov. 10	Nov. 11	Nov. 12	Nov. 13	Nov. 14
40 days.	Nov. 15	Nov. 16	Nov. 17	Nov. 18	Nov. 19
45 days.	Nov. 20	Nov. 21	Nov. 22	Nov. 23	Nov. 24
50 days.	Nov. 25	Nov. 26	Nov. 27	Nov. 28	Nov. 29
55 days.	Nov. 30	Dec. 1	Dec. 2	Dec. 3	Dec. 4
60 days.	Dec. 5	Dec. 6	Dec. 7	Dec. 8	Dec. 9
65 days.	Dec. 10	Dec. 11	Dec. 12	Dec. 13	Dec. 14
70 days.	Dec. 15	Dec. 16	Dec. 17	Dec. 18	Dec. 19
75 days.	Dec. 20	Dec. 21	Dec. 22	Dec. 23	Dec. 24
80 days.	Dec. 25	Dec. 26	Dec. 27	Dec. 28	Dec. 29
85 days.	Dec. 30	Dec. 31	Jan. 1	Jan. 2	Jan. 3
90 days.	Jan. 4	Jan. 5	Jan. 6	Jan. 7	Jan. 8
95 days.	Jan. 9	Jan. 10	Jan. 11	Jan. 12	Jan. 13
100 days.	Jan. 14	Jan. 15	Jan. 16	Jan. 17	Jan. 18
1 month.	Nov. 6	Nov. 7	Nov. 8	Nov. 9	Nov. 10
2 months.	Dec. 6	Dec. 7	Dec. 8	Dec. 9	Dec. 10
3 months.	Jan. 6	Jan. 7	Jan. 8	Jan. 9	Jan. 10
4 months.	Feb. 6	Feb. 7	Feb. 8	Feb. 9	Feb. 10
5 months.	Mar. 6	Mar. 7	Mar. 8	Mar. 9	Mar. 10
6 months.	Apr. 6	Apr. 7	Apr. 8	Apr. 9	Apr. 10
7 months.	May 6	May 7	May 8	May 9	May 10
8 months.	Jun. 6	Jun. 7	Jun. 8	Jun. 9	Jun. 10
9 months.	July 6	Jul. 7	Jul. 8	Jul. 9	Jul. 10
10 months.	Aug. 6	Aug. 7	Aug. 8	Aug. 9	Aug. 10
11 months.	Sep. 6	Sep. 7	Sep. 8	Sep. 9	Sep. 10
12 months.	Oct. 6	Oct. 7	Oct. 8	Oct. 9	Oct. 10

Time.	Oct'r 8.	Oct'r 9.	Oct'r 10.	Oct'r 11.	Oct'r 12.
5 days.	Oct. 16	Oct. 17	Oct. 18	Oct. 19	Oct. 20
10 days.	Oct. 21	Oct. 22	Oct. 23	Oct. 24	Oct. 25
15 days.	Oct. 26	Oct. 27	Oct. 28	Oct. 29	Oct. 30
20 days.	Oct. 31	Nov. 1	Nov. 2	Nov. 3	Nov. 4
25 days.	Nov. 5	Nov. 6	Nov. 7	Nov. 8	Nov. 9
30 days.	Nov. 10	Nov. 11	Nov. 12	Nov. 13	Nov. 14
35 days.	Nov. 15	Nov. 16	Nov. 17	Nov. 18	Nov. 19
40 days.	Nov. 20	Nov. 21	Nov. 22	Nov. 23	Nov. 24
45 days.	Nov. 25	Nov. 26	Nov. 27	Nov. 28	Nov. 29
50 days.	Nov. 30	Dec. 1	Dec. 2	Dec. 3	Dec. 4
55 days.	Dec. 5	Dec. 6	Dec. 7	Dec. 8	Dec. 9
60 days.	Dec. 10	Dec. 11	Dec. 12	Dec. 13	Dec. 14
65 days.	Dec. 15	Dec. 16	Dec. 17	Dec. 18	Dec. 19
70 days.	Dec. 20	Dec. 21	Dec. 22	Dec. 23	Dec. 24
75 days.	Dec. 25	Dec. 26	Dec. 27	Dec. 28	Dec. 29
80 days.	Dec. 30	Dec. 31	Jan. 1	Jan. 2	Jan. 3
85 days.	Jan. 4	Jan. 5	Jan. 6	Jan. 7	Jan. 8
90 days.	Jan. 9	Jan. 10	Jan. 11	Jan. 12	Jan. 13
95 days.	Jan. 14	Jan. 15	Jan. 16	Jan. 17	Jan. 18
100 days.	Jan. 19	Jan. 20	Jan. 21	Jan. 22	Jan. 23
1 month.	Nov. 11	Nov. 12	Nov. 13	Nov. 14	Nov. 15
2 months.	Dec. 11	Dec. 12	Dec. 13	Dec. 14	Dec. 15
3 months.	Jan. 11	Jan. 12	Jan. 13	Jan. 14	Jan. 15
4 months.	Feb. 11	Feb. 12	Feb. 13	Feb. 14	Feb. 15
5 months.	Mar. 11	Mar. 12	Mar. 13	Mar. 14	Mar. 15
6 months.	Apr. 11	Apr. 12	Apr. 13	Apr. 14	Apr. 15
7 months.	May 11	May 12	May 13	May 14	May 15
8 months.	Jun. 11	Jun. 12	Jun. 13	Jun. 14	Jun. 15
9 months.	July 11	Jul. 12	Jul. 13	Jul. 14	Jul. 15
10 months.	Aug. 11	Aug. 12	Aug. 13	Aug. 14	Aug. 15
11 months.	Sep. 11	Sep. 12	Sep. 13	Sep. 14	Sep. 15
12 months.	Oct. 11	Oct. 12	Oct. 13	Oct. 14	Oct. 15

Time.	Oct'r 13.	Oct'r 14.	Oct'r 15.	Oct'r 16.	Oct'r 17.
5 days.	Oct. 21	Oct. 22	Oct. 23	Oct. 24	Oct. 25
10 days.	Oct. 26	Oct. 27	Oct. 28	Oct. 29	Oct. 30
15 days.	Oct. 31	Nov. 1	Nov. 2	Nov. 3	Nov. 4
20 days.	Nov. 5	Nov. 6	Nov. 7	Nov. 8	Nov. 9
25 days.	Nov. 10	Nov. 11	Nov. 12	Nov. 13	Nov. 14
30 days.	Nov. 15	Nov. 16	Nov. 17	Nov. 18	Nov. 19
35 days.	Nov. 20	Nov. 21	Nov. 22	Nov. 23	Nov. 24
40 days.	Nov. 25	Nov. 26	Nov. 27	Nov. 28	Nov. 29
45 days.	Nov. 30	Dec. 1	Dec. 2	Dec. 3	Dec. 4
50 days.	Dec. 5	Dec. 6	Dec. 7	Dec. 8	Dec. 9
55 days.	Dec. 10	Dec. 11	Dec. 12	Dec. 13	Dec. 14
60 days.	Dec. 15	Dec. 16	Dec. 17	Dec. 18	Dec. 19
65 days.	Dec. 20	Dec. 21	Dec. 22	Dec. 23	Dec. 24
70 days.	Dec. 25	Dec. 26	Dec. 27	Dec. 28	Dec. 29
75 days.	Dec. 30	Dec. 31	Jan. 1	Jan. 2	Jan. 3
80 days.	Jan. 4	Jan. 5	Jan. 6	Jan. 7	Jan. 8
85 days.	Jan. 9	Jan. 10	Jan. 11	Jan. 12	Jan. 13
90 days.	Jan. 14	Jan. 15	Jan. 16	Jan. 17	Jan. 18
95 days.	Jan. 19	Jan. 20	Jan. 21	Jan. 22	Jan. 23
100 days.	Jan. 24	Jan. 25	Jan. 26	Jan. 27	Jan. 28
1 month.	Nov. 16	Nov. 17	Nov. 18	Nov. 19	Nov. 20
2 months.	Dec. 16	Dec. 17	Dec. 18	Dec. 19	Dec. 20
3 months.	Jan. 16	Jan. 17	Jan. 18	Jan. 19	Jan. 20
4 months.	Feb. 16	Feb. 17	Feb. 18	Feb. 19	Feb. 20
5 months.	Mar. 16	Mar. 17	Mar. 18	Mar. 19	Mar. 20
6 months.	Apr. 16	Apr. 17	Apr. 18	Apr. 19	Apr. 20
7 months.	May 16	May 17	May 18	May 19	May 20
8 months.	Jun. 16	Jun. 17	Jun. 18	Jun. 19	Jun. 20
9 months.	July 16	Jul. 17	Jul. 18	Jul. 19	Jul. 20
10 months.	Aug. 16	Aug. 17	Aug. 18	Aug. 19	Aug. 20
11 months.	Sep. 16	Sep. 17	Sep. 18	Sep. 19	Sep. 20
12 months.	Oct. 16	Oct. 17	Oct. 18	Oct. 19	Oct. 20

Time.	Oct'r 18.	Oct'r 19.	Oct'r 20.	Oct'r 21.	Oct'r 22.
5 days.	Oct. 26	Oct. 27	Oct. 28	Oct. 29	Oct. 30
10 days.	Oct. 31	Nov. 1	Nov. 2	Nov. 3	Nov. 4
15 days.	Nov. 5	Nov. 6	Nov. 7	Nov. 8	Nov. 9
20 days.	Nov. 10	Nov. 11	Nov. 12	Nov. 13	Nov. 14
25 days.	Nov. 15	Nov. 16	Nov. 17	Nov. 18	Nov. 19
30 days.	Nov. 20	Nov. 21	Nov. 22	Nov. 23	Nov. 24
35 days.	Nov. 25	Nov. 26	Nov. 27	Nov. 28	Nov. 29
40 days.	Nov. 30	Dec. 1	Dec. 2	Dec. 3	Dec. 4
45 days.	Dec. 5	Dec. 6	Dec. 7	Dec. 8	Dec. 9
50 days.	Dec. 10	Dec. 11	Dec. 12	Dec. 13	Dec. 14
55 days.	Dec. 15	Dec. 16	Dec. 17	Dec. 18	Dec. 19
60 days.	Dec. 20	Dec. 21	Dec. 22	Dec. 23	Dec. 24
65 days.	Dec. 25	Dec. 26	Dec. 27	Dec. 28	Dec. 29
70 days.	Dec. 30	Dec. 31	Jan. 1	Jan. 2	Jan. 3
75 days.	Jan. 4	Jan. 5	Jan. 6	Jan. 7	Jan. 8
80 days.	Jan. 9	Jan. 10	Jan. 11	Jan. 12	Jan. 13
85 days.	Jan. 14	Jan. 15	Jan. 16	Jan. 17	Jan. 18
90 days.	Jan. 19	Jan. 20	Jan. 21	Jan. 22	Jan. 23
95 days.	Jan. 24	Jan. 25	Jan. 26	Jan. 27	Jan. 28
100 days.	Jan. 29	Jan. 30	Jan. 31	Feb. 1	Feb. 2
1 month.	Nov. 21	Nov. 22	Nov. 23	Nov. 24	Nov. 25
2 months.	Dec. 21	Dec. 22	Dec. 23	Dec. 24	Dec. 25
3 months.	Jan. 21	Jan. 22	Jan. 23	Jan. 24	Jan. 25
4 months.	Feb. 21	Feb. 22	Feb. 23	Feb. 24	Feb. 25
5 months.	Mar. 21	Mar. 22	Mar. 23	Mar. 24	Mar. 25
6 months.	Apr. 21	Apr. 22	Apr. 23	Apr. 24	Apr. 25
7 months.	May 21	May 22	May 23	May 24	May 25
8 months.	Jun. 21	Jun. 22	Jun. 23	Jun. 24	Jun. 25
9 months.	July 21	Jul. 22	Jul. 23	Jul. 24	Jul. 25
10 months.	Aug. 21	Aug. 22	Aug. 23	Aug. 24	Aug. 25
11 months.	Sep. 21	Sep. 22	Sep. 23	Sep. 24	Sep. 25
12 months.	Oct. 21	Oct. 22	Oct. 23	Oct. 24	Oct. 25

Time.	Oct'r 23.	Oct'r 24.	Oct'r 25.	Oct'r 26.	Oct'r 27.
5 days.	Oct. 31	Nov. 1	Nov. 2	Nov. 3	Nov. 4
10 days.	Nov. 5	Nov. 6	Nov. 7	Nov. 8	Nov. 9
15 days.	Nov. 10	Nov. 11	Nov. 12	Nov. 13	Nov. 14
20 days.	Nov. 15	Nov. 16	Nov. 17	Nov. 18	Nov. 19
25 days.	Nov. 20	Nov. 21	Nov. 22	Nov. 23	Nov. 24
30 days.	Nov. 25	Nov. 26	Nov. 27	Nov. 28	Nov. 29
35 days.	Nov. 30	Dec. 1	Dec. 2	Dec. 3	Dec. 4
40 days.	Dec. 5	Dec. 6	Dec. 7	Dec. 8	Dec. 9
45 days.	Dec. 10	Dec. 11	Dec. 12	Dec. 13	Dec. 14
50 days.	Dec. 15	Dec. 16	Dec. 17	Dec. 18	Dec. 19
55 days.	Dec. 20	Dec. 21	Dec. 22	Dec. 23	Dec. 24
60 days.	Dec. 25	Dec. 26	Dec. 27	Dec. 28	Dec. 29
65 days.	Dec. 30	Dec. 31	Jan. 1	Jan. 2	Jan. 3
70 days.	Jan. 4	Jan. 5	Jan. 6	Jan. 7	Jan. 8
75 days.	Jan. 9	Jan. 10	Jan. 11	Jan. 12	Jan. 13
80 days.	Jan. 14	Jan. 15	Jan. 16	Jan. 17	Jan. 18
85 days.	Jan. 19	Jan. 20	Jan. 21	Jan. 22	Jan. 23
90 days.	Jan. 24	Jan. 25	Jan. 26	Jan. 27	Jan. 28
95 days.	Jan. 29	Jan. 30	Jan. 31	Feb. 1	Feb. 2
100 days.	Feb. 3	Feb. 4	Feb. 5	Feb. 6	Feb. 7
1 month.	Nov. 26	Nov. 27	Nov. 28	Nov. 29	Nov. 30
2 months.	Dec. 26	Dec. 27	Dec. 28	Dec. 29	Dec. 30
3 months.	Jan. 26	Jan. 27	Jan. 28	Jan. 29	Jan. 30
4 months.	Feb. 26	Feb. 27	Feb. 28	Mar. 1	Mar. 2
*4 mo's, L.Y.	Feb. 26	Feb. 27	Feb. 28	Feb. 29	Mar. 1
5 months.	Mar. 26	Mar. 27	Mar. 28	Mar. 29	Mar. 30
6 months.	Apr. 26	Apr. 27	Apr. 28	Apr. 29	Apr. 30
7 months.	May 26	May 27	May 28	May 29	May 30
8 months.	Jun. 26	Jun. 27	Jun. 28	Jun. 29	Jun. 30
9 months.	July 26	Jul. 27	Jul. 28	Jul. 29	Jul. 30
10 months.	Aug. 26	Aug. 27	Aug. 28	Aug. 29	Aug. 30
11 months.	Sep. 26	Sep. 27	Sep. 28	Sep. 29	Sep. 30
12 months.	Oct. 26	Oct. 27	Oct. 28	Oct. 29	Oct. 30

*Use this line for notes maturing in Leap Year.

Time.	Oct'r 28.	Oct'r 29.	Oct'r 30.	Oct'r 31.	Nov'r 1.
5 days.	Nov. 5	Nov. 6	Nov. 7	Nov. 8	Nov. 9
10 days.	Nov. 10	Nov. 11	Nov. 12	Nov. 13	Nov. 14
15 days.	Nov. 15	Nov. 16	Nov. 17	Nov. 18	Nov. 19
20 days.	Nov. 20	Nov. 21	Nov. 22	Nov. 23	Nov. 24
25 days.	Nov. 25	Nov. 26	Nov. 27	Nov. 28	Nov. 29
30 days.	Nov. 30	Dec. 1	Dec. 2	Dec. 3	Dec. 4
35 days.	Dec. 5	Dec. 6	Dec. 7	Dec. 8	Dec. 9
40 days.	Dec. 10	Dec. 11	Dec. 12	Dec. 13	Dec. 14
45 days.	Dec. 15	Dec. 16	Dec. 17	Dec. 18	Dec. 19
50 days.	Dec. 20	Dec. 21	Dec. 22	Dec. 23	Dec. 24
55 days.	Dec. 25	Dec. 26	Dec. 27	Dec. 28	Dec. 29
60 days.	Dec. 30	Dec. 31	Jan. 1	Jan. 2	Jan. 3
65 days.	Jan. 4	Jan. 5	Jan. 6	Jan. 7	Jan. 8
70 days.	Jan. 9	Jan. 10	Jan. 11	Jan. 12	Jan. 13
75 days.	Jan. 14	Jan. 15	Jan. 16	Jan. 17	Jan. 18
80 days.	Jan. 19	Jan. 20	Jan. 21	Jan. 22	Jan. 23
85 days.	Jan. 24	Jan. 25	Jan. 26	Jan. 27	Jan. 28
90 days.	Jan. 29	Jan. 30	Jan. 31	Feb. 1	Feb. 2
95 days.	Feb. 3	Feb. 4	Feb. 5	Feb. 6	Feb. 7
100 days.	Feb. 8	Feb. 9	Feb. 10	Feb. 11	Feb. 12
1 month.	Dec. 1	Dec. 2	Dec. 3	Dec. 3	Dec. 4
2 months.	Dec. 31	Jan. 1	Jan. 2	Jan. 3	Jan. 4
3 months.	Jan. 31	Feb. 1	Feb. 2	Feb. 3	Feb. 4
4 months.	Mar. 3	Mar. 3	Mar. 3	Mar. 3	Mar. 4
*4 mo's, I. Y.	Mar. 2	Mar. 3	Mar. 3	Mar. 3	Mar. 4
5 months.	Mar. 31	Apr. 1	Apr. 2	Apr. 3	Apr. 4
6 months.	May 1	May 2	May 3	May 3	May 4
7 months.	May 31	Jun. 1	Jun. 2	Jun. 3	Jun. 4
8 months.	July 1	Jul. 2	Jul. 3	Jul. 3	Jul. 4
9 months.	July 31	Aug. 1	Aug. 2	Aug. 3	Aug. 4
10 months.	Aug. 31	Sep. 1	Sep. 2	Sep. 3	Sep. 4
11 months.	Oct. 1	Oct. 2	Oct. 3	Oct. 3	Oct. 4
12 months.	Oct. 31	Nov. 1	Nov. 2	Nov. 3	Nov. 4

*Use this line for notes maturing in Leap Year.

Time.	Nov'r 2.	Nov'r 3.	Nov'r 4.	Nov'r 5.	Nov'r 6.
5 days.	Nov. 10	Nov. 11	Nov. 12	Nov. 13	Nov. 14
10 days.	Nov. 15	Nov. 16	Nov. 17	Nov. 18	Nov. 19
15 days.	Nov. 20	Nov. 21	Nov. 22	Nov. 23	Nov. 24
20 days.	Nov. 25	Nov. 26	Nov. 27	Nov. 28	Nov. 29
25 days.	Nov. 30	Dec. 1	Dec. 2	Dec. 3	Dec. 4
30 days.	Dec. 5	Dec. 6	Dec. 7	Dec. 8	Dec. 9
35 days.	Dec. 10	Dec. 11	Dec. 12	Dec. 13	Dec. 14
40 days.	Dec. 15	Dec. 16	Dec. 17	Dec. 18	Dec. 19
45 days.	Dec. 20	Dec. 21	Dec. 22	Dec. 23	Dec. 24
50 days.	Dec. 25	Dec. 26	Dec. 27	Dec. 28	Dec. 29
55 days.	Dec. 30	Dec. 31	Jan. 1	Jan. 2	Jan. 3
60 days.	Jan. 4	Jan. 5	Jan. 6	Jan. 7	Jan. 8
65 days.	Jan. 9	Jan. 10	Jan. 11	Jan. 12	Jan. 13
70 days.	Jan. 14	Jan. 15	Jan. 16	Jan. 17	Jan. 18
75 days.	Jan. 19	Jan. 20	Jan. 21	Jan. 22	Jan. 23
80 days.	Jan. 24	Jan. 25	Jan. 26	Jan. 27	Jan. 28
85 days.	Jan. 29	Jan. 30	Jan. 31	Feb. 1	Feb. 2
90 days.	Feb. 3	Feb. 4	Feb. 5	Feb. 6	Feb. 7
95 days.	Feb. 8	Feb. 9	Feb. 10	Feb. 11	Feb. 12
100 days.	Feb. 13	Feb. 14	Feb. 15	Feb. 16	Feb. 17
1 month.	Dec. 5	Dec. 6	Dec. 7	Dec. 8	Dec. 9
2 months.	Jan. 5	Jan. 6	Jan. 7	Jan. 8	Jan. 9
3 months.	Feb. 5	Feb. 6	Feb. 7	Feb. 8	Feb. 9
4 months.	Mar. 5	Mar. 6	Mar. 7	Mar. 8	Mar. 9
5 months.	Apr. 5	Apr. 6	Apr. 7	Apr. 8	Apr. 9
6 months.	May 5	May 6	May 7	May 8	May 9
7 months.	June 5	Jun. 6	Jun. 7	Jun. 8	Jun. 9
8 months.	July 5	Jul. 6	Jul. 7	Jul. 8	Jul. 9
9 months.	Aug. 5	Aug. 6	Aug. 7	Aug. 8	Aug. 9
10 months.	Sept. 5	Sep. 6	Sep. 7	Sep. 8	Sep. 9
11 months.	Oct. 5	Oct. 6	Oct. 7	Oct. 8	Oct. 9
12 months.	Nov. 5	Nov. 6	Nov. 7	Nov. 8	Nov. 9

Time.	Nov'r 7.	Nov'r 8.	Nov'r 9.	Nov'r 10.	Nov'r 11.
5 days.	Nov. 15	Nov. 16	Nov. 17	Nov. 18	Nov. 19
10 days.	Nov. 20	Nov. 21	Nov. 22	Nov. 23	Nov. 24
15 days.	Nov. 25	Nov. 26	Nov. 27	Nov. 28	Nov. 29
20 days.	Nov. 30	Dec. 1	Dec. 2	Dec. 3	Dec. 4
25 days.	Dec. 5	Dec. 6	Dec. 7	Dec. 8	Dec. 9
30 days.	Dec. 10	Dec. 11	Dec. 12	Dec. 13	Dec. 14
35 days.	Dec. 15	Dec. 16	Dec. 17	Dec. 18	Dec. 19
40 days.	Dec. 20	Dec. 21	Dec. 22	Dec. 23	Dec. 24
45 days.	Dec. 25	Dec. 26	Dec. 27	Dec. 28	Dec. 29
50 days.	Dec. 30	Dec. 31	Jan. 1	Jan. 2	Jan. 3
55 days.	Jan. 4	Jan. 5	Jan. 6	Jan. 7	Jan. 8
60 days.	Jan. 9	Jan. 10	Jan. 11	Jan. 12	Jan. 13
65 days.	Jan. 14	Jan. 15	Jan. 16	Jan. 17	Jan. 18
70 days.	Jan. 19	Jan. 20	Jan. 21	Jan. 22	Jan. 23
75 days.	Jan. 24	Jan. 25	Jan. 26	Jan. 27	Jan. 28
80 days.	Jan. 29	Jan. 30	Jan. 31	Feb. 1	Feb. 2
85 days.	Feb. 3	Feb. 4	Feb. 5	Feb. 6	Feb. 7
90 days.	Feb. 8	Feb. 9	Feb. 10	Feb. 11	Feb. 12
95 days.	Feb. 13	Feb. 14	Feb. 15	Feb. 16	Feb. 17
100 days.	Feb. 18	Feb. 19	Feb. 20	Feb. 21	Feb. 22
1 month.	Dec. 10	Dec. 11	Dec. 12	Dec. 13	Dec. 14
2 months.	Jan. 10	Jan. 11	Jan. 12	Jan. 13	Jan. 14
3 months.	Feb. 10	Feb. 11	Feb. 12	Feb. 13	Feb. 14
4 months.	Mar. 10	Mar. 11	Mar. 12	Mar. 13	Mar. 14
5 months.	Apr. 10	Apr. 11	Apr. 12	Apr. 13	Apr. 14
6 months.	May 10	May 11	May 12	May 13	May 14
7 months.	June 10	Jun. 11	Jun. 12	Jun. 13	Jun. 14
8 months.	July 10	Jul. 11	Jul. 12	Jul. 13	Jul. 14
9 months.	Aug. 10	Aug. 11	Aug. 12	Aug. 13	Aug. 14
10 months.	Sept. 10	Sep. 11	Sep. 12	Sep. 13	Sep. 14
11 months.	Oct. 10	Oct. 11	Oct. 12	Oct. 13	Oct. 14
12 months.	Nov. 10	Nov. 11	Nov. 12	Nov. 13	Nov. 14

Time.	Nov'r 12.	Nov'r 13.	Nov'r 14.	Nov'r 15.	Nov'r 16.
5 days.	Nov. 20	Nov. 21	Nov. 22	Nov. 23	Nov. 24
10 days.	Nov. 25	Nov. 26	Nov. 27	Nov. 28	Nov. 29
15 days.	Nov. 30	Dec. 1	Dec. 2	Dec. 3	Dec. 4
20 days.	Dec. 5	Dec. 6	Dec. 7	Dec. 8	Dec. 9
25 days.	Dec. 10	Dec. 11	Dec. 12	Dec. 13	Dec. 14
30 days.	Dec. 15	Dec. 16	Dec. 17	Dec. 18	Dec. 19
35 days.	Dec. 20	Dec. 21	Dec. 22	Dec. 23	Dec. 24
40 days.	Dec. 25	Dec. 26	Dec. 27	Dec. 28	Dec. 29
45 days.	Dec. 30	Dec. 31	Jan. 1	Jan. 2	Jan. 3
50 days.	Jan. 4	Jan. 5	Jan. 6	Jan. 7	Jan. 8
55 days.	Jan. 9	Jan. 10	Jan. 11	Jan. 12	Jan. 13
60 days.	Jan. 14	Jan. 15	Jan. 16	Jan. 17	Jan. 18
65 days.	Jan. 19	Jan. 20	Jan. 21	Jan. 22	Jan. 23
70 days.	Jan. 24	Jan. 25	Jan. 26	Jan. 27	Jan. 28
75 days.	Jan. 29	Jan. 30	Jan. 31	Feb. 1	Feb. 2
80 days.	Feb. 3	Feb. 4	Feb. 5	Feb. 6	Feb. 7
85 days.	Feb. 8	Feb. 9	Feb. 10	Feb. 11	Feb. 12
90 days.	Feb. 13	Feb. 14	Feb. 15	Feb. 16	Feb. 17
95 days.	Feb. 18	Feb. 19	Feb. 20	Feb. 21	Feb. 22
100 days.	Feb. 23	Feb. 24	Feb. 25	Feb 26	Feb. 27
1 month.	Dec. 15	Dec. 16	Dec. 17	Dec. 18	Dec. 19
2 months.	Jan. 15	Jan. 16	Jan. 17	Jan. 18	Jan. 19
3 months.	Feb. 15	Feb. 16	Feb. 17	Feb. 18	Feb. 19
4 months.	Mar. 15	Mar. 16	Mar. 17	Mar. 18	Mar. 19
5 months.	Apr. 15	Apr. 16	Apr. 17	Apr. 18	Apr. 19
6 months.	May 15	May 16	May 17	May 18	May 19
7 months.	June 15	Jun. 16	Jun. 17	Jun. 18	Jun. 19
8 months.	July 15	Jul. 16	Jul. 17	Jul. 18	Jul. 19
9 months.	Aug. 15	Aug. 16	Aug. 17	Aug. 18	Aug. 19
10 months.	Sept. 15	Sep. 16	Sep. 17	Sep. 18	Sep. 19
11 months.	Oct. 15	Oct. 16	Oct. 17	Oct. 18	Oct. 19
12 months.	Nov. 15	Nov. 16	Nov. 17	Nov. 18	Nov. 19

For Leap Year changes, see next page.

Time.	Nov'r 17.	Nov'r 18.	Nov'r 19.	Nov'r 20.	Nov'r 21.
5 days.	Nov. 25	Nov. 26	Nov. 27	Nov. 28	Nov. 29
10 days.	Nov. 30	Dec. 1	Dec. 2	Dec. 3	Dec. 4
15 days.	Dec. 5	Dec. 6	Dec. 7	Dec. 8	Dec. 9
20 days.	Dec. 10	Dec. 11	Dec. 12	Dec. 13	Dec. 14
25 days.	Dec. 15	Dec. 16	Dec. 17	Dec. 18	Dec. 19
30 days.	Dec. 20	Dec. 21	Dec. 22	Dec. 23	Dec. 24
35 days.	Dec. 25	Dec. 26	Dec. 27	Dec. 28	Dec. 29
40 days.	Dec. 30	Dec. 31	Jan. 1	Jan. 2	Jan. 3
45 days.	Jan. 4	Jan. 5	Jan. 6	Jan. 7	Jan. 8
50 days.	Jan. 9	Jan. 10	Jan. 11	Jan. 12	Jan. 13
55 days.	Jan. 14	Jan. 15	Jan. 16	Jan. 17	Jan. 18
60 days.	Jan. 19	Jan. 20	Jan. 21	Jan. 22	Jan. 23
65 days.	Jan. 24	Jan. 25	Jan. 26	Jan. 27	Jan. 28
70 days.	Jan. 29	Jan. 30	Jan. 31	Feb. 1	Feb. 2
75 days.	Feb. 3	Feb. 4	Feb. 5	Feb. 6	Feb. 7
80 days.	Feb. 8	Feb. 9	Feb. 10	Feb. 11	Feb. 12
85 days.	Feb. 13	Feb. 14	Feb. 15	Feb. 16	Feb. 17
90 days.	Feb. 18	Feb. 19	Feb. 20	Feb. 21	Feb. 22
95 days.	Feb. 23	Feb. 24	Feb. 25	Feb. 26	Feb. 27
100 days.	Feb. 28	Mar. 1	Mar. 2	Mar. 3	Mar. 4
1 month.	Dec. 20	Dec. 21	Dec. 22	Dec. 23	Dec. 24
2 months.	Jan. 20	Jan. 21	Jan. 22	Jan. 23	Jan. 24
3 months.	Feb. 20	Feb. 21	Feb. 22	Feb. 23	Feb. 24
4 months.	Mar. 20	Mar. 21	Mar. 22	Mar. 23	Mar. 24
5 months.	Apr. 20	Apr. 21	Apr. 22	Apr. 23	Apr. 24
6 months.	May 20	May 21	May 22	May 23	May 24
7 months.	June 20	Jun. 21	Jun. 22	Jun. 23	Jun. 24
8 months.	July 20	Jul. 21	Jul. 22	Jul. 23	Jul. 24
9 months.	Aug. 20	Aug. 21	Aug. 22	Aug. 23	Aug. 24
10 months.	Sept. 20	Sep. 21	Sep. 22	Sep. 23	Sep. 24
11 months.	Oct. 20	Oct. 21	Oct. 22	Oct. 23	Oct. 24
12 months.	Nov. 20	Nov. 21	Nov. 22	Nov. 23	Nov. 24

Changes when Notes mature in Leap-Year.

Time.	Nov'm'r 17.	Nov'm'r 18.	Nov'm'r 19.	Nov'm'r 20.	Nov'm'r 21.
100 days.	Feb. 28	Feb. 29	Mar. 1	Mar. 2	Mar. 3

For Leap Year changes, see next page.

Time.	Nov'r 22.	Nov'r 23.	Nov'r 24.	Nov'r 25.	Nov'r 26.
5 days.	Nov. 30	Dec. 1	Dec. 2	Dec. 3	Dec. 4
10 days.	Dec. 5	Dec. 6	Dec. 7	Dec. 8	Dec. 9
15 days.	Dec. 10	Dec. 11	Dec. 12	Dec. 13	Dec. 14
20 days.	Dec. 15	Dec. 16	Dec. 17	Dec. 18	Dec. 19
25 days.	Dec. 20	Dec. 21	Dec. 22	Dec. 23	Dec. 24
30 days.	Dec. 25	Dec. 26	Dec. 27	Dec. 28	Dec. 29
35 days.	Dec. 30	Dec. 31	Jan. 1	Jan. 2	Jan. 3
40 days.	Jan. 4	Jan. 5	Jan. 6	Jan. 7	Jan. 8
45 days.	Jan. 9	Jan. 10	Jan. 11	Jan. 12	Jan. 13
50 days.	Jan. 14	Jan. 15	Jan. 16	Jan. 17	Jan. 18
55 days.	Jan. 19	Jan. 20	Jan. 21	Jan. 22	Jan. 23
60 days.	Jan. 24	Jan. 25	Jan. 26	Jan. 27	Jan. 28
65 days.	Jan. 29	Jan. 30	Jan. 31	Feb. 1	Feb. 2
70 days.	Feb. 3	Feb. 4	Feb. 5	Feb. 6	Feb. 7
75 days.	Feb. 8	Feb. 9	Feb. 10	Feb. 11	Feb. 12
80 days.	Feb. 13	Feb. 14	Feb. 15	Feb. 16	Feb. 17
85 days.	Feb. 18	Feb. 19	Feb. 20	Feb. 21	Feb. 22
90 days.	Feb. 23	Feb. 24	Feb. 25	Feb. 26	Feb. 27
95 days.	Feb. 28	Mar. 1	Mar. 2	Mar. 3	Mar. 4
100 days.	Mar. 5	Mar. 6	Mar. 7	Mar. 8	Mar. 9
1 month.	Dec. 25	Dec. 26	Dec. 27	Dec. 28	Dec. 29
2 months.	Jan. 25	Jan. 26	Jan. 27	Jan. 28	Jan. 29
3 months.	Feb. 25	Feb. 26	Feb. 27	Feb. 28	Mar. 1
4 months.	Mar. 25	Mar. 26	Mar. 27	Mar. 28	Mar. 29
5 months.	Apr. 25	Apr. 26	Apr. 27	Apr. 28	Apr. 29
6 months.	May 25	May 26	May 27	May 28	May 29
7 months.	June 25	June 26	Jun. 27	Jun. 28	Jun. 29
8 months.	July 25	July 26	Jul. 27	Jul. 28	Jul. 29
9 months.	Aug. 25	Aug. 26	Aug. 27	Aug. 28	Aug. 29
10 months.	Sept. 25	Sep. 26	Sep. 27	Sep. 28	Sep. 29
11 months.	Oct. 25	Oct. 26	Oct. 27	Oct. 28	Oct. 29
12 months.	Nov. 25	Nov. 26	Nov. 27	Nov. 28	Nov. 29

Changes when Notes mature in Leap-Year.

Time.	Nov'm'r 22.	Nov'm'r 23.	Nov'm'r 24.	Nov'm'r 25.	Nov'm'r 26.
95 days.	Feb. 28	Feb. 29	Mar. 1	Mar. 2	Mar. 3
100 days.	Mar. 4	Mar. 5	Mar. 6	Mar. 7	Mar. 8
3 months.	Feb. 25	Feb. 26	Feb. 27	Feb. 28	Feb. 29

For Leap Year changes, see next page.

Time.	Nov'r 27.	Nov'r 28.	Nov'r 29.	Nov'r 30.	Dec'm'r 1.
5 days.	Dec. 5	Dec. 6	Dec. 7	Dec. 8	Dec. 9
10 days.	Dec. 10	Dec. 11	Dec. 12	Dec. 13	Dec. 14
15 days.	Dec. 15	Dec. 16	Dec. 17	Dec. 18	Dec. 19
20 days.	Dec. 20	Dec. 21	Dec. 22	Dec. 23	Dec. 24
25 days.	Dec. 25	Dec. 26	Dec. 27	Dec. 28	Dec. 29
30 days.	Dec. 30	Dec. 31	Jan. 1	Jan. 2	Jan. 3
35 days.	Jan. 4	Jan. 5	Jan. 6	Jan. 7	Jan. 8
40 days.	Jan. 9	Jan. 10	Jan. 11	Jan. 12	Jan. 13
45 days.	Jan. 14	Jan. 15	Jan. 16	Jan. 17	Jan. 18
50 days.	Jan. 19	Jan. 20	Jan. 21	Jan. 22	Jan. 23
55 days.	Jan. 24	Jan. 25	Jan. 26	Jan. 27	Jan. 28
60 days.	Jan. 29	Jan. 30	Jan. 31	Feb. 1	Feb. 2
65 days.	Feb. 3	Feb. 4	Feb. 5	Feb. 6	Feb. 7
70 days.	Feb. 8	Feb. 9	Feb. 10	Feb. 11	Feb. 12
75 days.	Feb. 13	Feb. 14	Feb. 15	Feb. 16	Feb. 17
80 days.	Feb. 18	Feb. 19	Feb. 20	Feb. 21	Feb. 22
85 days.	Feb. 23	Feb. 24	Feb. 25	Feb. 26	Feb. 27
90 days.	Feb. 28	Mar. 1	Mar. 2	Mar. 3	Mar. 4
95 days.	Mar. 5	Mar. 6	Mar. 7	Mar. 8	Mar. 9
100 days.	Mar. 10	Mar. 11	Mar. 12	Mar. 13	Mar. 14
1 month.	Dec. 30	Dec. 31	Jan. 1	Jan. 2	Jan. 4
2 months.	Jan. 30	Jan. 31	Feb. 1	Feb. 2	Feb. 4
3 months.	Mar. 2	Mar. 3	Mar. 3	Mar. 3	Mar. 4
4 months.	Mar. 30	Mar. 31	Apr. 1	Apr. 2	Apr. 4
5 months.	Apr. 30	May 1	May 2	May 3	May 4
6 months.	May 30	May 31	Jun. 1	Jun. 2	Jun. 4
7 months.	June 30	Jul. 1	Jul. 2	Jul. 3	Jul. 4
8 months.	July 30	July 31	Aug. 1	Aug. 2	Aug. 4
9 months.	Aug. 30	Aug. 31	Sep. 1	Sep. 2	Sep. 4
10 months.	Sept. 30	Oct. 1	Oct. 2	Oct. 3	Oct. 4
11 months.	Oct. 30	Oct. 31	Nov. 1	Nov. 2	Nov. 4
12 months.	Nov. 30	Dec. 1	Dec. 2	Dec. 3	Dec. 4

Changes when Notes mature in Leap-Year.

Time.	Nov'm'r 27.	Nov'm'r 28.	Nov'm'r 29.	Nov'm'r 30.	Dec'm'r 1.
90 days.	Feb. 28	Feb. 29	Mar. 1	Mar. 2	Mar. 3
95 days.	Mar. 4	Mar. 5	Mar. 6	Mar. 7	Mar. 8
100 days.	Mar. 9	Mar. 10	Mar. 11	Mar. 12	Mar. 13
3 months.	Mar. 1	Mar. 2	Mar. 3	Mar. 3	Mar. 4

For Leap Year changes, see next page.

Time.	Dec'm'r 2.	Dec'm'r 3.	Dec'm'r 4.	Dec'm'r 5.	Dec'm'r 6.
5 days.	Dec. 10	Dec. 11	Dec. 12	Dec. 13	Dec. 14
10 days.	Dec. 15	Dec. 16	Dec. 17	Dec. 18	Dec. 19
15 days.	Dec. 20	Dec. 21	Dec. 22	Dec. 23	Dec. 24
20 days.	Dec. 25	Dec. 26	Dec. 27	Dec. 28	Dec. 29
25 days.	Dec. 30	Dec. 31	Jan. 1	Jan. 2	Jan. 3
30 days.	Jan. 4	Jan. 5	Jan. 6	Jan. 7	Jan. 8
35 days.	Jan. 9	Jan. 10	Jan. 11	Jan. 12	Jan. 13
40 days.	Jan. 14	Jan. 15	Jan. 16	Jan. 17	Jan. 18
45 days.	Jan. 19	Jan. 20	Jan. 21	Jan. 22	Jan. 23
50 days.	Jan. 24	Jan. 25	Jan. 26	Jan. 27	Jan. 28
55 days.	Jan. 29	Jan. 30	Jan. 31	Feb. 1	Feb. 2
60 days.	Feb. 3	Feb. 4	Feb. 5	Feb. 6	Feb. 7
65 days.	Feb. 8	Feb. 9	Feb. 10	Feb. 11	Feb. 12
70 days.	Feb. 13	Feb. 14	Feb. 15	Feb. 16	Feb. 17
75 days.	Feb. 18	Feb. 19	Feb. 20	Feb. 21	Feb. 22
80 days.	Feb. 23	Feb. 24	Feb. 25	Feb. 26	Feb. 27
85 days.	Feb. 28	Mar. 1	Mar. 2	Mar. 3	Mar. 4
90 days.	Mar. 5	Mar. 6	Mar. 7	Mar. 8	Mar. 9
95 days.	Mar. 10	Mar. 11	Mar. 12	Mar. 13	Mar. 14
100 days.	Mar. 15	Mar. 16	Mar. 17	Mar. 18	Mar. 19
1 month.	Jan. 5	Jan. 6	Jan. 7	Jan. 8	Jan. 9
2 months.	Feb. 5	Feb. 6	Feb. 7	Feb. 8	Feb. 9
3 months.	Mar. 5	Mar. 6	Mar. 7	Mar. 8	Mar. 9
4 months.	Apr. 5	Apr. 6	Apr. 7	Apr. 8	Apr. 9
5 months.	May 5	May 6	May 7	May 8	May 9
6 months.	June 5	June 6	Jun. 7	Jun. 8	Jun. 9
7 months.	July 5	July 6	Jul. 7	Jul. 8	Jul. 9
8 months.	Aug. 5	Aug. 6	Aug. 7	Aug. 8	Aug. 9
9 months.	Sept. 5	Sep. 6	Sep. 7	Sep. 8	Sep. 9
10 months.	Oct. 5	Oct. 6	Oct. 7	Oct. 8	Oct. 9
11 months.	Nov. 5	Nov. 6	Nov. 7	Nov. 8	Nov. 9
12 months.	Dec. 5	Dec. 6	Dec. 7	Dec. 8	Dec. 9

Changes when Notes mature in Leap-Year.

Time.	Dec'm'r 2.	Dec'm'r 3.	Dec'm'r 4.	Dec'm'r 5.	Dec'm'r 6.
85 days.	Feb. 28	Feb. 29	Mar. 1	Mar. 2	Mar. 3
90 days.	Mar. 4	Mar. 5	Mar. 6	Mar. 7	Mar. 8
95 days.	Mar. 9	Mar. 10	Mar. 11	Mar. 12	Mar. 13
100 days.	Mar. 14	Mar. 15	Mar. 16	Mar. 17	Mar. 18

For Leap Year changes, see next page.

Time.	Dec'm'r 7.	Dec'm'r 8.	Dec'm'r 9.	Dec'm'r 10.	Dec'm'r 11.
5 days.	Dec. 15	Dec. 16	Dec. 17	Dec. 18	Dec. 19
10 days.	Dec. 20	Dec. 21	Dec. 22	Dec. 23	Dec. 24
15 days.	Dec. 25	Dec. 26	Dec. 27	Dec. 28	Dec. 29
20 days.	Dec. 30	Dec. 31	Jan. 1	Jan. 2	Jan. 3
25 days.	Jan. 4	Jan. 5	Jan. 6	Jan. 7	Jan. 8
30 days.	Jan. 9	Jan. 10	Jan. 11	Jan. 12	Jan. 13
35 days.	Jan. 14	Jan. 15	Jan. 16	Jan. 17	Jan. 18
40 days.	Jan. 19	Jan. 20	Jan. 21	Jan. 22	Jan. 23
45 days.	Jan. 24	Jan. 25	Jan. 26	Jan. 27	Jan. 28
50 days.	Jan. 29	Jan. 30	Jan. 31	Feb. 1	Feb. 2
55 days.	Feb. 3	Feb. 4	Feb. 5	Feb. 6	Feb. 7
60 days.	Feb. 8	Feb. 9	Feb. 10	Feb. 11	Feb. 12
65 days.	Feb. 13	Feb. 14	Feb. 15	Feb. 16	Feb. 17
70 days.	Feb. 18	Feb. 19	Feb. 20	Feb. 21	Feb. 22
75 days.	Feb. 23	Feb. 24	Feb. 25	Feb. 26	Feb. 27
80 days.	Feb. 28	Mar. 1	Mar. 2	Mar. 3	Mar. 4
85 days.	Mar. 5	Mar. 6	Mar. 7	Mar. 8	Mar. 9
90 days.	Mar. 10	Mar. 11	Mar. 12	Mar. 13	Mar. 14
95 days.	Mar. 15	Mar. 16	Mar. 17	Mar. 18	Mar. 19
100 days.	Mar. 20	Mar. 21	Mar. 22	Mar. 23	Mar. 24
1 month.	Jan. 10	Jan. 11	Jan. 12	Jan. 13	Jan. 14
2 months.	Feb. 10	Feb. 11	Feb. 12	Feb. 13	Feb. 14
3 months.	Mar. 10	Mar. 11	Mar. 12	Mar. 13	Mar. 14
4 months.	Apr. 10	Apr. 11	Apr. 12	Apr. 13	Apr. 14
5 months.	May 10	May 11	May 12	May 13	May 14
6 months.	June 10	June 11	Jun. 12	Jun. 13	Jun. 14
7 months.	July 10	July 11	Jul. 12	Jul. 13	Jul. 14
8 months.	Aug. 10	Aug. 11	Aug. 12	Aug. 13	Aug. 14
9 months.	Sept. 10	Sep. 11	Sep. 12	Sep. 13	Sep. 14
10 months.	Oct. 10	Oct. 11	Oct. 12	Oct. 13	Oct. 14
11 months.	Nov. 10	Nov. 11	Nov. 12	Nov. 13	Nov. 14
12 months.	Dec. 10	Dec. 11	Dec. 12	Dec. 13	Dec. 14

Changes when Notes mature in Leap-Year.

Time.	Dec'm'r 7.	Dec'm'r 8.	Dec'm'r 9.	Dec'm'r 10.	Dec'm'r 11.
80 days.	Feb. 28	Feb. 29	Mar. 1	Mar. 2	Mar. 3
85 days.	Mar. 4	Mar. 5	Mar. 6	Mar. 7	Mar. 8
90 days.	Mar. 9	Mar. 10	Mar. 11	Mar. 12	Mar. 13
95 days.	Mar. 14	Mar. 15	Mar. 16	Mar. 17	Mar. 18
100 days.	Mar. 19	Mar. 20	Mar. 21	Mar. 22	Mar. 23

For Leap Year changes, see next page.

Time.	Dec'm'r 12.	Dec'm'r 13.	Dec'm'r 14.	Dec'm'r 15.	Dec'm'r 16.
5 days.	Dec. 20	Dec. 21	Dec. 22	Dec. 23	Dec. 24
10 days.	Dec. 25	Dec. 26	Dec. 27	Dec. 28	Dec. 29
15 days.	Dec. 30	Dec. 31	Jan. 1	Jan. 2	Jan. 3
20 days.	Jan. 4	Jan. 5	Jan. 6	Jan. 7	Jan. 8
25 days.	Jan. 9	Jan. 10	Jan. 11	Jan. 12	Jan. 13
30 days.	Jan. 14	Jan. 15	Jan. 16	Jan. 17	Jan. 18
35 days.	Jan. 19	Jan. 20	Jan. 21	Jan. 22	Jan. 23
40 days.	Jan. 24	Jan. 25	Jan. 26	Jan. 27	Jan. 28
45 days.	Jan. 29	Jan. 30	Jan. 31	Feb. 1	Feb. 2
50 days.	Feb. 3	Feb. 4	Feb. 5	Feb. 6	Feb. 7
55 days.	Feb. 8	Feb. 9	Feb. 10	Feb. 11	Feb. 12
60 days.	Feb. 13	Feb. 14	Feb. 15	Feb. 16	Feb. 17
65 days.	Feb. 18	Feb. 19	Feb. 20	Feb. 21	Feb. 22
70 days.	Feb. 23	Feb. 24	Feb. 25	Feb. 26	Feb. 27
75 days.	Feb. 28	Mar. 1	Mar. 2	Mar. 3	Mar. 4
80 days.	Mar. 5	Mar. 6	Mar. 7	Mar. 8	Mar. 9
85 days.	Mar. 10	Mar. 11	Mar. 12	Mar. 13	Mar. 14
90 days.	Mar. 15	Mar. 16	Mar. 17	Mar. 18	Mar. 19
95 days.	Mar. 20	Mar. 21	Mar. 22	Mar. 23	Mar. 24
100 days.	Mar. 25	Mar. 26	Mar. 27	Mar. 28	Mar. 29
1 month.	Jan. 15	Jan. 16	Jan. 17	Jan. 18	Jan. 19
2 months.	Feb. 15	Feb. 16	Feb. 17	Feb. 18	Feb. 19
3 months.	Mar. 15	Mar. 16	Mar. 17	Mar. 18	Mar. 19
4 months.	Apr. 15	Apr. 16	Apr. 17	Apr. 18	Apr. 19
5 months.	May 15	May 16	May 17	May 18	May 19
6 months.	June 15	June 16	Jun. 17	Jun. 18	Jun. 19
7 months.	July 15	July 16	Jul. 17	Jul. 18	Jul. 19
8 months.	Aug. 15	Aug. 16	Aug. 17	Aug. 18	Aug. 19
9 months.	Sept. 15	Sep. 16	Sep. 17	Sep. 18	Sep. 19
10 months.	Oct. 15	Oct. 16	Oct. 17	Oct. 18	Oct. 19
11 months.	Nov. 15	Nov. 16	Nov. 17	Nov. 18	Nov. 19
12 months.	Dec. 15	Dec. 16	Dec. 17	Dec. 18	Dec. 19

Changes when Notes mature in Leap-Year.

Time.	Dec'm'r 12.	Dec'm'r 13.	Dec'm'r 14.	Dec'm'r 15.	Dec'm'r 16.
75 days.	Feb. 28	Feb. 29	Mar. 1	Mar. 2	Mar. 3
80 days.	Mar. 4	Mar. 5	Mar. 6	Mar. 7	Mar. 8
85 days.	Mar. 9	Mar. 10	Mar. 11	Mar. 12	Mar. 13
90 days.	Mar. 14	Mar. 15	Mar. 16	Mar. 17	Mar. 18
95 days.	Mar. 19	Mar. 20	Mar. 21	Mar. 22	Mar. 23
100 days.	Mar. 24	Mar. 25	Mar. 26	Mar. 27	Mar. 28

For Leap Year changes, see next page.

Time.	Dec'm'r 17.	Dec'm'r 18.	Dec'm'r 19.	Dec'm'r 20.	Dec'm'r 21.
5 days.	Dec. 25	Dec. 26	Dec. 27	Dec. 28	Dec. 29
10 days.	Dec. 30	Dec. 31	Jan. 1	Jan. 2	Jan. 3
15 days.	Jan. 4	Jan. 5	Jan. 6	Jan. 7	Jan. 8
20 days.	Jan. 9	Jan. 10	Jan. 11	Jan. 12	Jan. 13
25 days.	Jan. 14	Jan. 15	Jan. 16	Jan. 17	Jan. 18
30 days.	Jan. 19	Jan. 20	Jan. 21	Jan. 22	Jan. 23
35 days.	Jan. 24	Jan. 25	Jan. 26	Jan. 27	Jan. 28
40 days.	Jan. 29	Jan. 30	Jan. 31	Feb. 1	Feb. 2
45 days.	Feb. 3	Feb. 4	Feb. 5	Feb. 6	Feb. 7
50 days.	Feb. 8	Feb. 9	Feb. 10	Feb. 11	Feb. 12
55 days.	Feb. 13	Feb. 14	Feb. 15	Feb. 16	Feb. 17
60 days.	Feb. 18	Feb. 19	Feb. 20	Feb. 21	Feb. 22
65 days.	Feb. 23	Feb. 24	Feb. 25	Feb. 26	Feb. 27
70 days.	Feb. 28	Mar. 1	Mar. 2	Mar. 3	Mar. 4
75 days.	Mar. 5	Mar. 6	Mar. 7	Mar. 8	Mar. 9
80 days.	Mar. 10	Mar. 11	Mar. 12	Mar. 13	Mar. 14
85 days.	Mar. 15	Mar. 16	Mar. 17	Mar. 18	Mar. 19
90 days.	Mar. 20	Mar. 21	Mar. 22	Mar. 23	Mar. 24
95 days.	Mar. 25	Mar. 26	Mar. 27	Mar. 28	Mar. 29
100 days.	Mar. 30	Mar. 31	Apr. 1	Apr. 2	Apr. 3
1 month.	Jan. 20	Jan. 21	Jan. 22	Jan. 23	Jan. 24
2 months.	Feb. 20	Feb. 21	Feb. 22	Feb. 23	Feb. 24
3 months.	Mar. 20	Mar. 21	Mar. 22	Mar. 23	Mar. 24
4 months.	Apr. 20	Apr. 21	Apr. 22	Apr. 23	Apr. 24
5 months.	May 20	May 21	May 22	May 23	May 24
6 months.	June 20	June 21	Jun. 22	Jun. 23	Jun. 24
7 months.	July 20	July 21	Jul. 22	Jul. 23	Jul. 24
8 months.	Aug. 20	Aug. 21	Aug. 22	Aug. 23	Aug. 24
9 months.	Sept. 20	Sep. 21	Sep. 22	Sep. 23	Sep. 24
10 months.	Oct. 20	Oct. 21	Oct. 22	Oct. 23	Oct. 24
11 months.	Nov. 20	Nov. 21	Nov. 22	Nov. 23	Nov. 24
12 months.	Dec. 20	Dec. 21	Dec. 22	Dec. 23	Dec. 24

Changes when Notes mature in Leap-Year.

Time.	Dec'm'r 17.	Dec'm'r 18.	Dec'm'r 19.	Dec'm'r 20.	Dec'm'r 21.
70 days.	Feb. 28	Feb. 29	Mar. 1	Mar. 2	Mar. 3
75 days.	Mar. 4	Mar. 5	Mar. 6	Mar. 7	Mar. 8
80 days.	Mar. 9	Mar. 10	Mar. 11	Mar. 12	Mar. 13
85 days.	Mar. 14	Mar. 15	Mar. 16	Mar. 17	Mar. 18
90 days.	Mar. 19	Mar. 20	Mar. 21	Mar. 22	Mar. 23
95 days.	Mar. 24	Mar. 25	Mar. 26	Mar. 27	Mar. 28
100 days.	Mar. 29	Mar. 30	Mar. 31	Apr. 1	Apr. 2

For Leap Year changes, see next page.

Time.	Dec'm'r 22.	Dec'm'r 23.	Dec'm'r 24.	Dec'm'r 25.	Dec'm'r 26.
5 days.	Dec. 30	Dec. 31	Jan. 1	Jan. 2	Jan. 3
10 days.	Jan. 4	Jan. 5	Jan. 6	Jan. 7	Jan. 8
15 days.	Jan. 9	Jan. 10	Jan. 11	Jan. 12	Jan. 13
20 days.	Jan. 14	Jan. 15	Jan. 16	Jan. 17	Jan. 18
25 days.	Jan. 19	Jan. 20	Jan. 21	Jan. 22	Jan. 23
30 days.	Jan. 24	Jan. 25	Jan. 26	Jan. 27	Jan. 28
35 days.	Jan. 29	Jan. 30	Jan. 31	Feb. 1	Feb. 2
40 days.	Feb. 3	Feb. 4	Feb. 5	Feb. 6	Feb. 7
45 days.	Feb. 8	Feb. 9	Feb. 10	Feb. 11	Feb. 12
50 days.	Feb. 13	Feb. 14	Feb. 15	Feb. 16	Feb. 17
55 days.	Feb. 18	Feb. 19	Feb. 20	Feb. 21	Feb. 22
60 days.	Feb. 23	Feb. 24	Feb. 25	Feb. 26	Feb. 27
65 days.	Feb. 28	Mar. 1	Mar. 2	Mar. 3	Mar. 4
70 days.	Mar. 5	Mar. 6	Mar. 7	Mar. 8	Mar. 9
75 days.	Mar. 10	Mar. 11	Mar. 12	Mar. 13	Mar. 14
80 days.	Mar. 15	Mar. 16	Mar. 17	Mar. 18	Mar. 19
85 days.	Mar. 20	Mar. 21	Mar. 22	Mar. 23	Mar. 24
90 days.	Mar. 25	Mar. 26	Mar. 27	Mar. 28	Mar. 29
95 days.	Mar. 30	Mar. 31	Apr. 1	Apr. 2	Apr. 3
100 days.	Apr. 4	Apr. 5	Apr. 6	Apr. 7	Apr. 8
1 month.	Jan. 25	Jan. 26	Jan. 27	Jan. 28	Jan. 29
2 months.	Feb. 25	Feb. 26	Feb. 27	Feb. 28	Mar. 1
3 months.	Mar. 25	Mar. 26	Mar. 27	Mar. 28	Mar. 29
4 months.	Apr. 25	Apr. 26	Apr. 27	Apr. 28	Apr. 29
5 months.	May 25	May 26	May 27	May 28	May 29
6 months.	June 25	June 26	Jun. 27	Jun. 28	Jun. 29
7 months.	July 25	July 26	Jul. 27	Jul. 28	Jul. 29
8 months.	Aug. 25	Aug. 26	Aug. 27	Aug. 28	Aug. 29
9 months.	Sept. 25	Sep. 26	Sep. 27	Sep. 28	Sep. 29
10 months.	Oct. 25	Oct. 26	Oct. 27	Oct. 28	Oct. 29
11 months.	Nov. 25	Nov. 26	Nov. 27	Nov. 28	Nov. 29
12 months.	Dec. 25	Dec. 26	Dec. 27	Dec. 28	Dec. 29

Changes when Notes mature in Leap-Year.

Time.	Dec'm'r 22.	Dec'm'r 23.	Dec'm'r 24.	Dec'm'r 25.	Dec'm'r 26.
65 days.	Feb. 28	Feb. 29	Mar. 1	Mar. 2	Mar. 3
70 days.	Mar. 4	Mar. 5	Mar. 6	Mar. 7	Mar. 8
75 days.	Mar. 9	Mar. 10	Mar. 11	Mar. 12	Mar. 13
80 days.	Mar. 14	Mar. 15	Mar. 16	Mar. 17	Mar. 18
85 days.	Mar. 19	Mar. 20	Mar. 21	Mar. 22	Mar. 23
90 days.	Mar. 24	Mar. 25	Mar. 26	Mar. 27	Mar. 28
95 days.	Mar. 29	Mar. 30	Mar. 31	Apr. 1	Apr. 2
100 days.	Apr. 3	Apr. 4	Apr. 5	Apr. 6	Apr. 7
2 months.					Feb. 29

For Leap Year changes, see next page.

Time.	Dec'm'r 27.	Dec'm'r 28.	Dec'm'r 29.	Dec'm'r 30.	Dec'm'r 31.
5 days.	Jan. 4	Jan. 5	Jan. 6	Jan. 7	Jan. 8
10 days.	Jan. 9	Jan. 10	Jan. 11	Jan. 12	Jan. 13
15 days.	Jan. 14	Jan. 15	Jan. 16	Jan. 17	Jan. 18
20 days.	Jan. 19	Jan. 20	Jan. 21	Jan. 22	Jan. 23
25 days.	Jan. 24	Jan. 25	Jan. 26	Jan. 27	Jan. 28
30 days.	Jan. 29	Jan. 30	Jan. 31	Feb. 1	Feb. 2
35 days.	Feb. 3	Feb. 4	Feb. 5	Feb. 6	Feb. 7
40 days.	Feb. 8	Feb. 9	Feb. 10	Feb. 11	Feb. 12
45 days.	Feb. 13	Feb. 14	Feb. 15	Feb. 16	Feb. 17
50 days.	Feb. 18	Feb. 19	Feb. 20	Feb. 21	Feb. 22
55 days.	Feb. 23	Feb. 24	Feb. 25	Feb. 26	Feb. 27
60 days.	Feb. 28	Mar. 1	Mar. 2	Mar. 3	Mar. 4
65 days.	Mar. 5	Mar. 6	Mar. 7	Mar. 8	Mar. 9
70 days.	Mar. 10	Mar. 11	Mar. 12	Mar. 13	Mar. 14
75 days.	Mar. 15	Mar. 16	Mar. 17	Mar. 18	Mar. 19
80 days.	Mar. 20	Mar. 21	Mar. 22	Mar. 23	Mar. 24
85 days.	Mar. 25	Mar. 26	Mar. 27	Mar. 28	Mar. 29
90 days.	Mar. 30	Mar. 31	Apr. 1	Apr. 2	Apr. 3
95 days.	Apr. 4	Apr. 5	Apr. 6	Apr. 7	Apr. 8
100 days.	Apr. 9	Apr. 10	Apr. 11	Apr. 12	Apr. 13
1 month.	Jan. 30	Jan. 31	Feb. 1	Feb. 2	Feb. 3
2 months.	Mar. 2	Mar. 3	Mar. 3	Mar. 3	Mar. 3
3 months.	Mar. 30	Mar. 31	Apr. 1	Apr. 2	Apr. 3
4 months.	Apr. 30	May 1	May 2	May 3	May 3
5 months.	May 30	May 31	Jun. 1	Jun. 2	Jun. 3
6 months.	June 30	July 1	Jul. 2	Jul. 3	Jul. 3
7 months.	July 30	July 31	Aug. 1	Aug. 2	Aug. 3
8 months.	Aug. 30	Aug. 31	Sep. 1	Sep. 2	Sep. 3
9 months.	Sept. 30	Oct. 1	Oct. 2	Oct. 3	Oct. 3
10 months.	Oct. 30	Oct. 31	Nov. 1	Nov. 2	Nov. 3
11 months.	Nov. 30	Dec. 1	Dec. 2	Dec. 3	Dec. 3
12 months.	Dec. 30	Dec. 31	Jan. 1	Jan. 2	Jan. 3

Changes when Notes mature in Leap-Year.

Time.	Dec'm'r 27.	Dec'm'r 28.	Dec'm'r 29.	Dec'm'r 30.	Dec'm'r 31.
60 days.	Feb. 28	Feb. 29	Mar. 1	Mar. 2	Mar. 3
65 days.	Mar. 4	Mar. 5	Mar. 6	Mar. 7	Mar. 8
70 days.	Mar. 9	Mar. 10	Mar. 11	Mar. 12	Mar. 13
75 days.	Mar. 14	Mar. 15	Mar. 16	Mar. 17	Mar. 18
80 days.	Mar. 19	Mar. 20	Mar. 21	Mar. 22	Mar. 23
85 days.	Mar. 24	Mar. 25	Mar. 26	Mar. 27	Mar. 28
90 days.	Mar. 29	Mar. 30	Mar. 31	Apr. 1	Apr. 2
95 days.	Apr. 3	Apr. 4	Apr. 5	Apr. 6	Apr. 7
100 days.	Apr. 8	Apr. 9	Apr. 10	Apr. 11	Apr. 12
2 months.	Mar. 1	Mar. 2	Mar. 3	Mar. 3	Mar. 3

Date–Differential

Tables.

Examples :

     From January 5th to September 25th=264 days (see page 102.)

From September 20th to May 1st=224 days (see page 110.)

In case either of the above examples should include February 29th, add one day to the result.

Number of days from any day in JANUARY to any day in the year, the result including both dates.

From	To January						To February						To March					
	1	5	10	15	20	25	1	5	10	15	20	25	1	5	10	15	20	25
Jan'y 1	366	5	10	15	20	25	32	36	41	46	51	56	60	64	69	74	79	84
do. 5	362	366	6	11	16	21	28	32	37	42	47	52	56	60	65	70	75	80
do. 10	357	361	366	6	11	16	23	27	32	37	42	47	51	55	60	65	70	75
do. 15	352	356	361	366	6	11	18	22	27	32	37	42	46	50	55	60	65	70
do. 20	347	351	356	361	366	6	13	17	22	27	32	37	41	45	50	55	60	65
do. 25	342	346	351	356	361	366	8	12	17	22	27	32	36	40	45	50	55	60
do. 31	336	340	345	350	355	360	2	6	11	16	21	26	30	34	39	44	49	54

From	To April						To May						To June					
	1	5	10	15	20	25	1	5	10	15	20	25	1	5	10	15	20	25
Jan'y 1	91	95	100	105	110	115	121	125	130	135	140	145	152	156	161	166	171	176
do. 5	87	91	96	101	106	111	117	121	126	131	136	141	148	152	157	162	167	172
do. 10	82	86	91	96	101	106	112	116	121	126	131	136	143	147	152	157	162	167
do. 15	77	81	86	91	96	101	107	111	116	121	126	131	138	142	147	152	157	162
do. 20	72	76	81	86	91	96	102	106	111	116	121	126	133	137	142	147	152	157
do. 25	67	71	76	81	86	91	97	101	106	111	116	121	128	132	137	142	147	152
do. 31	61	65	70	75	80	85	91	95	100	105	110	115	122	126	131	136	141	146

From	To July						To August						To September					
	1	5	10	15	20	25	1	5	10	15	20	25	1	5	10	15	20	25
Jan'y 1	182	186	191	196	201	206	213	217	222	227	232	237	244	248	253	258	263	268
do. 5	178	182	187	192	197	202	209	213	218	223	228	233	240	244	249	254	259	264
do. 10	173	177	182	187	192	197	204	208	213	218	223	228	235	239	244	249	254	259
do. 15	168	172	177	182	187	192	199	203	208	213	218	223	230	234	239	244	249	254
do. 20	163	167	172	177	182	187	194	198	203	208	213	218	225	229	234	239	244	249
do. 25	158	162	167	172	177	182	189	193	198	203	208	213	220	224	229	234	239	244
do. 31	152	156	161	166	171	176	183	187	192	197	202	207	214	218	223	228	233	238

From	To October						To November						To December					
	1	5	10	15	20	25	1	5	10	15	20	25	1	5	10	15	20	25
Jan'y 1	274	278	283	288	293	298	305	309	314	319	324	329	335	339	344	349	354	359
do. 5	270	274	279	284	289	294	301	305	310	315	320	325	331	335	340	345	350	355
do. 10	265	269	274	279	284	289	296	300	305	310	315	320	326	330	335	340	345	350
do. 15	260	264	269	274	279	284	291	295	300	305	310	315	321	325	330	335	340	345
do. 20	255	259	264	269	274	279	286	290	295	300	305	310	316	320	325	330	335	340
do. 25	250	254	259	264	269	274	281	285	290	295	300	305	311	315	320	325	330	335
do. 31	244	248	253	258	263	268	275	279	284	289	294	299	305	309	314	319	324	329

In Leap-Year, add 1 day to the results given above, whenever the time between the two specified dates includes February 29th.

Number of days from any day in FEBRUARY to any day in the year, the result including both dates.

From	To February						To March						To April					
	1	5	10	15	20	25	1	5	10	15	20	25	1	5	10	15	20	25
Feb'y 1	366	5	10	15	20	25	29	33	38	43	48	53	60	64	69	74	79	84
do. 5	362	366	6	11	16	21	25	29	34	39	44	49	56	60	65	70	75	80
do. 10	357	361	366	6	11	16	20	24	29	34	39	44	51	55	60	65	70	75
do. 15	352	356	361	366	6	11	15	19	24	29	34	39	46	50	55	60	65	70
do. 20	347	351	356	361	366	6	10	14	19	24	29	34	41	45	50	55	60	65
do. 25	342	346	351	356	361	366	5	9	14	19	24	29	36	40	45	50	55	60
do. 28	339	343	348	353	358	363	2	6	11	16	21	26	33	37	42	47	52	57

From	To May						To June						To July					
	1	5	10	15	20	25	1	5	10	15	20	25	1	5	10	15	20	25
Feb'y 1	90	94	99	104	109	114	121	125	130	135	140	145	151	155	160	165	170	175
do. 5	86	90	95	100	105	110	117	121	126	131	136	141	147	151	156	161	166	171
do. 10	81	85	90	95	100	105	112	116	121	126	131	136	142	146	151	156	161	166
do. 15	76	80	85	90	95	100	107	111	116	121	126	131	137	141	146	151	156	161
do. 20	71	75	80	85	90	95	102	106	111	116	121	126	132	136	141	146	151	156
do. 25	66	70	75	80	85	90	97	101	106	111	116	121	127	131	136	141	146	151
do. 28	63	67	72	77	82	87	94	98	103	108	113	118	124	128	133	138	143	148

From	To August						To September						To October					
	1	5	10	15	20	25	1	5	10	15	20	25	1	5	10	15	20	25
Feb'y 1	182	186	191	196	201	206	213	217	222	227	232	237	243	247	252	257	262	267
do. 5	178	182	187	192	197	202	209	213	218	223	228	233	239	243	248	253	258	263
do. 10	173	177	182	187	192	197	204	208	213	218	223	228	234	238	243	248	253	258
do. 15	168	172	177	182	187	192	199	203	208	213	218	223	229	233	238	243	248	253
do. 20	163	167	172	177	182	187	194	198	203	208	213	218	224	228	233	238	243	248
do. 25	158	162	167	172	177	182	189	193	198	203	208	213	219	223	228	233	238	243
do. 28	155	159	164	169	174	179	186	190	195	200	205	210	216	220	225	230	235	240

From	To November						To December						To January					
	1	5	10	15	20	25	1	5	10	15	20	25	1	5	10	15	20	25
Feb'y 1	274	278	283	288	293	298	304	308	313	318	323	328	335	339	344	349	354	359
do. 5	270	274	279	284	289	294	300	304	309	314	319	324	331	335	340	345	350	355
do. 10	265	269	274	279	284	289	295	299	304	309	314	319	326	330	335	340	345	350
do. 15	260	264	269	274	279	284	290	294	299	304	309	314	321	325	330	335	340	345
do. 20	255	259	264	269	274	279	285	289	294	299	304	309	316	320	325	330	335	340
do. 25	250	254	259	264	269	274	280	284	289	294	299	304	311	315	320	325	330	335
do. 28	247	251	256	261	266	271	277	281	286	291	296	301	308	312	317	322	327	332

In Leap-Year, add 1 day to the results given above, whenever the time between the two specified dates includes February 29th.

Number of days from any day in MARCH to any day in the year, the result including both dates.

From	To March						To April						To May					
	1	5	10	15	20	25	1	5	10	15	20	25	1	5	10	15	20	25
M'ch 1	366	5	10	15	20	25	32	36	41	46	51	56	62	66	71	76	81	86
do. 5	362	366	6	11	16	21	28	32	37	42	47	52	58	62	67	72	77	82
do. 10	357	361	366	6	11	16	23	27	32	37	42	47	53	57	62	67	72	77
do. 15	352	356	361	366	6	11	18	22	27	32	37	42	48	52	57	62	67	72
do. 20	347	351	356	361	366	6	13	17	22	27	32	37	43	47	52	57	62	67
do. 25	342	346	351	356	361	366	8	12	17	22	27	32	38	42	47	52	57	62
do. 31	336	340	345	350	355	360	2	6	11	16	21	26	32	36	41	46	51	56

From	To June						To July						To August					
	1	5	10	15	20	25	1	5	10	15	20	25	1	5	10	15	20	25
M'ch 1	93	97	102	107	112	117	123	127	132	137	142	147	154	158	163	168	173	178
do. 5	89	93	98	103	108	113	119	123	128	133	138	143	150	154	159	164	169	174
do. 10	84	88	93	98	103	108	114	118	123	128	133	138	145	149	154	159	164	169
do. 15	79	83	88	93	98	103	109	113	118	123	128	133	140	144	149	154	159	164
do. 20	74	78	83	88	93	98	104	108	113	118	123	128	135	139	144	149	154	159
do. 25	69	73	78	83	88	93	99	103	108	113	118	123	130	134	139	144	149	154
do. 31	63	67	72	77	82	87	93	97	102	107	112	117	124	128	133	138	143	148

From	To September						To October						To November					
	1	5	10	15	20	25	1	5	10	15	20	25	1	5	10	15	20	25
M'ch 1	185	189	194	199	204	209	215	219	224	229	234	239	246	250	255	260	265	270
do. 5	181	185	190	195	200	205	211	215	220	225	230	235	242	246	251	256	261	266
do. 10	176	180	185	190	195	200	206	210	215	220	225	230	237	241	246	251	256	261
do. 15	171	175	180	185	190	195	201	205	210	215	220	225	232	236	241	246	251	256
do. 20	166	170	175	180	185	190	196	200	205	210	215	220	227	231	236	241	246	251
do. 25	161	165	170	175	180	185	191	195	200	205	210	215	222	226	231	236	241	246
do. 31	155	159	164	169	174	179	185	189	194	199	204	209	216	220	225	230	235	240

From	To December						To January						To February					
	1	5	10	15	20	25	1	5	10	15	20	25	1	5	10	15	20	25
M'ch 1	276	280	285	290	295	300	307	311	316	321	326	331	338	342	347	352	357	362
do. 5	272	276	281	286	291	296	303	307	312	317	322	327	334	338	343	348	353	358
do. 10	267	271	276	281	286	291	298	302	307	312	317	322	329	333	338	343	348	353
do. 15	262	266	271	276	281	286	293	297	302	307	312	317	324	328	333	338	343	348
do. 20	257	261	266	271	276	281	288	292	297	302	307	312	319	323	328	333	338	343
do. 25	252	256	261	266	271	276	283	287	292	297	302	307	314	318	323	328	333	338
do. 31	246	250	255	260	265	270	277	281	286	291	296	301	308	312	317	322	327	332

In Leap-Year, add 1 day to the results given above, whenever the time between the two specified dates includes February 29th.

Number of days from any day in APRIL to any day in the year, the result including both dates.

From	To April 1	5	10	15	20	25	To May 1	5	10	15	20	25	To June 1	5	10	15	20	25
April 1	366	5	10	15	20	25	31	35	40	45	50	55	62	66	71	76	81	86
do. 5	362	366	6	11	16	21	27	31	36	41	46	51	58	62	67	72	77	82
do. 10	357	361	366	6	11	16	22	26	31	36	41	46	53	57	62	67	72	77
do. 15	352	356	361	366	6	11	17	21	26	31	36	41	48	52	57	62	67	72
do. 20	347	351	356	361	366	6	12	16	21	26	31	36	43	47	52	57	62	67
do. 25	342	346	351	356	361	366	7	11	16	21	26	31	38	42	47	52	57	62
do. 30	337	341	346	351	356	361	2	6	11	16	21	26	33	37	42	47	52	57

From	To July 1	5	10	15	20	25	To August 1	5	10	15	20	25	To September 1	5	10	15	20	25
April 1	92	96	101	106	111	116	123	127	132	137	142	147	154	158	163	168	173	178
do. 5	88	92	97	102	107	112	119	123	128	133	138	143	150	154	159	164	169	174
do. 10	83	87	92	97	102	107	114	118	123	128	133	138	145	149	154	159	164	169
do. 15	78	82	87	92	97	102	109	113	118	123	128	133	140	144	149	154	159	164
do. 20	73	77	82	87	92	97	104	108	113	118	123	128	135	139	144	149	154	159
do. 25	68	72	77	82	87	92	99	103	108	113	118	123	130	134	139	144	149	154
do. 30	63	67	72	77	82	87	94	98	103	108	113	118	125	129	134	139	144	149

From	To October 1	5	10	15	20	25	To November 1	5	10	15	20	25	To December 1	5	10	15	20	25
April 1	184	188	193	198	203	208	215	219	224	229	234	239	245	249	254	259	264	269
do. 5	180	184	189	194	199	204	211	215	220	225	230	235	241	245	250	255	260	265
do. 10	175	179	184	189	194	199	206	210	215	220	225	230	236	240	245	250	255	260
do. 15	170	174	179	184	189	194	201	205	210	215	220	225	231	235	240	245	250	255
do. 20	165	169	174	179	184	189	196	200	205	210	215	220	226	230	235	240	245	250
do. 25	160	164	169	174	179	184	191	195	200	205	210	215	221	225	230	235	240	245
do. 30	155	159	164	169	174	179	186	190	195	200	205	210	216	220	225	230	235	240

From	To January 1	5	10	15	20	25	To February 1	5	10	15	20	25	To March 1	5	10	15	20	25
April 1	276	280	285	290	295	300	307	311	316	321	326	331	335	339	344	349	354	359
do. 5	272	276	281	286	291	296	303	307	312	317	322	327	331	335	340	345	350	355
do. 10	267	271	276	281	286	291	298	302	307	312	317	322	326	330	335	340	345	350
do. 15	262	266	271	276	281	286	293	297	302	307	312	317	321	325	330	335	340	345
do. 20	257	261	266	271	276	281	288	292	297	302	307	312	316	320	325	330	335	340
do. 25	252	256	261	266	271	276	283	287	292	297	302	307	311	315	320	325	330	335
do. 30	247	251	256	261	266	271	278	282	287	292	297	302	306	310	315	320	325	330

In Leap-Year, add 1 day to the results given above, whenever the time between the two specified dates includes February 29th.

Number of days from any day in MAY to any day in the year. the result including both dates.

From	To May						To June						To July					
	1	5	10	15	20	25	1	5	10	15	20	25	1	5	10	15	20	25
May 1	366	5	10	15	20	25	32	36	41	46	51	56	62	66	71	76	81	86
do. 5	362	366	6	11	16	21	28	32	37	42	47	52	58	62	67	72	77	82
do. 10	357	361	366	6	11	16	23	27	32	37	42	47	53	57	62	67	72	77
do. 15	352	356	361	366	6	11	18	22	27	32	37	42	48	52	57	62	67	72
do. 20	347	351	356	361	366	6	13	17	22	27	32	37	43	47	52	57	62	67
do. 25	342	346	351	356	361	366	8	12	17	22	27	32	38	42	47	52	57	62
do. 31	336	340	345	350	355	360	2	6	11	16	21	26	32	36	41	46	51	56

From	To August						To September						To October					
	1	5	10	15	20	25	1	5	10	15	20	25	1	5	10	15	20	25
May 1	93	97	102	107	112	117	124	128	133	138	143	148	154	158	163	168	173	178
do. 5	89	93	98	103	108	113	120	124	129	134	139	144	150	154	159	164	169	174
do. 10	84	88	93	98	103	108	115	119	124	129	134	139	145	149	154	159	164	169
do. 15	79	83	88	93	98	103	110	114	119	124	129	134	140	144	149	154	159	164
do. 20	74	78	83	88	93	98	105	109	114	119	124	129	135	139	144	149	154	159
do. 25	69	73	78	83	88	93	100	104	109	114	119	124	130	134	139	144	149	154
do. 31	63	67	72	77	82	87	94	98	103	108	113	118	124	128	133	138	143	148

From	To November						To December						To January					
	1	5	10	15	20	25	1	5	10	15	20	25	1	5	10	15	20	25
May 1	185	189	194	199	204	209	215	219	224	229	234	239	246	250	255	260	265	270
do. 5	181	185	190	195	200	205	211	215	220	225	230	235	242	246	251	256	261	266
do. 10	176	180	185	190	195	200	206	210	215	220	225	230	237	241	246	251	256	261
do. 15	171	175	180	185	190	195	201	205	210	215	220	225	232	236	241	246	251	256
do. 20	166	170	175	180	185	190	196	200	205	210	215	220	227	231	236	241	246	251
do. 25	161	165	170	175	180	185	191	195	200	205	210	215	222	226	231	236	241	246
do. 31	155	159	164	169	174	179	185	189	194	199	204	209	216	220	225	230	235	240

From	To February						To March						To April					
	1	5	10	15	20	25	1	5	10	15	20	25	1	5	10	15	20	25
May 1	277	281	286	291	296	301	305	309	314	319	324	329	336	340	345	350	355	360
do. 5	273	277	282	287	292	297	301	305	310	315	320	325	332	336	341	346	351	356
do. 10	268	272	277	282	287	292	296	300	305	310	315	320	327	331	336	341	346	351
do. 15	263	267	272	277	282	287	291	295	300	305	310	315	322	326	331	336	341	346
do. 20	258	262	267	272	277	282	286	290	295	300	305	310	317	321	326	331	336	341
do. 25	253	257	262	267	272	277	281	285	290	295	300	305	312	316	321	326	331	336
do. 31	247	251	256	261	266	271	275	279	284	289	294	299	306	310	315	320	325	330

In Leap-Year, add 1 day to the results given above, whenever the time between the two specified dates includes February 29th.

Number of days from any day in JUNE to any day in the year, the result including both dates.

From	To June						To July						To August					
	1	5	10	15	20	25	1	5	10	15	20	25	1	5	10	15	20	25
June 1	366	5	10	15	20	25	31	35	40	45	50	55	62	66	71	76	81	86
do. 5	362	366	6	11	16	21	27	31	36	41	46	51	58	62	67	72	77	82
do. 10	357	361	366	6	11	16	22	26	31	36	41	46	53	57	62	67	72	77
do. 15	352	356	361	366	6	11	17	21	26	31	36	41	48	52	57	62	67	72
do. 20	347	351	356	361	366	6	12	16	21	26	31	36	43	47	52	57	62	67
do. 25	342	346	351	356	361	366	7	11	16	21	26	31	38	42	47	52	57	62
do. 30	337	341	346	351	356	361	2	6	11	16	21	26	33	37	42	47	52	57

From	To September						To October						To November					
	1	5	10	15	20	25	1	5	10	15	20	25	1	5	10	15	20	25
June 1	93	97	102	107	112	117	123	127	132	137	142	147	154	158	163	168	173	178
do. 5	89	93	98	103	108	113	119	123	128	133	138	143	150	154	159	164	169	174
do. 10	84	88	93	98	103	108	114	118	123	128	133	138	145	149	154	159	164	169
do. 15	79	83	88	93	98	103	109	113	118	123	128	133	140	144	149	154	159	164
do. 20	74	78	83	88	93	98	104	108	113	118	123	128	135	139	144	149	154	159
do. 25	69	73	78	83	88	93	99	103	108	113	118	123	130	134	139	144	149	154
do. 30	64	68	73	78	83	88	94	98	103	108	113	118	125	129	134	139	144	149

From	To December						To January						To February					
	1	5	10	15	20	25	1	5	10	15	20	25	1	5	10	15	20	25
June 1	184	188	193	198	203	208	215	219	224	229	234	239	246	250	255	260	265	270
do. 5	180	184	189	194	199	204	211	215	220	225	230	235	242	246	251	256	261	266
do. 10	175	179	184	189	194	199	206	210	215	220	225	230	237	241	246	251	256	261
do. 15	170	174	179	184	189	194	201	205	210	215	220	225	232	236	241	246	251	256
do. 20	165	169	174	179	184	189	196	200	205	210	215	220	227	231	236	241	246	251
do. 25	160	164	169	174	179	184	191	195	200	205	210	215	222	226	231	236	241	246
do. 30	155	159	164	169	174	179	186	190	195	200	205	210	217	221	226	231	236	241

From	To March						To April						To May					
	1	5	10	15	20	25	1	5	10	15	20	25	1	5	10	15	20	25
June 1	274	278	283	288	293	298	305	309	314	319	324	329	335	339	344	349	354	359
do. 5	270	274	279	284	289	294	301	305	310	315	320	325	331	335	340	345	350	355
do. 10	265	269	274	279	284	289	296	300	305	310	315	320	326	330	335	340	345	350
do. 15	260	264	269	274	279	284	291	295	300	305	310	315	321	325	330	335	340	345
do. 20	255	259	264	269	274	279	286	290	295	300	305	310	316	320	325	330	335	340
do. 25	250	254	259	264	269	274	281	285	290	295	300	305	311	315	320	325	330	335
do. 30	245	249	254	259	264	269	276	280	285	290	295	300	306	310	315	320	325	330

In Leap-Year, add 1 day to the results given above, whenever the time between the two specified dates includes February 29th.

Number of days from any day in JULY to any day in the year, the result including both dates.

From	To July						To August						To September					
	1	5	10	15	20	25	1	5	10	15	20	25	1	5	10	15	20	25
July 1	366	5	10	15	20	25	32	36	41	46	51	56	63	67	72	77	82	87
do. 5	362	366	6	11	16	21	28	32	37	42	47	52	59	63	68	73	78	83
do. 10	357	361	366	6	11	16	23	27	32	37	42	47	54	58	63	68	73	78
do. 15	352	356	361	366	6	11	18	22	27	32	37	42	49	53	58	63	68	73
do. 20	347	351	356	361	366	6	13	17	22	27	32	37	44	48	53	58	63	68
do. 25	342	346	351	356	361	366	8	12	17	22	27	32	39	43	48	53	58	63
do. 31	336	340	345	350	355	360	2	6	11	16	21	26	33	37	42	47	52	57

From	To October						To November						To December					
	1	5	10	15	20	25	1	5	10	15	20	25	1	5	10	15	20	25
July 1	93	97	102	107	112	117	124	128	133	138	143	148	154	158	163	168	173	178
do. 5	89	93	98	103	108	113	120	124	129	134	139	144	150	154	159	164	169	174
do. 10	84	88	93	98	103	108	115	119	124	129	134	139	145	149	154	159	164	169
do. 15	79	83	88	93	98	103	110	114	119	124	129	134	140	144	149	154	159	164
do. 20	74	78	83	88	93	98	105	109	114	119	124	129	135	139	144	149	154	159
do. 25	69	73	78	83	88	93	100	104	109	114	119	124	130	134	139	144	149	154
do. 31	63	67	72	77	82	87	94	98	103	108	113	118	124	128	133	138	143	148

From	To January						To February						To March					
	1	5	10	15	20	25	1	5	10	15	20	25	1	5	10	15	20	25
July 1	185	189	194	199	204	209	216	220	225	230	235	240	244	248	253	258	263	268
do. 5	181	185	190	195	200	205	212	216	221	226	231	236	240	244	249	254	259	264
do. 10	176	180	185	190	195	200	207	211	216	221	226	231	235	239	244	249	254	259
do. 15	171	175	180	185	190	195	202	206	211	216	221	226	230	234	239	244	249	254
do. 20	166	170	175	180	185	190	197	201	206	211	216	221	225	229	234	239	244	249
do. 25	161	165	170	175	180	185	192	196	201	206	211	216	220	224	229	234	239	244
do. 31	155	159	164	169	174	179	186	190	195	200	205	210	214	218	223	228	233	238

From	To April						To May						To June					
	1	5	10	15	20	25	1	5	10	15	20	25	1	5	10	15	20	25
July 1	275	279	284	289	294	299	305	309	314	319	324	329	336	340	345	350	355	360
do. 5	271	275	280	285	290	295	301	305	310	315	320	325	332	336	341	346	351	356
do. 10	266	270	275	280	285	290	296	300	305	310	315	320	327	331	336	341	346	351
do. 15	261	265	270	275	280	285	291	295	300	305	310	315	322	326	331	336	341	346
do. 20	256	260	265	270	275	280	286	290	295	300	305	310	317	321	326	331	336	341
do. 25	251	255	260	265	270	275	281	285	290	295	300	305	312	316	321	326	331	336
do. 31	245	249	254	259	264	269	275	279	284	289	294	299	306	310	315	320	325	330

In Leap-Year, add 1 day to the results given above, whenever the time between the two specified dates includes February 29th.

Number of days from any day in AUGUST to any day in the year, the result including both dates.

From	To August						To September						To October					
	1	5	10	15	20	25	1	5	10	15	20	25	1	5	10	15	20	25
Aug. 1	366	5	10	15	20	25	32	36	41	46	51	56	62	66	71	76	81	86
do. 5	362	366	6	11	16	21	28	32	37	42	47	52	58	62	67	72	77	82
do. 10	357	361	366	6	11	16	23	27	32	37	42	47	53	57	62	67	72	77
do. 15	352	356	361	366	6	11	18	22	27	32	37	42	48	52	57	62	67	72
do. 20	347	351	356	361	366		13	17	22	27	32	37	43	47	52	57	62	67
do. 25	342	346	351	356	361	366	8	12	17	22	27	32	38	42	47	52	57	62
do. 31	336	340	345	350	355	360	2	6	11	16	21	26	32	36	41	46	51	56

From	To November						To December						To January					
	1	5	10	15	20	25	1	5	10	15	20	25	1	5	10	15	20	25
Aug. 1	93	97	102	107	112	117	123	127	132	137	142	147	154	158	163	168	173	178
do. 5	89	93	98	103	108	113	119	123	128	133	138	143	150	154	159	164	169	174
do. 10	84	88	93	98	103	108	114	118	123	128	133	138	145	149	154	159	164	169
do. 15	79	83	88	93	98	103	109	113	118	123	128	133	140	144	149	154	159	164
do. 20	74	78	83	88	93	98	104	108	113	118	123	128	135	139	144	149	154	159
do. 25	69	73	78	83	88	93	99	103	108	113	118	123	130	134	139	144	149	154
do. 31	63	67	72	77	82	87	93	97	102	107	112	117	124	128	133	138	143	148

From	To February						To March						To April					
	1	5	10	15	20	25	1	5	10	15	20	25	1	5	10	15	20	25
Aug. 1	185	189	194	199	204	209	213	217	222	227	232	237	244	248	253	258	263	268
do. 5	181	185	190	195	200	205	209	213	218	223	228	233	240	244	249	254	259	264
do. 10	176	180	185	190	195	200	204	208	213	218	223	228	235	239	244	249	254	259
do. 15	171	175	180	185	190	195	199	203	208	213	218	223	230	234	239	244	249	254
do. 20	166	170	175	180	185	190	194	198	203	208	213	218	225	229	234	239	244	249
do. 25	161	165	170	175	180	185	189	193	198	203	208	213	220	224	229	234	239	244
do. 31	155	159	164	169	174	179	183	187	192	197	202	207	214	218	223	228	233	238

From	To May						To June						To July					
	1	5	10	15	20	25	1	5	10	15	20	25	1	5	10	15	20	25
Aug. 1	274	278	283	288	293	298	305	309	314	319	324	329	335	339	344	349	354	359
do. 5	270	274	279	284	289	294	301	305	310	315	320	325	331	335	340	345	350	355
do. 10	265	269	274	279	284	289	296	300	305	310	315	320	326	330	335	340	345	350
do. 15	260	264	269	274	279	284	291	295	300	305	310	315	321	325	330	335	340	345
do. 20	255	259	264	269	274	279	286	290	295	300	305	310	316	320	325	330	335	340
do. 25	250	254	259	264	269	274	281	285	290	295	300	305	311	315	320	325	330	335
do. 31	244	248	253	258	263	268	275	279	284	289	294	299	305	309	314	319	324	329

In Leap-Year, add 1 day to the results given above, whenever the time between the two specified dates includes February 29th.

Number of days from any day in SEPTEMBER to any day in the year, the result including both dates.

From	To September						To October						To November					
	1	5	10	15	20	25	1	5	10	15	20	25	1	5	10	15	20	25
Sept. 1	366	5	10	15	20	25	31	35	40	45	50	55	62	66	71	76	81	86
do. 5	362	366	6	11	16	21	27	31	36	41	46	51	58	62	67	72	77	82
do. 10	357	361	366	6	11	16	22	26	31	36	41	46	53	57	62	67	72	77
do. 15	352	356	361	366	6	11	17	21	26	31	36	41	48	52	57	62	67	72
do. 20	347	351	356	361	366	6	12	16	21	26	31	36	43	47	52	57	62	67
do. 25	342	346	351	356	361	366	7	11	16	21	26	31	38	42	47	52	57	62
do. 30	337	341	346	351	356	361	2	6	11	16	21	26	33	37	42	47	52	57

From	To December						To January						To February					
	1	5	10	15	20	25	1	5	10	15	20	25	1	5	10	15	20	25
Sept. 1	92	96	101	106	111	116	123	127	132	137	142	147	154	158	163	168	173	178
do. 5	88	92	97	102	107	112	119	123	128	133	138	143	150	154	159	164	169	174
do. 10	83	87	92	97	102	107	114	118	123	128	133	138	145	149	154	159	164	169
do. 15	78	82	87	92	97	102	109	113	118	123	128	133	140	144	149	154	159	164
do. 20	73	77	82	87	92	97	104	108	113	118	123	128	135	139	144	149	154	159
do. 25	68	72	77	82	87	92	99	103	108	113	118	123	130	134	139	144	149	154
do. 30	63	67	72	77	82	87	94	98	103	108	113	118	125	129	134	139	144	149

From	To March						To April						To May					
	1	5	10	15	20	25	1	5	10	15	20	25	1	5	10	15	20	25
Sept. 1	182	186	191	196	201	206	213	217	222	227	232	237	243	247	252	257	262	267
do. 5	178	182	187	192	197	202	209	213	218	223	228	233	239	243	248	253	258	263
do. 10	173	177	182	187	192	197	204	208	213	218	223	228	234	238	243	248	253	258
do. 15	168	172	177	182	187	192	199	203	208	213	218	223	229	233	238	243	248	253
do. 20	163	167	172	177	182	187	194	198	203	208	213	218	224	228	233	238	243	248
do. 25	158	162	167	172	177	182	189	193	198	203	208	213	219	223	228	233	238	243
do. 30	153	157	162	167	172	177	184	188	193	198	203	208	214	218	223	228	233	238

From	To June						To July						To August					
	1	5	10	15	20	25	1	5	10	15	20	25	1	5	10	15	20	25
Sept. 1	274	278	283	288	293	298	304	308	313	318	323	328	335	339	344	349	354	359
do. 5	270	274	279	284	289	294	300	304	309	314	319	324	331	335	340	345	350	355
do. 10	265	269	274	279	284	289	295	299	304	309	314	319	326	330	335	340	345	350
do. 15	260	264	269	274	279	284	290	294	299	304	309	314	321	325	330	335	340	345
do. 20	255	259	264	269	274	279	285	289	294	299	304	309	316	320	325	330	335	340
do. 25	250	254	259	264	269	274	280	284	289	294	299	304	311	315	320	325	330	335
do. 30	245	249	254	259	264	269	275	279	284	289	294	299	306	310	315	320	325	330

In Leap-Year, add 1 day to the results given above, whenever the time between the two specified dates includes February 29th.

Number of days from any day in OCTOBER to any day in the year, the result including both dates.

From	To October						To November						To December					
	1	5	10	15	20	25	1	5	10	15	20	25	1	5	10	15	20	25
Oct. 1	366	5	10	15	20	25	32	36	41	46	51	56	62	66	71	76	81	86
do. 5	362	366	6	11	16	21	28	32	37	42	47	52	58	62	67	72	77	82
do. 10	357	361	366	6	11	16	23	27	32	37	42	47	53	57	62	67	72	77
do. 15	352	356	361	366	6	11	18	22	27	32	37	42	48	52	57	62	67	72
do. 20	347	351	356	361	366	6	13	17	22	27	32	37	43	47	52	57	62	67
do. 25	342	346	351	356	361	366	8	12	17	22	27	32	38	42	47	52	57	62
do. 31	336	340	345	350	355	360	2	6	11	16	21	26	32	36	41	46	51	56

From	To January						To February						To March					
	1	5	10	15	20	25	1	5	10	15	20	25	1	5	10	15	20	25
Oct. 1	93	97	102	107	112	117	124	128	133	138	143	148	152	156	161	166	171	176
do. 5	89	93	98	103	108	113	120	124	129	134	139	144	148	152	157	162	167	172
do. 10	84	88	93	98	103	108	115	119	124	129	134	139	143	147	152	157	162	167
do. 15	79	83	88	93	98	103	110	114	119	124	129	134	138	142	147	152	157	162
do. 20	74	78	83	88	93	98	105	109	114	119	124	129	133	137	142	147	152	157
do. 25	69	73	78	83	88	93	100	104	109	114	119	124	128	132	137	142	147	152
do. 31	63	67	72	77	82	87	94	98	103	108	113	118	122	126	131	136	141	146

From	To April						To May						To June					
	1	5	10	15	20	25	1	5	10	15	20	25	1	5	10	15	20	25
Oct. 1	183	187	192	197	202	207	213	217	222	227	232	237	244	248	253	258	263	268
do. 5	179	183	188	193	198	203	209	213	218	223	228	233	240	244	249	254	259	264
do. 10	174	178	183	188	193	198	204	208	213	218	223	228	235	239	244	249	254	259
do. 15	169	173	178	183	188	193	199	203	208	213	218	223	230	234	239	244	249	254
do. 20	164	168	173	178	183	188	194	198	203	208	213	218	225	229	234	239	244	249
do. 25	159	163	168	173	178	183	189	193	198	203	208	213	220	224	229	234	239	244
do. 31	153	157	162	167	172	177	183	187	192	197	202	207	214	218	223	228	233	238

From	To July						To August						To September					
	1	5	10	15	20	25	1	5	10	15	20	25	1	5	10	15	20	25
Oct. 1	274	278	283	288	293	298	305	309	314	319	324	329	336	340	345	350	355	360
do. 5	270	274	279	284	289	294	301	305	310	315	320	325	332	336	341	346	351	356
do. 10	265	269	274	279	284	289	296	300	305	310	315	320	327	331	336	341	346	351
do. 15	260	264	269	274	279	284	291	295	300	305	310	315	322	326	331	336	341	346
do. 20	255	259	264	269	274	279	286	290	295	300	305	310	317	321	326	331	336	341
do. 25	250	254	259	264	269	274	281	285	290	295	300	305	312	316	321	326	331	336
do. 31	244	248	253	258	263	268	275	279	284	289	294	299	306	310	315	320	325	330

In Leap-Year, add 1 day to the results given above, whenever the time between the two specified dates includes February 29th.

Number of days from any day in NOVEMBER to any day in the year, the result including both dates.

From	To November						To December						To January					
	1	5	10	15	20	25	1	5	10	15	20	25	1	5	10	15	20	25
Nov. 1	366	5	10	15	20	25	31	35	40	45	50	55	62	66	71	76	81	86
do. 5	362	366	6	11	16	21	27	31	36	41	46	51	58	62	67	72	77	82
do. 10	357	361	366	6	11	16	22	26	31	36	41	46	53	57	62	67	72	77
do. 15	352	356	361	366	6	11	17	21	26	31	36	41	48	52	57	62	67	72
do. 20	347	351	356	361	366	6	12	16	21	26	31	36	43	47	52	57	62	67
do. 25	342	346	351	356	361	366	7	11	16	21	26	31	38	42	47	52	57	62
do. 30	337	341	346	351	356	361	2	6	11	16	21	26	33	37	42	47	52	57

From	To February						To March						To April					
	1	5	10	15	20	25	1	5	10	15	20	25	1	5	10	15	20	25
Nov. 1	93	97	102	107	112	117	121	125	130	135	140	145	152	156	161	166	171	176
do. 5	89	93	98	103	108	113	117	121	126	131	136	141	148	152	157	162	167	172
do. 10	84	88	93	98	103	108	112	116	121	126	131	136	143	147	152	157	162	167
do. 15	79	83	88	93	98	103	107	111	116	121	126	131	138	142	147	152	157	162
do. 20	74	78	83	88	93	98	102	106	111	116	121	126	133	137	142	147	152	157
do. 25	69	73	78	83	88	93	97	101	106	111	116	121	128	132	137	142	147	152
do. 30	64	68	73	78	83	88	92	96	101	106	111	116	123	127	132	137	142	147

From	To May						To June						To July					
	1	5	10	15	20	25	1	5	10	15	20	25	1	5	10	15	20	25
Nov. 1	182	186	191	196	201	206	213	217	222	227	232	237	243	247	252	257	262	267
do. 5	178	182	187	192	197	202	209	213	218	223	228	233	239	243	248	253	258	263
do. 10	173	177	182	187	192	197	204	208	213	218	223	228	234	238	243	248	253	258
do. 15	168	172	177	182	187	192	199	203	208	213	218	223	229	233	238	243	248	253
do. 20	163	167	172	177	182	187	194	198	203	208	213	218	224	228	233	238	243	248
do. 25	158	162	167	172	177	182	189	193	198	203	208	213	219	223	228	233	238	243
do. 30	153	157	162	167	172	177	184	188	193	198	203	208	214	218	223	228	233	238

From	To August						To September						To October					
	1	5	10	15	20	25	1	5	10	15	20	25	1	5	10	15	20	25
Nov. 1	274	278	283	288	293	298	305	309	314	319	324	329	335	339	344	349	354	359
do. 5	270	274	279	284	289	294	301	305	310	315	320	325	331	335	340	345	350	355
do. 10	265	269	274	279	284	289	296	300	305	310	315	320	326	330	335	340	345	350
do. 15	260	264	269	274	279	284	291	295	300	305	310	315	321	325	330	335	340	345
do. 20	255	259	264	269	274	279	286	290	295	300	305	310	316	320	325	330	335	340
do. 25	250	254	259	264	269	274	281	285	290	295	300	305	311	315	320	325	330	335
do. 30	245	249	254	259	264	269	276	280	285	290	295	300	306	310	315	320	325	330

In Leap-Year, add 1 day to the results given above, whenever the time between the two specified dates includes February 29th.

Number of days from any day in DECEMBER to any day in the year, the result including both dates.

From	To December						To January						To February					
	1	5	10	15	20	25	1	5	10	15	20	25	1	5	10	15	20	25
Dec. 1	366	5	10	15	20	25	32	36	41	46	51	56	63	67	72	77	82	87
do. 5	362	366	6	11	16	21	28	32	37	42	47	52	59	63	68	73	78	83
do. 10	357	361	366	6	11	16	23	27	32	37	42	47	54	58	63	68	73	78
do. 15	352	356	361	366	6	11	18	22	27	32	37	42	49	53	58	63	68	73
do. 20	347	351	356	361	366	6	13	17	22	27	32	37	44	48	53	58	63	68
do. 25	342	346	351	356	361	366	8	12	17	22	27	32	39	43	48	53	58	63
do. 31	336	340	345	350	355	360	2	6	11	16	21	26	33	37	42	47	52	57

From	To March						To April						To May					
	1	5	10	15	20	25	1	5	10	15	20	25	1	5	10	15	20	25
Dec. 1	91	95	100	105	110	115	122	126	131	136	141	146	152	156	161	166	171	176
do. 5	87	91	96	101	106	111	118	122	127	132	137	142	148	152	157	162	167	172
do. 10	82	86	91	96	101	106	113	117	122	127	132	137	143	147	152	157	162	167
do. 15	77	81	86	91	96	101	108	112	117	122	127	132	138	142	147	152	157	162
do. 20	72	76	81	86	91	96	103	107	112	117	122	127	133	137	142	147	152	157
do. 25	67	71	76	81	86	91	98	102	107	112	117	122	128	132	137	142	147	152
do. 31	61	65	70	75	80	85	92	96	101	106	111	116	122	126	131	136	141	146

From	To June						To July						To August					
	1	5	10	15	20	25	1	5	10	15	20	25	1	5	10	15	20	25
Dec. 1	183	187	192	197	202	207	213	217	222	227	232	237	244	248	253	258	263	268
do. 5	179	183	188	193	198	203	209	213	218	223	228	233	240	244	249	254	259	264
do. 10	174	178	183	188	193	198	204	208	213	218	223	228	235	239	244	249	254	259
do. 15	169	173	178	183	188	193	199	203	208	213	218	223	230	234	239	244	249	254
do. 20	164	168	173	178	183	188	194	198	203	208	213	218	225	229	234	239	244	249
do. 25	159	163	168	173	178	183	189	193	198	203	208	213	220	224	229	234	239	244
do. 31	153	157	162	167	172	177	183	187	192	197	202	207	214	218	223	228	233	238

From	To September						To October						To November					
	1	5	10	15	20	25	1	5	10	15	20	25	1	5	10	15	20	25
Dec. 1	275	279	284	289	294	299	305	309	314	319	324	329	336	340	345	350	355	360
do. 5	271	275	280	285	290	295	301	305	310	315	320	325	332	336	341	346	351	356
do. 10	266	270	275	280	285	290	296	300	305	310	315	320	327	331	336	341	346	351
do. 15	261	265	270	275	280	285	291	295	300	305	310	315	322	326	331	336	341	346
do. 20	256	260	265	270	275	280	286	290	295	300	305	310	317	321	326	331	336	341
do. 25	251	255	260	265	270	275	281	285	290	295	300	305	312	316	321	326	331	336
do. 31	245	249	254	259	264	269	275	279	284	289	294	299	306	310	315	320	325	330

In Leap-Year, add 1 day to the results given above, whenever the time between the two specified dates includes February 29th.

Note~Maturity Tables,

without grace.

For use in States where Three Days' Grace are
NOT ALLOWED.

WITHOUT GRACE.
For Leap Year changes, see next page.

Time.	January 1.	January 2.	January 3.	January 4.	January 5.
5 days.	Jan. 6	Jan. 7	Jan. 8	Jan. 9	Jan. 10
10 days.	Jan. 11	Jan. 12	Jan. 13	Jan. 14	Jan. 15
15 days.	Jan. 16	Jan. 17	Jan. 18	Jan. 19	Jan. 20
20 days.	Jan. 21	Jan. 22	Jan. 23	Jan. 24	Jan. 25
25 days.	Jan. 26	Jan. 27	Jan. 28	Jan. 29	Jan. 30
30 days.	Jan. 31	Feb. 1	Feb. 2	Feb. 3	Feb. 4
35 days.	Feb. 5	Feb. 6	Feb. 7	Feb. 8	Feb. 9
40 days.	Feb. 10	Feb. 11	Feb. 12	Feb. 13	Feb. 14
45 days.	Feb. 15	Feb. 16	Feb. 17	Feb. 18	Feb. 19
50 days.	Feb. 20	Feb. 21	Feb. 22	Feb. 23	Feb. 24
55 days.	Feb. 25	Feb. 26	Feb. 27	Feb. 28	Mar. 1
60 days.	Mar. 2	Mar. 3	Mar. 4	Mar. 5	Mar. 6
65 days.	Mar. 7	Mar. 8	Mar. 9	Mar. 10	Mar. 11
70 days.	Mar. 12	Mar. 13	Mar. 14	Mar. 15	Mar. 16
75 days.	Mar. 17	Mar. 18	Mar. 19	Mar. 20	Mar. 21
80 days.	Mar. 22	Mar. 23	Mar. 24	Mar. 25	Mar. 26
85 days.	Mar. 27	Mar. 28	Mar. 29	Mar. 30	Mar. 31
90 days.	Apr. 1	Apr. 2	Apr. 3	Apr. 4	Apr. 5
95 days.	Apr. 6	Apr. 7	Apr. 8	Apr. 9	Apr. 10
100 days.	Apr. 11	Apr. 12	Apr. 13	Apr. 14	Apr. 15
1 month.	Feb. 1	Feb. 2	Feb. 3	Feb. 4	Feb. 5
2 months.	Mar. 1	Mar. 2	Mar. 3	Mar. 4	Mar. 5
3 months.	Apr. 1	Apr. 2	Apr. 3	Apr. 4	Apr. 5
4 months.	May 1	May 2	May 3	May 4	May 5
5 months.	Jun. 1	Jun. 2	Jun. 3	June 4	Jun. 5
6 months.	Jul. 1	Jul. 2	Jul. 3	July 4	July 5
7 months.	Aug. 1	Aug. 2	Aug. 3	Aug. 4	Aug. 5
8 months.	Sep. 1	Sep. 2	Sep. 3	Sept. 4	Sep. 5
9 months.	Oct. 1	Oct. 2	Oct. 3	Oct. 4	Oct. 5
10 months.	Nov. 1	Nov. 2	Nov. 3	Nov. 4	Nov. 5
11 months.	Dec. 1	Dec. 2	Dec. 3	Dec. 4	Dec. 5
12 months.	Jan. 1	Jan. 2	Jan. 3	Jan. 4	Jan. 5

The above Tables are WITHOUT three days' grace.

(WITHOUT GRACE.)
Changes when Notes mature in Leap-Year.

Time.	January 1.	January 2.	January 3.	January 4.	January 5.
55 days.	Feb. 25	Feb. 26	Feb. 27	Feb. 28	Feb. 29
60 days.	Mar. 1	Mar. 2	Mar. 3	Mar. 4	Mar. 5
65 days.	Mar. 6	Mar, 7	Mar. 8	Mar. 9	Mar. 10
70 days.	Mar. 11	Mar. 12	Mar. 13	Mar. 14	Mar. 15
75 days.	Mch 16	Mch 17	Mch 18	Mch 19	Mch 20
80 days.	Mar. 21	Mar. 22	Mar. 23	Mar. 24	Mar. 25
85 days.	Mar. 26	Mar. 27	Mar. 28	Mar. 29	Mar. 30
90 days.	Mar. 31	Apr. 1	Apr. 2	Apr. 3	Apr. 4
95 days.	Apr. 5	Apr. 6	Apr. 7	Apr. 8	Apr. 9
100 days.	Apr. 10	Apr. 11	Apr. 12	Apr. 13	Apr. 14

The above Tables are for use in States where three days' grace are NOT allowed.

WITHOUT GRACE.
For Leap Year changes, see next page.

Time.	January 6.	January 7.	January 8.	January 9.	January 10.
5 days.	Jan. 11	Jan. 12	Jan. 13	Jan. 14	Jan. 15
10 days.	Jan. 16	Jan. 17	Jan. 18	Jan. 19	Jan. 20
15 days.	Jan. 21	Jan. 22	Jan. 23	Jan. 24	Jan. 25
20 days.	Jan. 26	Jan. 27	Jan. 28	Jan. 29	Jan. 30
25 days.	Jan. 31	Feb. 1	Feb. 2	Feb. 3	Feb. 4
30 days.	Feb. 5	Feb. 6	Feb. 7	Feb. 8	Feb. 9
35 days.	Feb. 10	Feb. 11	Feb. 12	Feb. 13	Feb. 14
40 days.	Feb. 15	Feb. 16	Feb. 17	Feb. 18	Feb. 19
45 days.	Feb. 20	Feb. 21	Feb. 22	Feb. 23	Feb. 24
50 days.	Feb. 25	Feb. 26	Feb. 27	Feb. 28	Mar. 1
55 days.	Mar. 2	Mar. 3	Mar. 4	Mar. 5	Mar. 6
60 days.	Mar. 7	Mar. 8	Mar. 9	Mar. 10	Mar. 11
65 days.	Mar. 12	Mar. 13	Mar. 14	Mar. 15	Mar. 16
70 days.	Mar. 17	Mar. 18	Mar. 19	Mar. 20	Mar. 21
75 days.	Mar. 22	Mar. 23	Mar. 24	Mar. 25	Mar. 26
80 days.	Mar. 27	Mar. 28	Mar. 29	Mar. 30	Mar. 31
85 days.	Apr. 1	Apr. 2	Apr. 3	Apr. 4	Apr. 5
90 days.	Apr. 6	Apr. 7	Apr. 8	Apr. 9	Apr. 10
95 days.	Apr. 11	Apr. 12	Apr. 13	Apr. 14	Apr. 15
100 days.	Apr. 16	Apr. 17	Apr. 18	Apr. 19	Apr. 20
1 month.	Feb. 6	Feb. 7	Feb. 8	Feb. 9	Feb. 10
2 months.	Mar. 6	Mar. 7	Mar. 8	Mar. 9	Mar. 10
3 months.	Apr. 6	Apr. 7	Apr. 8	Apr. 9	Apr. 10
4 months.	May 6	May 7	May 8	May 9	May 10
5 months.	Jun. 6	Jun. 7	Jun. 8	June 9	Jun. 10
6 months.	Jul. 6	Jul. 7	Jul. 8	July 9	July 10
7 months.	Aug. 6	Aug. 7	Aug. 8	Aug. 9	Aug. 10
8 months.	Sep. 6	Sep. 7	Sep. 8	Sept. 9	Sep. 10
9 months.	Oct. 6	Oct. 7	Oct. 8	Oct. 9	Oct. 10
10 months.	Nov. 6	Nov. 7	Nov. 8	Nov. 9	Nov. 10
11 months.	Dec. 6	Dec. 7	Dec. 8	Dec. 9	Dec. 10
12 months.	Jan. 6	Jan. 7	Jan. 8	Jan. 9	Jan. 10

The above Tables are WITHOUT three days' grace.

(WITHOUT GRACE.)

Changes when Notes mature in Leap-Year.

Time.	January 6.	January 7.	January 8.	January 9.	January 10.
50 days.	Feb. 25	Feb. 26	Feb. 27	Feb. 28	Feb. 29
55 days.	Mar. 1	Mar. 2	Mar. 3	Mar. 4	Mar. 5
60 days.	Mar. 6	Mar. 7	Mar. 8	Mar. 9	Mar. 10
65 days.	Mar. 11	Mar. 12	Mar. 13	Mar. 14	Mar. 15
70 days.	Mch 16	Mch 17	Mch 18	Mch 19	Mch 20
75 days.	Mar. 21	Mar. 22	Mar. 23	Mar. 24	Mar. 25
80 days.	Mar. 26	Mar. 27	Mar. 28	Mar. 29	Mar. 30
85 days.	Mar. 31	Apr. 1	Apr. 2	Apr. 3	Apr. 4
90 days.	Apr. 5	Apr. 6	Apr. 7	Apr. 8	Apr. 9
95 days.	Apr. 10	Apr. 11	Apr. 12	Apr. 13	Apr. 14
100 days.	Apr. 15	Apr. 16	Apr. 17	Apr. 18	Apr. 19

The above Tables are for use in States where three days' grace are NOT allowed.

WITHOUT GRACE.
For Leap Year changes, see next page.

Time.	January 11.	January 12.	January 13.	January 14.	January 15.
5 days.	Jan. 16	Jan. 17	Jan. 18	Jan. 19	Jan. 20
10 days.	Jan. 21	Jan. 22	Jan. 23	Jan. 24	Jan. 25
15 days.	Jan. 26	Jan. 27	Jan. 28	Jan. 29	Jan. 30
20 days.	Jan. 31	Feb. 1	Feb. 2	Feb. 3	Feb. 4
25 days.	Feb. 5	Feb. 6	Feb. 7	Feb. 8	Feb. 9
30 days.	Feb. 10	Feb. 11	Feb. 12	Feb. 13	Feb. 14
35 days.	Feb. 15	Feb. 16	Feb. 17	Feb. 18	Feb. 19
40 days.	Feb. 20	Feb. 21	Feb. 22	Feb. 23	Feb. 24
45 days.	Feb. 25	Feb. 26	Feb. 27	Feb. 28	Mar. 1
50 days.	Mar. 2	Mar. 3	Mar. 4	Mar. 5	Mar. 6
55 days.	Mar. 7	Mar. 8	Mar. 9	Mar. 10	Mar. 11
60 days.	Mar. 12	Mar. 13	Mar. 14	Mar. 15	Mar. 16
65 days.	Mar. 17	Mar. 18	Mar. 19	Mar. 20	Mar. 21
70 days.	Mar. 22	Mar. 23	Mar. 24	Mar. 25	Mar. 26
75 days.	Mar. 27	Mar. 28	Mar. 29	Mar. 30	Mar. 31
80 days.	Apr. 1	Apr. 2	Apr. 3	Apr. 4	Apr. 5
85 days.	Apr. 6	Apr. 7	Apr. 8	Apr. 9	Apr. 10
90 days.	Apr. 11	Apr. 12	Apr. 13	Apr. 14	Apr. 15
95 days.	Apr. 16	Apr. 17	Apr. 18	Apr. 19	Apr. 20
100 days.	Apr. 21	Apr. 22	Apr. 23	Apr. 24	Apr. 25
1 month.	Feb. 11	Feb. 12	Feb. 13	Feb. 14	Feb. 15
2 months.	Mar. 11	Mar. 12	Mar. 13	Mar. 14	Mar. 15
3 months.	Apr. 11	Apr. 12	Apr. 13	Apr. 14	Apr. 15
4 months.	May 11	May 12	May 13	May 14	May 15
5 months.	Jun. 11	Jun. 12	Jun. 13	June 14	Jun. 15
6 months.	Jul. 11	Jul. 12	Jul. 13	July 14	July 15
7 months.	Aug. 11	Aug. 12	Aug. 13	Aug. 14	Aug. 15
8 months.	Sep. 11	Sep. 12	Sep. 13	Sept. 14	Sep. 15
9 months.	Oct. 11	Oct. 12	Oct. 13	Oct. 14	Oct. 15
10 months.	Nov. 11	Nov. 12	Nov. 13	Nov. 14	Nov. 15
11 months.	Dec. 11	Dec. 12	Dec. 13	Dec. 14	Dec. 15
12 months.	Jan. 11	Jan. 12	Jan. 13	Jan. 14	Jan. 15

The above Tables are WITHOUT three days' grace.

(WITHOUT GRACE.)

Changes when Notes mature in Leap-Year.

Time.	January 11.	January 12.	January 13.	January 14.	January 15.
45 days.	Feb. 25	Feb. 26	Feb. 27	Feb. 28	Feb. 29
50 days.	Mar. 1	Mar. 2	Mar. 3	Mar. 4	Mar. 5
55 days.	Mar. 6	Mar. 7	Mar. 8	Mar. 9	Mar. 10
60 days.	Mar. 11	Mar. 12	Mar. 13	Mar. 14	Mar. 15
65 days.	Mch 16	Mch 17	Mch 18	Mch 19	Mch 20
70 days.	Mar. 21	Mar. 22	Mar. 23	Mar. 24	Mar. 25
75 days.	Mar. 26	Mar. 27	Mar. 28	Mar. 29	Mar. 30
80 days.	Mar. 31	Apr. 1	Apr. 2	Apr. 3	Apr. 4
85 days.	Apr. 5	Apr. 6	Apr. 7	Apr. 8	Apr. 9
90 days.	Apr. 10	Apr. 11	Apr. 12	Apr. 13	Apr. 14
95 days.	Apr. 15	Apr. 16	Apr. 17	Apr. 18	Apr. 19
100 days.	Apr. 20	Apr. 21	Apr. 22	Apr. 23	Apr. 24

The above Tables are for use in States where three days' grace are NOT allowed.

NOTE MATURITY TABLES.
WITHOUT GRACE.
For Leap Year changes, see next page.

Time.	January 16.	January 17.	January 18.	January 19.	January 20.
5 days.	Jan. 21	Jan. 22	Jan. 23	Jan. 24	Jan. 25
10 days.	Jan. 26	Jan. 27	Jan. 28	Jan. 29	Jan. 30
15 days.	Jan. 31	Feb. 1	Feb. 2	Feb. 3	Feb. 4
20 days.	Feb. 5	Feb. 6	Feb. 7	Feb. 8	Feb. 9
25 days.	Feb. 10	Feb. 11	Feb. 12	Feb. 13	Feb. 14
30 days.	Feb. 15	Feb. 16	Feb. 17	Feb. 18	Feb. 19
35 days.	Feb. 20	Feb. 21	Feb. 22	Feb. 23	Feb. 24
40 days.	Feb. 25	Feb. 26	Feb. 27	Feb. 28	Mar. 1
45 days.	Mar. 2	Mar. 3	Mar. 4	Mar. 5	Mar. 6
50 days.	Mar. 7	Mar. 8	Mar. 9	Mar. 10	Mar. 11
55 days.	Mar. 12	Mar. 13	Mar. 14	Mar. 15	Mar. 16
60 days.	Mar. 17	Mar. 18	Mar. 19	Mar. 20	Mar. 21
65 days.	Mar. 22	Mar. 23	Mar. 24	Mar. 25	Mar. 26
70 days.	Mar. 27	Mar. 28	Mar. 29	Mar. 30	Mar. 31
75 days.	Apr. 1	Apr. 2	Apr. 3	Apr. 4	Apr. 5
80 days.	Apr. 6	Apr. 7	Apr. 8	Apr. 9	Apr. 10
85 days.	Apr. 11	Apr. 12	Apr. 13	Apr. 14	Apr. 15
90 days.	Apr. 16	Apr. 17	Apr. 18	Apr. 19	Apr. 20
95 days.	Apr. 21	Apr. 22	Apr. 23	Apr. 24	Apr. 25
100 days.	Apr. 26	Apr. 27	Apr. 28	Apr. 29	Apr. 30
1 month.	Feb. 16	Feb. 17	Feb. 18	Feb. 19	Feb. 20
2 months.	Mar. 16	Mar. 17	Mar. 18	Mar. 19	Mar. 20
3 months.	Apr. 16	Apr. 17	Apr. 18	Apr. 19	Apr. 20
4 months.	May 16	May 17	May 18	May 19	May 20
5 months.	Jun. 16	Jun. 17	Jun. 18	June 19	Jun. 20
6 months.	Jul. 16	Jul. 17	Jul. 18	July 19	July 20
7 months.	Aug. 16	Aug. 17	Aug. 18	Aug. 19	Aug. 20
8 months.	Sep. 16	Sep. 17	Sep. 18	Sept. 19	Sep. 20
9 months.	Oct. 16	Oct. 17	Oct. 18	Oct. 19	Oct. 20
10 months.	Nov. 16	Nov. 17	Nov. 18	Nov. 19	Nov. 20
11 months.	Dec. 16	Dec. 17	Dec. 18	Dec. 19	Dec. 20
12 months.	Jan. 16	Jan. 17	Jan. 18	Jan. 19	Jan. 20

The above Tables are WITHOUT three days' grace.

(WITHOUT GRACE.)
Changes when Notes mature in Leap-Year.

Time.	January 16.	January 17.	January 18.	January 19.	January 20.
40 days.	Feb. 25	Feb. 26	Feb. 27	Feb. 28	Feb. 29
45 days.	Mar. 1	Mar. 2	Mar. 3	Mar. 4	Mar. 5
50 days.	Mar. 6	Mar. 7	Mar. 8	Mar. 9	Mar. 10
55 days.	Mar. 11	Mar. 12	Mar. 13	Mar. 14	Mar. 15
60 days.	Mch 16	Mch 17	Mch 18	Mch 19	Mch 20
65 days.	Mar. 21	Mar. 22	Mar. 23	Mar. 24	Mar. 25
70 days.	Mar. 26	Mar. 27	Mar. 28	Mar. 29	Mar. 30
75 days.	Mar. 31	Apr. 1	Apr. 2	Apr. 3	Apr. 4
80 days.	Apr. 5	Apr. 6	Apr. 7	Apr. 8	Apr. 9
85 days.	Apr. 10	Apr. 11	Apr. 12	Apr. 13	Apr. 14
90 days.	Apr. 15	Apr. 16	Apr. 17	Apr. 18	Apr. 19
95 days.	Apr. 20	Apr. 21	Apr. 22	Apr. 23	Apr. 24
100 days.	Apr. 25	Apr. 26	Apr. 27	Apr. 28	Apr. 29

The above Tables are for use in States where three days'
grace are NOT allowed.

WITHOUT GRACE.
For Leap Year changes, see next page.

Time.	January 21.	January 22.	January 23.	January 24.	January 25.
5 days.	Jan. 26	Jan. 27	Jan. 28	Jan. 29	Jan. 30
10 days.	Jan. 31	Feb. 1	Feb. 2	Feb. 3	Feb. 4
15 days.	Feb. 5	Feb. 6	Feb. 7	Feb. 8	Feb. 9
20 days.	Feb. 10	Feb. 11	Feb. 12	Feb. 13	Feb. 14
25 days.	Feb. 15	Feb. 16	Feb. 17	Feb. 18	Feb. 19
30 days.	Feb. 20	Feb. 21	Feb. 22	Feb. 23	Feb. 24
35 days.	Feb. 25	Feb. 26	Feb. 27	Feb. 28	Mar. 1
40 days.	Mar. 2	Mar. 3	Mar. 4	Mar. 5	Mar. 6
45 days.	Mar. 7	Mar. 8	Mar. 9	Mar. 10	Mar. 11
50 days.	Mar. 12	Mar. 13	Mar. 14	Mar. 15	Mar. 16
55 days.	Mar. 17	Mar. 18	Mar. 19	Mar. 20	Mar. 21
60 days.	Mar. 22	Mar. 23	Mar. 24	Mar. 25	Mar. 26
65 days.	Mar. 27	Mar. 28	Mar. 29	Mar. 30	Mar. 31
70 days.	Apr. 1	Apr. 2	Apr. 3	Apr. 4	Apr. 5
75 days.	Apr. 6	Apr. 7	Apr. 8	Apr. 9	Apr. 10
80 days.	Apr. 11	Apr. 12	Apr. 13	Apr. 14	Apr. 15
85 days.	Apr. 16	Apr. 17	Apr. 18	Apr. 19	Apr. 20
90 days.	Apr. 21	Apr. 22	Apr. 23	Apr. 24	Apr. 25
95 days.	Apr. 26	Apr. 27	Apr. 28	Apr. 29	Apr. 30
100 days.	May 1	May 2	May 3	May 4	May 5
1 month.	Feb. 21	Feb. 22	Feb. 23	Feb. 24	Feb. 25
2 months.	Mar. 21	Mar. 22	Mar. 23	Mar. 24	Mar. 25
3 months.	Apr. 21	Apr. 22	Apr. 23	Apr. 24	Apr. 25
4 months.	May 21	May 22	May 23	May 24	May 25
5 months.	Jun. 21	Jun. 22	Jun. 23	June 24	Jun. 25
6 months.	Jul. 21	Jul. 22	Jul. 23	July 24	July 25
7 months.	Aug. 21	Aug. 22	Aug. 23	Aug. 24	Aug. 25
8 months.	Sep. 21	Sep. 22	Sep. 23	Sept. 24	Sep. 25
9 months.	Oct. 21	Oct. 22	Oct. 23	Oct. 24	Oct. 25
10 months.	Nov. 21	Nov. 22	Nov. 23	Nov. 24	Nov. 25
11 months.	Dec. 21	Dec. 22	Dec. 23	Dec. 24	Dec. 25
12 months.	Jan. 21	Jan. 22	Jan. 23	Jan. 24	Jan. 25

The above Tables are WITHOUT three days' grace.

(WITHOUT GRACE.)

Changes when Notes mature in Leap-Year.

Time.	January 21.	January 22.	January 23.	January 24.	January 25.
35 days.	Feb. 25	Feb. 26	Feb. 27	Feb. 28	Feb. 29
40 days.	Mar. 1	Mar. 2	Mar. 3	Mar. 4	Mar. 5
45 days.	Mar. 6	Mar, 7	Mar. 8	Mar. 9	Mar. 10
50 days.	Mar. 11	Mar. 12	Mar. 13	Mar. 14	Mar. 15
55 days.	Mch 16	Mch 17	Mch 18	Mch 19	Mch 20
60 days.	Mar. 21	Mar. 22	Mar. 23	Mar. 24	Mar. 25
65 days.	Mar. 26	Mar. 27	Mar. 28	Mar. 29	Mar. 30
70 days.	Mar. 31	Apr. 1	Apr. 2	Apr. 3	Apr. 4
75 days.	Apr. 5	Apr. 6	Apr. 7	Apr. 8	Apr. 9
80 days.	Apr. 10	Apr. 11	Apr. 12	Apr. 13	Apr. 14
85 days.	Apr. 15	Apr. 16	Apr. 17	Apr. 18	Apr. 19
90 days.	Apr. 20	Apr. 21	Apr. 22	Apr. 23	Apr. 24
95 days.	Apr. 25	Apr. 26	Apr. 27	Apr. 28	Apr. 29
100 days.	Apr. 30	May 1	May 2	May 3	May 4

The above Tables are for use in States where three days' grace are NOT allowed.

WITHOUT GRACE.

For Leap Year changes, see next page.

Time.	January 26.	January 27.	January 28.	January 29.	January 30.
5 days.	Jan. 31	Feb. 1	Feb. 2	Feb. 3	Feb. 4
10 days.	Feb. 5	Feb. 6	Feb. 7	Feb. 8	Feb. 9
15 days.	Feb. 10	Feb. 11	Feb. 12	Feb. 13	Feb. 14
20 days.	Feb. 15	Feb. 16	Feb. 17	Feb. 18	Feb. 19
25 days.	Feb. 20	Feb. 21	Feb. 22	Feb. 23	Feb. 24
30 days.	Feb. 25	Feb. 26	Feb. 27	Feb. 28	Mar. 1
35 days.	Mar. 2	Mar. 3	Mar. 4	Mar. 5	Mar. 6
40 days.	Mar. 7	Mar. 8	Mar. 9	Mar. 10	Mar. 11
45 days.	Mar. 12	Mar. 13	Mar. 14	Mar. 15	Mar. 16
50 days.	Mar. 17	Mar. 18	Mar. 19	Mar. 20	Mar. 21
55 days.	Mar. 22	Mar. 23	Mar. 24	Mar. 25	Mar. 26
60 days.	Mar. 27	Mar. 28	Mar. 29	Mar. 30	Mar. 31
65 days.	Apr. 1	Apr. 2	Apr. 3	Apr. 4	Apr. 5
70 days.	Apr. 6	Apr. 7	Apr. 8	Apr. 9	Apr. 10
75 days.	Apr. 11	Apr. 12	Apr. 13	Apr. 14	Apr. 15
80 days.	Apr. 16	Apr. 17	Apr. 18	Apr. 19	Apr. 20
85 days.	Apr. 21	Apr. 22	Apr. 23	Apr. 24	Apr. 25
90 days.	Apr. 26	Apr. 27	Apr. 28	Apr. 29	Apr. 30
95 days.	May 1	May 2	May 3	May 4	May 5
100 days.	May 6	May 7	May 8	May 9	May 10
1 month.	Feb. 26	Feb. 27	Feb. 28	Feb. 28	Feb. 28
*1 mo., L. Y.	Feb. 26	Feb. 27	Feb. 28	Feb. 29	Feb. 29
2 months.	Mar. 26	Mar. 27	Mar. 28	Mar. 29	Mar. 30
3 months.	Apr. 26	Apr. 27	Apr. 28	Apr. 29	Apr. 30
4 months.	May 26	May 27	May 28	May 28	May 30
5 months.	Jun. 26	Jun. 27	Jun. 28	June 29	Jun. 30
6 months.	Jul. 26	Jul. 27	Jul. 28	July 29	July 30
7 months.	Aug. 26	Aug. 27	Aug. 28	Aug. 29	Aug. 30
8 months.	Sep. 26	Sep. 27	Sep. 28	Sept. 29	Sep. 30
9 months.	Oct. 26	Oct. 27	Oct. 28	Oct. 29	Oct. 30
10 months.	Nov. 26	Nov. 27	Nov. 28	Nov. 29	Nov. 30
11 months.	Dec. 26	Dec. 27	Dec. 28	Dec. 29	Dec. 30
12 months.	Jan. 26	Jan. 27	Jan. 28	Jan. 29	Jan. 30

*Use this line for Notes maturing in Leap Year.

The above Tables are WITHOUT three days' grace.

(WITHOUT GRACE.)

Changes when Notes mature in Leap-Year.

Time.	January 26.	January 27.	January 28.	January 29.	January 30.
30 days.	Feb. 25	Feb. 26	Feb. 27	Feb. 28	Feb. 29
35 days.	Mar. 1	Mar. 2	Mar. 3	Mar. 4	Mar. 5
40 days.	Mar. 6	Mar. 7	Mar. 8	Mar. 9	Mar. 10
45 days.	Mar. 11	Mar. 12	Mar. 13	Mar. 14	Mar. 15
50 days.	Mch 16	Mch 17	Mch 18	Mch 19	Mch 20
55 days.	Mar. 21	Mar. 22	Mar. 23	Mar. 24	Mar. 25
60 days.	Mar. 26	Mar. 27	Mar. 28	Mar. 29	Mar. 30
65 days.	Mar. 31	Apr. 1	Apr. 2	Apr. 3	Apr. 4
70 days.	Apr. 5	Apr. 6	Apr. 7	Apr. 8	Apr. 9
75 days.	Apr. 10	Apr. 11	Apr. 12	Apr. 13	Apr. 14
80 days.	Apr. 15	Apr. 16	Apr. 17	Apr. 18	Apr. 19
85 days.	Apr. 20	Apr. 21	Apr. 22	Apr. 23	Apr. 24
90 days.	Apr. 25	Apr. 26	Apr. 27	Apr. 28	Apr. 29
95 days.	Apr. 30	May 1	May 2	May 3	May 4
100 days.	May 5	May 6	May 7	May 8	May 9
1 month.	Feb. 26	Feb. 27	Feb. 28	Feb. 29	Feb. 29

The above Tables are for use in States where three days' grace are NOT allowed.

WITHOUT GRACE.

For Leap Year changes, see next page.

Time.	January 31.	Febr'y 1.	Febr'y 2.	Febr'y 3.	Febr'y 4.
5 days.	Feb. 5	Feb. 6	Feb. 7	Feb. 8	Feb. 9
10 days.	Feb. 10	Feb. 11	Feb. 12	Feb. 13	Feb. 14
15 days.	Feb. 15	Feb. 16	Feb. 17	Feb. 18	Feb. 19
20 days.	Feb. 20	Feb. 21	Feb. 22	Feb. 23	Feb. 24
25 days.	Feb. 25	Feb. 26	Feb. 27	Feb. 28	Mar. 1
30 days.	Mar. 2	Mar. 3	Mar. 4	Mar. 5	Mar. 6
35 days.	Mar. 7	Mar. 8	Mar. 9	Mar. 10	Mar. 11
40 days.	Mar. 12	Mar. 13	Mar. 14	Mar. 15	Mar. 16
45 days.	Mar. 17	Mar. 18	Mar. 19	Mar. 20	Mar. 21
50 days.	Mar. 22	Mar. 23	Mar. 24	Mar. 25	Mar. 26
55 days.	Mar. 27	Mar. 28	Mar. 29	Mar. 30	Mar. 31
60 days.	Apr. 1	Apr. 2	Apr. 3	Apr. 4	Apr. 5
65 days.	Apr. 6	Apr. 7	Apr. 8	Apr. 9	Apr. 10
70 days.	Apr. 11	Apr. 12	Apr. 13	Apr. 14	Apr. 15
75 days.	Apr. 16	Apr. 17	Apr. 18	Apr. 19	Apr. 20
80 days.	Apr. 21	Apr. 22	Apr. 23	Apr. 24	Apr. 25
85 days.	Apr. 26	Apr. 27	Apr. 28	Apr. 29	Apr. 30
90 days.	May 1	May 2	May 3	May 4	May 5
95 days.	May 6	May 7	May 8	May 9	May 10
100 days.	May 11	May 12	May 13	May 14	May 15
1 month.	Feb. 28	Mar. 1	Mar. 2	Mar. 3	Mar. 4
*1 mo., L. Y.	Feb. 29	Mar. 1	Mar. 2	Mar. 3	Mar. 4
2 months.	Mar. 31	Apr. 1	Apr. 2	Apr. 3	Apr. 4
3 months.	Apr. 30	May 1	May 2	May 3	May 4
4 months.	May 31	Jun. 1	Jun. 2	June 3	Jun. 4
5 months.	Jun. 30	Jul. 1	Jul. 2	July 3	July 4
6 months.	Jul. 31	Aug. 1	Aug. 2	Aug. 3	Aug. 4
7 months.	Aug. 31	Sep. 1	Sep. 2	Sept. 3	Sep. 4
8 months.	Sep. 30	Oct. 1	Oct. 2	Oct. 3	Oct. 4
9 months.	Oct. 31	Nov. 1	Nov. 2	Nov. 3	Nov. 4
10 months.	Nov. 30	Dec. 1	Dec. 2	Dec. 3	Dec. 4
11 months.	Dec. 31	Jan. 1	Jan. 2	Jan. 3	Jan. 4
12 months.	Jan. 31	Feb. 1	Feb. 2	Feb. 3	Feb. 4

*Use this line for Notes maturing in Leap Year.

The above Tables are WITHOUT three days' grace.

(WITHOUT GRACE.)
Changes when Notes mature in Leap-Year.

Time.	January 31.	Febr'y 1.	Febr'y 2.	Febr'y 3.	Febr'y 4.
25 days.	Feb. 25	Feb. 26	Feb. 27	Feb. 28	Feb. 29
30 days.	Mar. 1	Mar. 2	Mar. 3	Mar. 4	Mar. 5
35 days.	Mar. 6	Mar. 7	Mar. 8	Mar. 9	Mar. 10
40 days.	Mar. 11	Mar. 12	Mar. 13	Mar. 14	Mar. 15
45 days.	Mch 16	Mch 17	Mch 18	Mch 19	Mch 20
50 days.	Mar. 21	Mar. 22	Mar. 23	Mar. 24	Mar. 25
55 days.	Mar. 26	Mar. 27	Mar. 28	Mar. 29	Mar. 30
60 days.	Mar. 31	Apr. 1	Apr. 2	Apr. 3	Apr. 4
65 days.	Apr. 5	Apr. 6	Apr. 7	Apr. 8	Apr. 9
70 days.	Apr. 10	Apr. 11	Apr. 12	Apr. 13	Apr. 14
75 days.	Apr. 15	Apr. 16	Apr. 17	Apr. 18	Apr. 19
80 days.	Apr. 20	Apr. 21	Apr. 22	Apr. 23	Apr. 24
85 days.	Apr. 25	Apr. 26	Apr. 27	Apr. 28	Apr. 29
90 days.	Apr. 30	May 1	May 2	May 3	May 4
95 days.	May 5	May 6	May 7	May 8	May 9
100 days.	May 10	May 11	May 12	May 13	May 14
1 month.	Feb. 29	Mar. 1	Mar. 2	Mar. 3	Mar. 4

The above Tables are WITHOUT three days' grace.

WITHOUT GRACE.

For Leap Year changes, see next page.

Time.	Febr'y 5.	Febr'y 6.	Febr'y 7.	Febr'y 8.	Febr'y 9.
5 days.	Feb. 10	Feb. 11	Feb. 12	Feb. 13	Feb. 14
10 days.	Feb. 15	Feb. 16	Feb. 17	Feb. 18	Feb. 19
15 days.	Feb. 20	Feb. 21	Feb. 22	Feb. 23	Feb. 24
20 days.	Feb. 25	Feb. 26	Feb. 27	Feb. 28	Mar. 1
25 days.	Mar. 2	Mar. 3	Mar. 4	Mar. 5	Mar. 6
30 days.	Mar. 7	Mar. 8	Mar. 9	Mar. 10	Mar. 11
35 days.	Mar. 12	Mar. 13	Mar. 14	Mar. 15	Mar. 16
40 days.	Mar. 17	Mar. 18	Mar. 19	Mar. 20	Mar. 21
45 days.	Mar. 22	Mar. 23	Mar. 24	Mar. 25	Mar. 26
50 days.	Mar. 27	Mar. 28	Mar. 29	Mar. 30	Mar. 31
55 days.	Apr. 1	Apr. 2	Apr. 3	Apr. 4	Apr. 5
60 days.	Apr. 6	Apr. 7	Apr. 8	Apr. 9	Apr. 10
65 days.	Apr. 11	Apr. 12	Apr. 13	Apr. 14	Apr. 15
70 days.	Apr. 16	Apr. 17	Apr. 18	Apr. 19	Apr. 20
75 days.	Apr. 21	Apr. 22	Apr. 23	Apr. 24	Apr. 25
80 days.	Apr. 26	Apr. 27	Apr. 28	Apr. 29	Apr. 30
85 days.	May 1	May 2	May 3	May 4	May 5
90 days.	May 6	May 7	May 8	May 9	May 10
95 days.	May 11	May 12	May 13	May 14	May 15
100 days.	May 16	May 17	May 18	May 19	May 20
1 month.	Mar. 5	Mar. 6	Mar. 7	Mar. 8	Mar. 9
2 months.	Apr. 5	Apr. 6	Apr. 7	Apr. 8	Apr. 9
3 months.	May 5	May 6	May 7	May 8	May 9
4 months.	Jun. 5	Jun. 6	Jun. 7	June 8	Jun. 9
5 months.	Jul. 5	Jul. 6	Jul. 7	July 8	July 9
6 months.	Aug. 5	Aug. 6	Aug. 7	Aug. 8	Aug. 9
7 months.	Sep. 5	Sep. 6	Sep. 7	Sept. 8	Sep. 9
8 months.	Oct. 5	Oct. 6	Oct. 7	Oct. 8	Oct. 9
9 months.	Nov. 5	Nov. 6	Nov. 7	Nov. 8	Nov. 9
10 months.	Dec. 5	Dec. 6	Dec. 7	Dec. 8	Dec. 9
11 months.	Jan. 5	Jan. 6	Jan. 7	Jan. 8	Jan. 9
12 months.	Feb. 5	Feb. 6	Feb. 7	Feb. 8	Feb. 9

The above Tables are WITHOUT three days' grace.

(WITHOUT GRACE.)

Changes when Notes mature in Leap-Year.

Time.	Febr'y 5.	Febr'y 6.	Febr'y 7.	Febr'y 8.	Febr'y 9.
20 days.	Feb. 25	Feb. 26	Feb. 27	Feb. 28	Feb. 29
25 days.	Mar. 1	Mar. 2	Mar. 3	Mar. 4	Mar. 5
30 days.	Mar. 6	Mar, 7	Mar. 8	Mar. 9	Mar. 10
35 days.	Mar. 11	Mar. 12	Mar. 13	Mar. 14	Mar. 15
40 days.	Mch 16	Mch 17	Mch 18	Mch 19	Mch 20
45 days.	Mar. 21	Mar. 22	Mar. 23	Mar. 24	Mar. 25
50 days.	Mar. 26	Mar. 27	Mar. 28	Mar. 29	Mar. 30
55 days.	Mar. 31	Apr. 1	Apr. 2	Apr. 3	Apr. 4
60 days.	Apr. 5	Apr. 6	Apr. 7	Apr. 8	Apr. 9
65 days.	Apr. 10	Apr. 11	Apr. 12	Apr. 13	Apr. 14
70 days.	Apr. 15	Apr. 16	Apr. 17	Apr. 18	Apr. 19
75 days.	Apr. 20	Apr. 21	Apr. 22	Apr. 23	Apr. 24
80 days.	Apr. 25	Apr. 26	Apr. 27	Apr. 28	Apr. 29
85 days.	Apr. 30	May 1	May 2	May 3	May 4
90 days.	May 5	May 6	May 7	May 8	May 9
95 days.	May 10	May 11	May 12	May 13	May 14
100 days.	May 15	May 16	May 17	May 18	May 19

The above Tables are WITHOUT three days' grace.

WITHOUT GRACE.
For Leap Year changes, see next page.

Time.	Febr'y 10.	Febr'y 11.	Febr'y 12.	Febr'y 13.	Febr'y 14.
5 days.	Feb. 15	Feb. 16	Feb. 17	Feb. 18	Feb. 19
10 days.	Feb. 20	Feb. 21	Feb. 22	Feb. 23	Feb. 24
15 days.	Feb. 25	Feb. 26	Feb. 27	Feb. 28	Mar. 1
20 days.	Mar. 2	Mar. 3	Mar. 4	Mar. 5	Mar. 6
25 days.	Mar. 7	Mar. 8	Mar. 9	Mar. 10	Mar. 11
30 days.	Mar. 12	Mar. 13	Mar. 14	Mar. 15	Mar. 16
35 days.	Mar. 17	Mar. 18	Mar. 19	Mar. 20	Mar. 21
40 days.	Mar. 22	Mar. 23	Mar. 24	Mar. 25	Mar. 26
45 days.	Mar. 27	Mar. 28	Mar. 29	Mar. 30	Mar. 31
50 days.	Apr. 1	Apr. 2	Apr. 3	Apr. 4	Apr. 5
55 days.	Apr. 6	Apr. 7	Apr. 8	Apr. 9	Apr. 10
60 days.	Apr. 11	Apr. 12	Apr. 13	Apr. 14	Apr. 15
65 days.	Apr. 16	Apr. 17	Apr. 18	Apr. 19	Apr. 20
70 days.	Apr. 21	Apr. 22	Apr. 23	Apr. 24	Apr. 25
75 days.	Apr. 26	Apr. 27	Apr. 28	Apr. 29	Apr. 30
80 days.	May 1	May 2	May 3	May 4	May 5
85 days.	May 6	May 7	May 8	May 9	May 10
90 days.	May 11	May 12	May 13	May 14	May 15
95 days.	May 16	May 17	May 18	May 19	May 20
100 days.	May 21	May 22	May 23	May 24	May 25
1 month.	Mar. 10	Mar. 11	Mar. 12	Mar. 13	Mar. 14
2 months.	Apr. 10	Apr. 11	Apr. 12	Apr. 13	Apr. 14
3 months.	May 10	May 11	May 12	May 13	May 14
4 months.	Jun. 10	Jun. 11	Jun. 12	June 13	Jun. 14
5 months.	Jul. 10	Jul. 11	Jul. 12	July 13	July 14
6 months.	Aug. 10	Aug. 11	Aug. 12	Aug. 13	Aug. 14
7 months.	Sep. 10	Sep. 11	Sep. 12	Sept. 13	Sep. 14
8 months.	Oct. 10	Oct. 11	Oct. 12	Oct. 13	Oct. 14
9 months.	Nov. 10	Nov. 11	Nov. 12	Nov. 13	Nov. 14
10 months.	Dec. 10	Dec. 11	Dec. 12	Dec. 13	Dec. 14
11 months.	Jan. 10	Jan. 11	Jan. 12	Jan. 13	Jan. 14
12 months.	Feb. 10	Feb. 11	Feb. 12	Feb. 13	Feb. 14

The above Tables are WITHOUT three days' grace.

(WITHOUT GRACE.)

Changes when Notes mature in Leap-Year.

Time.	Febr'y 10.	Febr'y 11.	Febr'y 12.	Febr'y 13.	Febr'y 14.
15 days.	Feb. 25	Feb. 26	Feb. 27	Feb. 28	Feb. 29
20 days.	Mar. 1	Mar. 2	Mar. 3	Mar. 4	Mar. 5
25 days.	Mar. 6	Mar. 7	Mar. 8	Mar. 9	Mar. 10
30 days.	Mar. 11	Mar. 12	Mar. 13	Mar. 14	Mar. 15
35 days.	Mch 16	Mch 17	Mch 18	Mch 19	Mch 20
40 days.	Mar. 21	Mar. 22	Mar. 23	Mar. 24	Mar. 25
45 days.	Mar. 26	Mar. 27	Mar. 28	Mar. 29	Mar. 30
50 days.	Mar. 31	Apr. 1	Apr. 2	Apr. 3	Apr. 4
55 days.	Apr. 5	Apr. 6	Apr. 7	Apr. 8	Apr. 9
60 days.	Apr. 10	Apr. 11	Apr. 12	Apr. 13	Apr. 14
65 days.	Apr. 15	Apr. 16	Apr. 17	Apr. 18	Apr. 19
70 days.	Apr. 20	Apr. 21	Apr. 22	Apr. 23	Apr. 24
75 days.	Apr. 25	Apr. 26	Apr. 27	Apr. 28	Apr. 29
80 days.	Apr. 30	May 1	May 2	May 3	May 4
85 days.	May 5	May 6	May 7	May 8	May 9
90 days.	May 10	May 11	May 12	May 13	May 14
95 days.	May 15	May 16	May 17	May 18	May 19
100 days.	May 20	May 21	May 22	May 23	May 24

The above Tables are WITHOUT three days' grace.

NOTE-MATURITY TABLES.
(WITHOUT GRACE.)
For Leap-Year changes, see next page.

Time.	Febr'y 15.	Febr'y 16.	Febr'y 17.	Febr'y 18.	Febr'y 19.
5 days.	Feb. 20	Feb. 21	Feb. 22	Feb. 23	Feb. 24
10 days.	Feb. 25	Feb. 26	Feb. 27	Feb. 28	Mar. 1
15 days.	Mar. 2	Mar. 3	Mar. 4	Mar. 5	Mar. 6
20 days.	Mar. 7	Mar. 8	Mar. 9	Mar. 10	Mar. 11
25 days.	Mar. 12	Mar. 13	Mar. 14	Mar. 15	Mar. 16
30 days.	Mar. 17	Mar. 18	Mar. 19	Mar. 20	Mar. 21
35 days.	Mar. 22	Mar. 23	Mar. 24	Mar. 25	Mar. 26
40 days.	Mar. 27	Mar. 28	Mar. 29	Mar. 30	Mar. 31
45 days.	Apr. 1	Apr. 2	Apr. 3	Apr. 4	Apr. 5
50 days.	Apr. 6	Apr. 7	Apr. 8	Apr. 9	Apr. 10
55 days.	Apr. 11	Apr. 12	Apr. 13	Apr. 14	Apr. 15
60 days.	Apr. 16	Apr. 17	Apr. 18	Apr. 19	Apr. 20
65 days.	Apr. 21	Apr. 22	Apr. 23	Apr. 24	Apr. 25
70 days.	Apr. 26	Apr. 27	Apr. 28	Apr. 29	Apr. 30
75 days.	May 1	May 2	May 3	May 4	May 5
80 days.	May 6	May 7	May 8	May 9	May 10
85 days.	May 11	May 12	May 13	May 14	May 15
90 days.	May 16	May 17	May 18	May 19	May 20
95 days.	May 21	May 22	May 23	May 24	May 25
100 days.	May 26	May 27	May 28	May 29	May 30
1 month.	Mch 15	Mch 16	Mch 17	Mch 18	Mch 19
2 months.	Apr. 15	Apr. 16	Apr. 17	Apr. 18	Apr. 19
3 months.	May 15	May 16	May 17	May 18	May 19
4 months.	June 15	June 16	June 17	June 18	June 19
5 months.	July 15	July 16	July 17	July 18	July 19
6 months.	Aug. 15	Aug. 16	Aug. 17	Aug. 18	Aug. 19
7 months.	Sep. 15	Sep. 16	Sep. 17	Sep. 18	Sep. 19
8 months.	Oct. 15	Oct. 16	Oct. 17	Oct. 18	Oct. 19
9 months.	Nov. 15	Nov. 16	Nov. 17	Nov. 18	Nov. 19
10 months.	Dec. 15	Dec. 16	Dec. 17	Dec. 18	Dec. 19
11 months.	Jan. 15	Jan. 16	Jan. 17	Jan. 18	Jan. 19
12 months.	Feb. 15	Feb. 16	Feb. 17	Feb. 18	Feb. 19

The above tables are **without three days' grace.**

(WITHOUT GRACE.)

Changes when notes are DATED in Leap-Year.

Time.	Febr'y 15.	Febr'y 16.	Febr'y 17.	Febr'y 18.	Febr'y 19.
10 days.	Feb. 25	Feb. 26	Feb. 27	Feb. 28	Feb. 29
15 days.	Mar. 1	Mar. 2	Mar. 3	Mar. 4	Mar. 5
20 days.	Mar. 6	Mar. 7	Mar. 8	Mar. 9	Mar. 10
25 days.	Mar. 11	Mar. 12	Mar. 13	Mar. 14	Mar. 15
30 days.	Mar. 16	Mar. 17	Mar. 18	Mar. 19	Mar. 20
35 days.	Mar. 21	Mar. 22	Mar. 23	Mar. 24	Mar. 25
40 days.	Mar. 26	Mar. 27	Mar. 28	Mar. 29	Mar. 30
45 days.	Mar. 31	Apr. 1	Apr. 2	Apr. 3	Apr. 4
50 days.	Apr. 5	Apr. 6	Apr. 7	Apr. 8	Apr. 9
55 days.	Apr. 10	Apr. 11	Apr. 12	Apr. 13	Apr. 14
60 days.	Apr. 15	Apr. 16	Apr. 17	Apr. 18	Apr. 19
65 days.	Apr. 20	Apr. 21	Apr. 22	Apr. 23	Apr. 24
70 days.	Apr. 25	Apr. 26	Apr. 27	Apr. 28	Apr. 29
75 days.	Apr. 30	May 1	May 2	May 3	May 4
80 days.	May 5	May 6	May 7	May 8	May 9
85 days.	May 10	May 11	May 12	May 13	May 14
90 days.	May 15	May 16	May 17	May 18	May 19
95 days.	May 20	May 21	May 22	May 23	May 24
100 days.	May 25	May 26	May 27	May 28	May 29

The above tables are **without three days' grace·**

(WITHOUT GRACE.)
For Leap-Year changes, see next page.

Time.	Febr'y 20.	Febr'y 21.	Febr'y 22.	Febr'y 23.	Febr'y 24.
5 days.	Feb. 25	Feb. 26	Feb. 27	Feb. 28	Mar. 1
10 days.	Mar. 2	Mar. 3	Mar. 4	Mar. 5	Mar. 6
15 days.	Mar. 7	Mar. 8	Mar. 9	Mar. 10	Mar. 11
20 days.	Mar. 12	Mar. 13	Mar. 14	Mar. 15	Mar. 16
25 days.	Mar. 17	Mar. 18	Mar. 19	Mar. 20	Mar. 21
30 days.	Mar. 22	Mar. 23	Mar. 24	Mar. 25	Mar. 26
35 days.	Mar. 27	Mar. 28	Mar. 29	Mar. 30	Mar. 31
40 days.	Apr. 1	Apr. 2	Apr. 3	Apr. 4	Apr. 5
45 days.	Apr. 6	Apr. 7	Apr. 8	Apr. 9	Apr. 10
50 days.	Apr. 11	Apr. 12	Apr. 13	Apr. 14	Apr. 15
55 days.	Apr. 16	Apr. 17	Apr. 18	Apr. 19	Apr. 20
60 days.	Apr. 21	Apr. 22	Apr. 23	Apr. 24	Apr. 25
65 days.	Apr. 26	Apr. 27	Apr. 28	Apr. 29	Apr. 30
70 days.	May 1	May 2	May 3	May 4	May 5
75 days.	May 6	May 7	May 8	May 9	May 10
80 days.	May 11	May 12	May 13	May 14	May 15
85 days.	May 16	May 17	May 18	May 19	May 20
90 days.	May 21	May 22	May 23	May 24	May 25
95 days.	May 26	May 27	May 28	May 29	May 30
100 days.	May 31	June 1	June 2	June 3	June 4
1 month.	Mch 20	Mch 21	Mch 22	Mch 23	Mch 24
2 months.	Apr. 20	Apr. 21	Apr. 22	Apr. 23	Apr. 24
3 months.	May 20	May 21	May 22	May 23	May 24
4 months.	June 20	June 21	June 22	June 23	June 24
5 months.	July 20	July 21	July 22	July 23	July 24
6 months.	Aug. 20	Aug. 21	Aug. 22	Aug. 23	Aug. 24
7 months.	Sep. 20	Sep. 21	Sep. 22	Sep. 23	Sep. 24
8 months.	Oct. 20	Oct. 21	Oct. 22	Oct. 23	Oct. 24
9 months.	Nov. 20	Nov. 21	Nov. 22	Nov. 23	Nov. 24
10 months.	Dec. 20	Dec. 21	Dec. 22	Dec. 23	Dec. 24
11 months.	Jan. 20	Jan. 21	Jan. 22	Jan. 23	Jan. 24
12 months.	Feb. 20	Feb. 21	Feb. 22	Feb. 23	Feb. 24

The above tables are **without three days' grace.**

(WITHOUT GRACE.)

Changes when notes are DATED in Leap-Year.

Time.	Febr'y 20.	Febr'y 21.	Febr'y 22.	Febr'y 23.	Febr'y 24.
5 days.	Feb. 25	Feb. 26	Feb. 27	Feb. 28	Feb. 29
10 days.	Mar. 1	Mar. 2	Mar. 3	Mar. 4	Mar. 5
15 days.	Mar. 6	Mar. 7	Mar. 8	Mar. 9	Mar. 10
20 days.	Mar. 11	Mar. 12	Mar. 13	Mar. 14	Mar. 15
25 days.	Mar. 16	Mar. 17	Mar. 18	Mar. 19	Mar. 20
30 days.	Mar. 21	Mar. 22	Mar. 23	Mar. 24	Mar. 25
35 days.	Mar. 26	Mar. 27	Mar. 28	Mar. 29	Mar. 30
40 days.	Mar. 31	Apr. 1	Apr. 2	Apr. 3	Apr. 4
45 days.	Apr. 5	Apr. 6	Apr. 7	Apr. 8	Apr. 9
50 days.	Apr. 10	Apr. 11	Apr. 12	Apr. 13	Apr. 14
55 days.	Apr. 15	Apr. 16	Apr. 17	Apr. 18	Apr. 19
60 days.	Apr. 20	Apr. 21	Apr. 22	Apr. 23	Apr. 24
65 days.	Apr. 25	Apr. 26	Apr. 27	Apr. 28	Apr. 29
70 days.	Apr. 30	May 1	May 2	May 3	May 4
75 days.	May 5	May 6	May 7	May 8	May 9
80 days.	May 10	May 11	May 12	May 13	May 14
85 days.	May 15	May 16	May 17	May 18	May 19
90 days.	May 20	May 21	May 22	May 23	May 24
95 days.	May 25	May 26	May 27	May 28	May 29
100 days.	May 30	May 31	June 1	June 2	June 3

The above tables are **without three days' grace.**

(WITHOUT GRACE.)

For Leap-Year changes, see next page.

Time.	Febr'y 25.	Febr'y 26.	Febr'y 27.	Febr'y 28.	March 1.
5 days.	Mar. 2	Mar. 3	Mar. 4	Mar. 5	Mar. 6
10 days.	Mar. 7	Mar. 8	Mar. 9	Mar. 10	Mar. 11
15 days.	Mar. 12	Mar. 13	Mar. 14	Mar. 15	Mar. 16
20 days.	Mar. 17	Mar. 18	Mar. 19	Mar. 20	Mar. 21
25 days.	Mar. 22	Mar. 23	Mar. 24	Mar. 25	Mar. 26
30 days.	Mar. 27	Mar. 28	Mar. 29	Mar. 30	Mar. 31
35 days.	Apr. 1	Apr. 2	Apr. 3	Apr. 4	Apr. 5
40 days.	Apr. 6	Apr. 7	Apr. 8	Apr. 9	Apr. 10
45 days.	Apr 11	Apr. 12	Apr. 13	Apr. 14	Apr. 15
50 days.	Apr. 16	Apr. 17	Apr. 18	Apr. 19	Apr. 20
55 days.	Apr. 21	Apr. 22	Apr. 23	Apr. 24	Apr. 25
60 days.	Apr. 26	Apr. 27	Apr. 28	Apr. 29	Apr. 30
65 days.	May 1	May 2	May 3	May 4	May 5
70 days.	May 6	May 7	May 8	May 9	May 10
75 days.	May 11	May 12	May 13	May 14	May 15
80 days.	May 16	May 17	May 18	May 19	May 20
85 days.	May 21	May 22	May 23	May 24	May 25
90 days.	May 26	May 27	May 28	May 29	May 30
95 days.	May 31	June 1	June 2	June 3	June 4
100 days.	June 5	June 6	June 7	June 8	June 9
1 month.	Mch 25	Mch 26	Mch 27	Mch 28	Apr. 1
2 months.	Apr. 25	Apr. 26	Apr. 27	Apr. 28	May 1
3 months.	May 25	May 26	May 27	May 28	June 1
4 months.	June 25	June 26	June 27	June 28	July 1
5 months.	July 25	July 26	July 27	July 28	Aug. 1
6 months.	Aug. 25	Aug. 26	Aug. 27	Aug. 28	Sep. 1
7 months.	Sep. 25	Sep. 26	Sep. 27	Sep. 28	Oct. 1
8 months.	Oct. 25	Oct. 26	Oct. 27	Oct. 28	Nov. 1
9 months.	Nov. 25	Nov. 26	Nov. 27	Nov. 28	Dec. 1
10 months.	Dec. 25	Dec. 26	Dec. 27	Dec. 28	Jan. 1
11 months.	Jan. 25	Jan. 26	Jan. 27	Jan. 28	Feb. 1
12 months.	Feb. 25	Feb. 26	Feb. 27	Feb. 28	Mch 1

The above tables are **without three days' grace.**

(WITHOUT GRACE.)

Changes when notes are DATED in Leap-Year.

Time.	Febr'y 25.	Febr'y 26.	Febr'y 27.	Febr'y 28.	Febr'y 29.
5 days.	Mar. 1	Mar. 2	Mar. 3	Mar. 4	Mar. 5
10 days.	Mar. 6	Mar. 7	Mar. 8	Mar. 9	Mar. 10
15 days.	Mar. 11	Mar. 12	Mar. 13	Mar. 14	Mar. 15
20 days.	Mar. 16	Mar. 17	Mar. 18	Mar. 19	Mar. 20
25 days.	Mar. 21	Mar. 22	Mar. 23	Mar. 24	Mar. 25
30 days.	Mar. 26	Mar. 27	Mar. 28	Mar. 29	Mar. 30
35 days.	Mar. 31	Apr. 1	Apr. 2	Apr. 3	Apr. 4
40 days.	Apr. 5	Apr. 6	Apr. 7	Apr. 8	Apr. 9
45 days.	Apr. 10	Apr. 11	Apr. 12	Apr. 13	Apr. 14
50 days.	Apr. 15	Apr. 16	Apr. 17	Apr. 18	Apr. 19
55 days.	Apr. 20	Apr. 21	Apr. 22	Apr. 23	Apr. 24
60 days.	Apr. 25	Apr. 26	Apr. 27	Apr. 28	Apr. 29
65 days.	Apr. 30	May 1	May 2	May 3	May 4
70 days.	May 5	May 6	May 7	May 8	May 9
75 days.	May 10	May 11	May 12	May 13	May 14
80 days.	May 15	May 16	May 17	May 18	May 19
85 days.	May 20	May 21	May 22	May 23	May 24
90 days.	May 25	May 26	May 27	May 28	May 29
95 days.	May 30	May 31	June 1	June 2	June 3
100 days.	June 4	June 5	June 6	June 7	June 8
1 month.	Mar. 25	Mar. 26	Mar. 27	Mar. 28	Mar. 29
2 months.	Apr. 25	Apr. 26	Apr. 27	Apr. 28	Apr. 29
3 months.	May 25	May 26	May 27	May 28	May 29
4 months.	June 25	June 26	June 27	June 28	June 29
5 months.	July 25	July 26	July 27	July 28	July 29
6 months.	Aug. 25	Aug. 26	Aug. 27	Aug. 28	Aug. 29
7 months.	Sep. 25	Sep. 26	Sep. 27	Sep. 28	Sep. 29
8 months.	Oct. 25	Oct. 26	Oct. 27	Oct. 28	Oct. 29
9 months.	Nov. 25	Nov. 26	Nov. 27	Nov. 28	Nov. 29
10 months.	Dec. 25	Dec. 26	Dec. 27	Dec. 28	Dec. 29
11 months.	Jan. 25	Jan. 26	Jan. 27	Jan. 28	Jan. 29
12 months.	Feb. 25	Feb. 26	Feb. 27	Feb. 28	Feb. 28
*12 mo's, L.Y	Feb. 25	Feb. 26	Feb. 27	Feb. 28	

*Use this line for notes dated in an ordinary year, and maturing in Leap Year.

The above tables are **without three days' grace·**

NOTE-MATURITY TABLES.
(WITHOUT GRACE.)

Time.	March 2.	March 3.	March 4.	March 5.	March 6.
5 days.	Mar. 7	Mar. 8	Mar. 9	Mar. 10	Mar. 11
10 days.	Mar. 12	Mar. 13	Mar. 14	Mar. 15	Mar. 16
15 days.	Mar. 17	Mar. 18	Mar. 19	Mar. 20	Mar. 21
20 days.	Mar. 22	Mar. 23	Mar. 24	Mar. 25	Mar. 26
25 days.	Mar. 27	Mar. 28	Mar. 29	Mar. 30	Mar. 31
30 days.	Apr. 1	Apr. 2	Apr. 3	Apr. 4	Apr. 5
35 days.	Apr. 6	Apr. 7	Apr. 8	Apr. 9	Apr. 10
40 days.	Apr. 11	Apr. 12	Apr. 13	Apr. 14	Apr. 15
45 days.	Apr. 16	Apr. 17	Apr. 18	Apr. 19	Apr. 20
50 days.	Apr. 21	Apr. 22	Apr. 23	Apr. 24	Apr. 25
55 days.	Apr. 26	Apr. 27	Apr. 28	Apr. 29	Apr. 30
60 days.	May 1	May 2	May 3	May 4	May 5
65 days.	May 6	May 7	May 8	May 9	May 10
70 days.	May 11	May 12	May 13	May 14	May 15
75 days.	May 16	May 17	May 18	May 19	May 20
80 days.	May 21	May 22	May 23	May 24	May 25
85 days.	May 26	May 27	May 28	May 29	May 30
90 days.	May 31	June 1	June 2	June 3	June 4
95 days.	Jnne 5	June 6	June 7	June 8	June 9
100 days.	June 10	June 11	June 12	June 13	June 14
1 month.	Apr. 2	Apr. 3	Apr. 4	Apr. 5	Apr. 6
2 months.	May 2	May 3	May 4	May 5	May 6
3 months.	June 2	June 3	June 4	June 5	June 6
4 months.	July 2	July 3	July 4	July 5	July 6
5 months.	Aug. 2	Aug. 3	Aug. 4	Aug. 5	Aug. 6
6 months.	Sep. 2	Sep. 3	Sep. 4	Sep. 5	Sep. 6
7 months.	Oct. 2	Oct. 3	Oct. 4	Oct. 5	Oct. 6
8 months.	Nov. 2	Nov. 3	Nov. 4	Nov. 5	Nov. 6
9 months.	Dec. 2	Dec. 3	Dec. 4	Dec. 5	Dec. 6
10 months.	Jan. 2	Jan. 3	Jan. 4	Jan. 5	Jan. 6
11 months.	Feb. 2	Feb. 3	Feb. 4	Feb. 5	Feb. 6
12 months.	Mch 2	Mch 3	Mch 4	Mch 5	Mch 6

The above tables are **without three days' grace**.

(WITHOUT GRACE.)

Time.	March 7.	March 8.	March 9.	March 10.	March 11.
5 days.	Mar. 12	Mar. 13	Mar. 14	Mar. 15	Mar. 16
10 days.	Mar. 17	Mar. 18	Mar. 19	Mar. 20	Mar. 21
15 days.	Mar. 22	Mar. 23	Mar. 24	Mar. 25	Mar. 26
20 days.	Mar. 27	Mar. 28	Mar. 29	Mar. 30	Mar. 31
25 days.	Apr. 1	Apr. 2	Apr. 3	Apr. 4	Apr. 5
30 days.	Apr. 6	Apr. 7	Apr. 8	Apr. 9	Apr. 10
35 days.	Apr. 11	Apr. 12	Apr. 13	Apr. 14	Apr. 15
40 days.	Apr. 16	Apr. 17	Apr. 18	Apr. 19	Apr. 20
45 days.	Apr. 21	Apr. 22	Apr. 23	Apr. 24	Apr. 25
50 days.	Apr. 26	Apr. 27	Apr. 28	Apr. 29	Apr. 30
55 days.	May 1	May 2	May 3	May 4	May 5
60 days.	May 6	May 7	May 8	May 9	May 10
65 days.	May 11	May 12	May 13	May 14	May 15
70 days.	May 16	May 17	May 18	May 19	May 20
75 days.	May 21	May 22	May 23	May 24	May 25
80 days.	May 26	May 27	May 28	May 29	May 30
85 days.	May 31	June 1	June 2	June 3	June 4
90 days.	June 5	June 6	June 7	June 8	June 9
95 days.	June 10	June 11	June 12	June 13	June 14
100 days.	June 15	June 16	June 17	June 18	Jun. 19
1 month.	Apr. 7	Apr. 8	Apr. 9	Apr. 10	Apr. 11
2 months.	May 7	May 8	May 9	May 10	May 11
3 months.	June 7	June 8	June 9	June 10	June 11
4 months.	July 7	July 8	July 9	July 10	July 11
5 months.	Aug. 7	Aug. 8	Aug. 9	Aug. 10	Aug 11
6 months.	Sep. 7	Sep. 8	Sep. 9	Sep. 10	Sep. 11
7 months.	Oct. 7	Oct. 8	Oct. 9	Oct. 10	Oct. 11
8 months.	Nov. 7	Nov. 8	Nov. 9	Nov. 10	Nov. 11
9 months.	Dec. 7	Dec. 8	Dec. 9	Dec. 10	Dec. 11
10 months.	Jan. 7	Jan. 8	Jan. 9	Jan. 10	Jan. 11
11 months.	Feb. 7	Feb. 8	Feb. 9	Feb. 10	Feb. 11
12 months.	Mch 7	Mch 8	Mch 9	Mch 10	Mch 11

The above tables are **without three days' grace.**

(WITHOUT GRACE.)

Time.	March 12.	March 13.	March 14.	March 15.	March 16.
5 days.	Mar. 17	Mar. 18	Mar. 19	Mar. 20	Mar. 21
10 days.	Mar. 22	Mar. 23	Mar. 24	Mar. 25	Mar. 26
15 days.	Mar. 27	Mar. 28	Mar. 29	Mar. 30	Mar. 31
20 days.	Apr. 1	Apr. 2	Apr. 3	Apr. 4	Apr. 5
25 days.	Apr. 6	Apr. 7	Apr. 8	Apr. 9	Apr. 10
30 days.	Apr. 11	Apr. 12	Apr. 13	Apr. 14	Apr. 15
35 days.	Apr. 16	Apr. 17	Apr. 18	Apr. 19	Apr. 20
40 days.	Apr. 21	Apr. 22	Apr. 23	Apr. 24	Apr. 25
45 days.	Apr. 26	Apr. 27	Apr. 28	Apr. 29	Apr. 30
50 days.	May 1	May 2	May 3	May 4	May 5
55 days.	May 6	May 7	May 8	May 9	May 10
60 days.	May 11	May 12	May 13	May 14	May 15
65 days.	May 16	May 17	May 18	May 19	May 20
70 days.	May 21	May 22	May 23	May 24	May 25
75 days.	May 26	May 27	May 28	May 29	May 30
80 days.	May 31	June 1	June 2	June 3	June 4
85 days.	Jnne 5	June 6	June 7	June 8	June 9
90 days.	June 10	June 11	June 12	June 13	June 14
95 days.	June 15	June 16	June 17	June 18	Jun. 19
100 days.	Jun. 20	Jun. 21	Jun. 22	Jun. 23	Jun. 24
1 month.	Apr. 12	Apr. 13	Apr. 14	Apr. 15	Apr. 16
2 months.	May 12	May 13	May 14	May 15	May 16
3 months.	June 12	June 13	June 14	June 15	June 16
4 mouths.	July 12	July 13	July 14	July 15	July 16
5 months.	Aug. 12	Aug. 13	Aug. 14	Aug. 15	Aug. 16
6 months.	Sep. 12	Sep. 13	Sep. 14	Sep. 15	Sep. 16
7 months.	Oct. 12	Oct. 13	Oct. 14	Oct. 15	Oct. 16
8 mouths.	Nov. 12	Nov. 13	Nov. 14	Nov. 15	Nov. 16
9 months.	Dec. 12	Dec. 13	Dec. 14	Dec. 15	Dec. 16
10 months.	Jan. 12	Jan. 13	Jan. 14	Jan. 15	Jan. 16
11 months.	Feb. 12	Feb. 13	Feb. 14	Feb. 15	Feb. 16
12 months.	Mch 12	Mch 13	Mch 14	Mch 15	Mch 16

The above tables are without three days' grace.

(WITHOUT GRACE.)

Time.	March 17.	March 18.	March 19.	March 20.	March 21.
5 days.	Mar. 22	Mar. 23	Mar. 24	Mar. 25	Mar. 26
10 days.	Mar. 27	Mar. 28	Mar. 29	Mar. 30	Mar. 31
15 days.	Apr. 1	Apr. 2	Apr. 3	Apr. 4	Apr. 5
20 days.	Apr. 6	Apr. 7	Apr. 8	Apr. 9	Apr. 10
25 days.	Apr. 11	Apr. 12	Apr. 13	Apr. 14	Apr. 15
30 days.	Apr. 16	Apr. 17	Apr. 18	Apr. 19	Apr. 20
35 days.	Apr. 21	Apr. 22	Apr. 23	Apr. 24	Apr. 25
40 days.	Apr. 26	Apr. 27	Apr. 28	Apr. 29	Apr. 30
45 days.	May 1	May 2	May 3	May 4	May 5
50 days.	May 6	May 7	May 8	May 9	May 10
55 days.	May 11	May 12	May 13	May 14	May 15
60 days.	May 16	May 17	May 18	May 19	May 20
65 days.	May 21	May 22	May 23	May 24	May 25
70 days.	May 26	May 27	May 28	May 29	May 30
75 days.	May 31	June 1	June 2	June 3	June 4
80 days.	Jnne 5	June 6	June 7	June 8	June 9
85 days.	June 10	June 11	June 12	June 13	June 14
90 days.	June 15	June 16	June 17	June 18	Jun. 19
95 days.	Jun. 20	Jun. 21	Jun. 22	Jun. 23	Jun. 24
100 days.	Jun. 25	Jun. 26	Jun. 27	Jun. 28	Jun. 29
1 month.	Apr. 17	Apr. 18	Apr. 19	Apr. 20	Apr. 21
2 months.	May 17	May 18	May 19	May 20	May 21
3 months.	June 17	June 18	June 19	June 20	June 21
4 months.	July 17	July 18	July 19	July 20	July 21
5 months.	Aug. 17	Aug. 18	Aug. 19	Aug. 20	Aug. 21
6 months.	Sep. 17	Sep. 18	Sep. 19	Sep. 20	Sep. 21
7 months.	Oct. 17	Oct. 18	Oct. 19	Oct. 20	Oct. 21
8 months.	Nov. 17	Nov. 18	Nov. 19	Nov. 20	Nov. 21
9 months.	Dec. 17	Dec. 18	Dec. 19	Dec. 20	Dec. 21
10 months.	Jan. 17	Jan. 18	Jan. 19	Jan. 20	Jan. 21
11 months.	Feb. 17	Feb. 18	Feb. 19	Feb. 20	Feb. 21
12 months.	Mch 17	Mch 18	Mch 19	Mch 20	Mch 21

The above tables are **without three davs' grace.**

(WITHOUT GRACE.)

Time.	March 22.	March 23.	March 24.	March 25.	March 26.
5 days.	Mar. 27	Mar. 28	Mar. 29	Mar. 30	Mar. 31
10 days.	Apr. 1	Apr. 2	Apr. 3	Apr. 4	Apr. 5
15 days.	Apr. 6	Apr. 7	Apr. 8	Apr. 9	Apr. 10
20 days.	Apr. 11	Apr. 12	Apr. 13	Apr. 14	Apr. 15
25 days.	Apr. 16	Apr. 17	Apr. 18	Apr. 19	Apr. 20
30 days.	Apr. 21	Apr. 22	Apr. 23	Apr. 24	Apr. 25
35 days.	Apr. 26	Apr. 27	Apr. 28	Apr. 29	Apr. 30
40 days.	May 1	May 2	May 3	May 4	May 5
45 days.	May 6	May 7	May 8	May 9	May 10
50 days.	May 11	May 12	May 13	May 14	May 15
55 days.	May 16	May 17	May 18	May 19	May 20
60 days.	May 21	May 22	May 23	May 24	May 25
65 days.	May 26	May 27	May 28	May 29	May 30
70 days.	May 31	June 1	June 2	June 3	June 4
75 days.	Jnne 5	June 6	June 7	June 8	June 9
80 days.	June 10	June 11	June 12	June 13	June 14
85 days.	June 15	June 16	June 17	June 18	Jun. 19
90 days.	Jun. 20	Jun. 21	Jun. 22	Jun. 23	Jun. 24
95 days.	Jun. 25	Jun. 26	Jun. 27	Jun. 28	Jun. 29
100 days.	Jun. 30	July 1	July 2	July 3	July 4
1 month.	Apr. 22	Apr. 23	Apr. 24	Apr. 25	Apr. 26
2 months.	May 22	May 23	May 24	May 25	May 26
3 months.	June 22	June 23	June 24	June 25	June 26
4 months.	July 22	July 23	July 24	July 25	July 26
5 months.	Aug. 22	Aug. 23	Aug. 24	Aug. 25	Aug. 26
6 months.	Sep. 22	Sep. 23	Sep. 24	Sep. 25	Sep. 26
7 months.	Oct. 22	Oct. 23	Oct. 24	Oct. 25	Oct. 26
8 months.	Nov. 22	Nov. 23	Nov. 24	Nov. 25	Nov. 26
9 months.	Dec. 22	Dec. 23	Dec. 24	Dec. 25	Dec. 26
10 months.	Jan. 22	Jan. 23	Jan. 24	Jan. 25	Jan. 26
11 months.	Feb. 22	Feb. 23	Feb. 24	Feb. 25	Feb. 26
12 months.	Mch 22	Mch 23	Mch 24	Mch 25	Mch 26

The above tables are **without three days' grace.**

(WITHOUT GRACE.)

Time.	March 27.	March 28.	March 29.	March 30.	March 31.
5 days.	Apr. 1	Apr. 2	Apr. 3	Apr. 4	Apr. 5
10 days.	Apr. 6	Apr. 7	Apr. 8	Apr. 9	Apr. 10
15 days.	Apr. 11	Apr. 12	Apr. 13	Apr. 14	Apr. 15
20 days.	Apr. 16	Apr. 17	Apr. 18	Apr. 19	Apr. 20
25 days.	Apr. 21	Apr. 22	Apr. 23	Apr. 24	Apr. 25
30 days.	Apr. 26	Apr. 27	Apr. 28	Apr. 29	Apr. 30
35 days.	May 1	May 2	May 3	May 4	May 5
40 days.	May 6	May 7	May 8	May 9	May 10
45 days.	May 11	May 12	May 13	May 14	May 15
50 days.	May 16	May 17	May 18	May 19	May 20
55 days.	May 21	May 22	May 23	May 24	May 25
60 days.	May 26	May 27	May 28	May 29	May 30
65 days.	May 31	June 1	June 2	June 3	June 4
70 days.	June 5	June 6	June 7	June 8	June 9
75 days.	June 10	June 11	June 12	June 13	June 14
80 days.	June 15	June 16	June 17	June 18	Jun. 19
85 days.	Jun. 20	Jun. 21	Jun. 22	Jun. 23	Jun. 24
90 days.	Jun. 25	Jun. 26	Jun. 27	Jun. 28	Jun. 29
95 days.	Jun. 30	July 1	July 2	July 3	July 4
100 days.	July 5	July 6	July 7	July 8	July 9
1 month.	Apr. 27	Apr. 28	Apr. 29	Apr. 30	Apr. 30
2 months.	May 27	May 28	May 29	May 30	May 31
3 months.	June 27	June 28	June 29	June 30	June 30
4 months.	July 27	July 28	July 29	July 30	July 31
5 months.	Aug. 27	Aug. 28	Aug. 29	Aug. 30	Aug. 31
6 months.	Sep. 27	Sep. 28	Sep. 29	Sep. 30	Sep. 30
7 months.	Oct. 27	Oct. 28	Oct. 29	Oct. 30	Oct. 31
8 months.	Nov. 27	Nov. 28	Nov. 29	Nov. 30	Nov. 30
9 months.	Dec. 27	Dec. 28	Dec. 29	Dec. 30	Dec. 31
10 months.	Jan. 27	Jan. 28	Jan. 29	Jan. 30	Jan. 31
11 months.	Feb. 27	Feb. 28	Feb. 28	Feb. 28	Feb. 28
*11 mo's, L.Y	Feb. 27	Feb. 28	Feb. 29	Feb. 29	Feb. 29
12 months.	Mch 27	Mch 28	Mch 29	Mch 30	Mch 31

*Use this line for Notes maturing in Leap Year.

The above tables are **without three days' grace**.

(WITHOUT GRACE.)

Time.	April 1.	April 2.	April 3.	April 4.	April 5.
5 days.	Apr. 6	Apr. 7	Apr. 8	Apr. 9	Apr. 10
10 days.	Apr. 11	Apr. 12	Apr. 13	Apr. 14	Apr. 15
15 days.	Apr. 16	Apr. 17	Apr. 18	Apr. 19	Apr. 20
20 days.	Apr. 21	Apr. 22	Apr. 23	Apr. 24	Apr. 25
25 days.	Apr. 26	Apr. 27	Apr. 28	Apr. 29	Apr. 30
30 days.	May 1	May 2	May 3	May 4	May 5
35 days.	May 6	May 7	May 8	May 9	May 10
40 days.	May 11	May 12	May 13	May 14	May 15
45 days.	May 16	May 17	May 18	May 19	May 20
50 days.	May 21	May 22	May 23	May 24	May 25
55 days.	May 26	May 27	May 28	May 29	May 30
60 days.	May 31	June 1	June 2	June 3	June 4
65 days.	Jnne 5	June 6	June 7	June 8	June 9
70 days.	June 10	June 11	June 12	June 13	June 14
75 days.	June 15	June 16	June 17	June 18	Jun. 19
80 days.	Jun. 20	Jun. 21	Jun. 22	Jun. 23	Jun. 24
85 days.	Jun. 25	Jun. 26	Jun. 27	Jun. 28	Jun. 29
90 days.	Jun. 30	July 1	July 2	July 3	July 4
95 days.	July 5	July 6	July 7	July 8	July 9
100 days.	July 10	July 11	July 12	July 13	July 14
1 month.	May 1	May 2	May 3	May 4	May 5
2 months.	June 1	June 2	June 3	June 4	June 5
3 months.	July 1	July 2	July 3	July 4	July 5
4 months.	Aug. 1	Aug. 2	Aug. 3	Aug. 4	Aug. 5
5 months.	Sep. 1	Sep. 2	Sep. 3	Sep. 4	Sep. 5
6 months.	Oct. 1	Oct. 2	Oct. 3	Oct. 4	Oct. 5
7 months.	Nov. 1	Nov. 2	Nov. 3	Nov. 4	Nov. 5
8 months.	Dec. 1	Dec. 2	Dec. 3	Dec. 4	Dec. 5
9 months.	Jan. 1	Jan. 2	Jan. 3	Jan. 4	Jan. 5
10 months.	Feb. 1	Feb. 2	Feb. 3	Feb. 4	Feb. 5
11 months.	Mch 1	Mch 2	Mch 3	Mch 4	Mch 5
12 months.	Apr. 1	Apr. 2	Apr. 3	Apr. 4	Apr. 5

The above tables are **without three days' grace.**

Time.	April 6.	April 7.	April 8.	April 9.	April 10.
5 days.	Apr. 11	Apr. 12	Apr. 13	Apr. 14	Apr. 15
10 days.	Apr. 16	Apr. 17	Apr. 18	Apr. 19	Apr. 20
15 days.	Apr. 21	Apr. 22	Apr. 23	Apr. 24	Apr. 25
20 days.	Apr. 26	Apr. 27	Apr. 28	Apr. 29	Apr. 30
25 days.	May 1	May 2	May 3	May 4	May 5
30 days.	May 6	May 7	May 8	May 9	May 10
35 days.	May 11	May 12	May 13	May 14	May 15
40 days.	May 16	May 17	May 18	May 19	May 20
45 days.	May 21	May 22	May 23	May 24	May 25
50 days.	May 26	May 27	May 28	May 29	May 30
55 days.	May 31	June 1	June 2	June 3	June 4
60 days.	Jnne 5	June 6	June 7	June 8	June 9
65 days.	June 10	June 11	June 12	June 13	June 14
70 days.	June 15	June 16	June 17	June 18	Jun. 19
75 days.	Jun. 20	Jun. 21	Jun. 22	Jun. 23	Jun. 24
80 days.	Jun. 25	Jun. 26	Jun. 27	Jun. 28	Jun. 29
85 days.	Jun. 30	July 1	July 2	July 3	July 4
90 days.	July 5	July 6	July 7	July 8	July 9
95 days.	July 10	July 11	July 12	July 13	July 14
100 days.	July 15	July 16	July 17	July 18	July 19
1 month.	May 6	May 7	May 8	May 9	May 10
2 months.	June 6	June 7	June 8	June 9	June 10
3 months.	July 6	July 7	July 8	July 9	July 10
4 months.	Aug. 6	Aug. 7	Aug. 8	Aug. 9	Aug. 10
5 months.	Sep. 6	Sep. 7	Sep. 8	Sep. 9	Sep. 10
6 months.	Oct. 6	Oct. 7	Oct. 8	Oct. 9	Oct. 10
7 months.	Nov. 6	Nov. 7	Nov. 8	Nov. 9	Nov. 10
8 months.	Dec. 6	Dec. 7	Dec. 8	Dec. 9	Dec. 10
9 months.	Jan. 6	Jan. 7	Jan. 8	Jan. 9	Jan. 10
10 months.	Feb. 6	Feb. 7	Feb. 8	Feb. 9	Feb. 10
11 months.	Mch 6	Mch 7	Mch 8	Mch 9	Mch 10
12 months.	Apr. 6	Apr. 7	Apr. 8	Apr. 9	Apr. 10

The above tables are WITHOUT three days' grace.

(WITHOUT GRACE.)

Time.	April 11.	April 12.	April 13.	April 14.	April 15.
5 days.	Apr. 16	Apr. 17	Apr. 18	Apr. 19	Apr. 20
10 days.	Apr. 21	Apr. 22	Apr. 23	Apr. 24	Apr. 25
15 days.	Apr. 26	Apr. 27	Apr. 28	Apr. 29	Apr. 30
20 days.	May 1	May 2	May 3	May 4	May 5
25 days.	May 6	May 7	May 8	May 9	May 10
30 days.	May 11	May 12	May 13	May 14	May 15
35 days.	May 16	May 17	May 18	May 19	May 20
40 days.	May 21	May 22	May 23	May 24	May 25
45 days.	May 26	May 27	May 28	May 29	May 30
50 days.	May 31	June 1	June 2	June 3	June 4
55 days.	Jnne 5	June 6	June 7	June 8	June 9
60 days.	June 10	June 11	June 12	June 13	June 14
65 days.	June 15	June 16	June 17	June 18	Jun. 19
70 days.	Jun. 20	Jun. 21	Jun. 22	Jun. 23	Jun. 24
75 days.	Jun. 25	Jun. 26	Jun. 27	Jun. 28	Jun. 29
80 days.	Jun. 30	July 1	July 2	July 3	July 4
85 days.	July 5	July 6	July 7	July 8	July 9
90 days.	July 10	July 11	July 12	July 13	July 14
95 days.	July 15	July 16	July 17	July 18	July 19
100 days.	July 20	July 21	July 22	July 23	July 24
1 month.	May 11	May 12	May 13	May 14	May 15
2 months.	June 11	June 12	June 13	June 14	June 15
3 months.	July 11	July 12	July 13	July 14	July 15
4 months.	Aug. 11	Aug. 12	Aug. 13	Aug. 14	Aug. 15
5 months.	Sep. 11	Sep. 12	Sep. 13	Sep. 14	Sep. 15
6 months.	Oct. 11	Oct. 12	Oct. 13	Oct. 14	Oct. 15
7 months.	Nov. 11	Nov. 12	Nov. 13	Nov. 14	Nov. 15
8 months.	Dec. 11	Dec. 12	Dec. 13	Dec. 14	Dec. 15
9 months.	Jan. 11	Jan. 12	Jan. 13	Jan. 14	Jan. 15
10 months.	Feb. 11	Feb. 12	Feb. 13	Feb. 14	Feb, 15
11 months.	Mch 11	Mch 12	Mch 13	Mch 14	Mch 15
12 months.	Apr. 11	Apr. 12	Apr. 13	Apr. 14	Apr. 15

The above tables are WITHOUT three days' grace.

Time.	April 16.	April 17.	April 18.	April 19.	April 20.
5 days.	Apr. 21	Apr. 22	Apr. 23	Apr. 24	Apr. 25
10 days.	Apr. 26	Apr. 27	Apr. 28	Apr. 29	Apr. 30
15 days.	May 1	May 2	May 3	May 4	May 5
20 days.	May 6	May 7	May 8	May 9	May 10
25 days.	May 11	May 12	May 13	May 14	May 15
30 days.	May 16	May 17	May 18	May 19	May 20
35 days.	May 21	May 22	May 23	May 24	May 25
40 days.	May 26	May 27	May 28	May 29	May 30
45 days.	May 31	June 1	June 2	June 3	June 4
50 days.	June 5	June 6	June 7	June 8	June 9
55 days.	June 10	June 11	June 12	June 13	June 14
60 days.	June 15	June 16	June 17	June 18	Jun. 19
65 days.	Jun. 20	Jun. 21	Jun. 22	Jun. 23	Jun. 24
70 days.	Jun. 25	Jun. 26	Jun. 27	Jun. 28	Jun. 29
75 days.	Jun. 30	July 1	July 2	July 3	July 4
80 days.	July 5	July 6	July 7	July 8	July 9
85 days.	July 10	July 11	July 12	July 13	July 14
90 days.	July 15	July 16	July 17	July 18	July 19
95 days.	July 20	July 21	July 22	July 23	July 24
100 days.	July 25	July 26	July 27	July 28	July 29
1 month.	May 16	May 17	May 18	May 19	May 20
2 months.	June 16	June 17	June 18	June 19	June 20
3 months.	July 16	July 17	July 18	July 19	July 20
4 months.	Aug. 16	Aug. 17	Aug. 18	Aug. 19	Aug. 20
5 months.	Sep. 16	Sep. 17	Sep. 18	Sep. 19	Sep. 20
6 months.	Oct. 16	Oct. 17	Oct. 18	Oct. 19	Oct. 20
7 months.	Nov. 16	Nov. 17	Nov. 18	Nov. 19	Nov. 20
8 months.	Dec. 16	Dec. 17	Dec. 18	Dec. 19	Dec. 20
9 months.	Jan. 16	Jan. 17	Jan. 18	Jan. 19	Jan. 20
10 months.	Feb. 16	Feb. 17	Feb. 18	Feb. 19	Feb. 20
11 months.	Mch 16	Mch 17	Mch 18	Mch 19	Mch 20
12 months.	Apr. 16	Apr. 17	Apr. 18	Apr. 19	Apr. 20

The above tables are WITHOUT three days' grace.

Time.	April 21.	April 22.	April 23.	April 24.	April 25.
5 days.	Apr. 26	Apr. 27	Apr. 28	Apr. 29	Apr. 30
10 days.	May 1	May 2	May 3	May 4	May 5
15 days.	May 6	May 7	May 8	May 9	May 10
20 days.	May 11	May 12	May 13	May 14	May 15
25 days.	May 16	May 17	May 18	May 19	May 20
30 days.	May 21	May 22	May 23	May 24	May 25
35 days.	May 26	May 27	May 28	May 29	May 30
40 days.	May 31	June 1	June 2	June 3	June 4
45 days.	Jnne 5	June 6	June 7	June 8	June 9
50 days.	June 10	June 11	June 12	June 13	June 14
55 days.	June 15	June 16	June 17	June 18	Jun. 19
60 days.	Jun. 20	Jun. 21	Jun. 22	Jun. 23	Jun. 24
65 days.	Jun. 25	Jun. 26	Jun. 27	Jun. 28	Jun. 29
70 days.	Jun. 30	July 1	July 2	July 3	July 4
75 days.	July 5	July 6	July 7	July 8	July 9
80 days.	July 10	July 11	July 12	July 13	July 14
85 days.	July 15	July 16	July 17	July 18	July 19
90 days.	July 20	July 21	July 22	July 23	July 24
95 days.	July 25	July 26	July 27	July 28	July 29
100 days.	July 30	July 31	Aug. 1	Aug. 2	Aug. 3
1 month.	May 21	May 22	May 23	May 24	May 25
2 months.	June 21	June 22	June 23	June 24	June 25
3 months.	July 21	July 22	July 23	July 24	July 25
4 months.	Aug. 21	Aug. 22	Aug. 23	Aug. 24	Aug. 25
5 months.	Sep. 21	Sep. 22	Sep. 23	Sep. 24	Sep. 25
6 months.	Oct. 21	Oct. 22	Oct. 23	Oct. 24	Oct. 25
7 months.	Nov. 21	Nov. 22	Nov. 23	Nov. 24	Nov. 25
8 months.	Dec. 21	Dec. 22	Dec. 23	Dec. 24	Dec. 25
9 months.	Jan. 21	Jan. 22	Jan. 23	Jan. 24	Jan. 25
10 months.	Feb. 21	Feb. 22	Feb. 23	Feb. 24	Feb. 25
11 months.	Mch 21	Mch 22	Mch 23	Mch 24	Mch 25
12 months.	Apr. 21	Apr. 22	Apr. 23	Apr. 24	Apr. 25

The above tables are WITHOUT three days' grace.

Time.	April 26.	April 27.	April 28.	April 29.	April 30.
5 days.	May 1	May 2	May 3	May 4	May 5
10 days.	May 6	May 7	May 8	May 9	May 10
15 days.	May 11	May 12	May 13	May 14	May 15
20 days.	May 16	May 17	May 18	May 19	May 20
25 days.	May 21	May 22	May 23	May 24	May 25
30 days.	May 26	May 27	May 28	May 29	May 30
35 days.	May 31	June 1	June 2	June 3	June 4
40 days.	June 5	June 6	June 7	June 8	June 9
45 days.	June 10	June 11	June 12	June 13	June 14
50 days.	June 15	June 16	June 17	June 18	June 19
55 days.	June 20	June 21	June 22	June 23	June 24
60 days.	June 25	June 26	June 27	June 28	June 29
65 days.	June 30	July 1	July 2	July 3	July 4
70 days.	July 5	July 6	July 7	July 8	July 9
75 days.	July 10	July 11	July 12	July 13	July 14
80 days.	July 15	July 16	July 17	July 18	July 19
85 days.	July 20	July 21	July 22	July 23	July 24
90 days.	July 25	July 26	July 27	July 28	July 29
95 days.	July 30	July 31	Aug. 1	Aug. 2	Aug. 3
100 days.	Aug. 4	Aug. 5	Aug. 6	Aug. 7	Aug. 8
1 month.	May 26	May 27	May 28	May 29	May 30
2 months.	Jun. 26	June 27	June 28	June 29	June 30
3 months.	Jul. 26	July 27	Jul. 28	July 29	July 30
4 months.	Aug. 26	Aug. 27	Aug. 28	Aug. 29	Aug. 30
5 months.	Sep. 26	Sep. 27	Sep. 28	Sep. 29	Sep. 30
6 months.	Oct. 26	Oct. 27	Oct. 28	Oct. 29	Oct. 30
7 months.	Nov. 26	Nov. 27	Nov. 28	Nov. 29	Nov. 30
8 months.	Dec. 26	Dec. 27	Dec. 28	Dec. 29	Dec. 30
9 months.	Jan. 26	Jan. 27	Jan. 28	Jan. 29	Jan. 30
10 months.	Feb. 26	Feb. 27	Feb. 28	Feb. 28	Feb. 28
*10 mo's, L. Y	Feb. 26	Feb. 27	Feb. 28	Feb. 29	Feb. 29
11 months.	Mar. 26	Mar. 27	Mar. 28	Mar. 29	Mar. 30
12 months.	Apr. 26	Apr. 27	Apr. 28	Apr. 29	Apr. 30

*Use this line for notes maturing in Leap-Year.

The above Tables are for use in States where three days' grace are NOT allowed.

(WITHOUT GRACE.)

Time.	May 1.	May 2.	May 3.	May 4.	May 5.
5 days.	May 6	May 7	May 8	May 9	May 10
10 days.	May 11	May 12	May 13	May 14	May 15
15 days.	May 16	May 17	May 18	May 19	May 20
20 days.	May 21	May 22	May 23	May 24	May 25
25 days.	May 26	May 27	May 28	May 29	May 30
30 days.	May 31	June 1	June 2	June 3	June 4
35 days.	June 5	June 6	June 7	June 8	June 9
40 days.	June 10	June 11	June 12	June 13	June 14
45 days.	June 15	June 16	June 17	June 18	June 19
50 days.	June 20	June 21	June 22	June 23	June 24
55 days.	June 25	June 26	June 27	June 28	June 29
60 days.	June 30	July 1	July 2	July 3	July 4
65 days.	July 5	July 6	July 7	July 8	July 9
70 days.	July 10	July 11	July 12	July 13	July 14
75 days.	July 15	July 16	July 17	July 18	July 19
80 days.	July 20	July 21	July 22	July 23	July 24
85 days.	July 25	July 26	July 27	July 28	July 29
90 days.	July 30	July 31	Aug. 1	Aug. 2	Aug. 3
95 days.	Aug. 4	Aug. 5	Aug. 6	Aug. 7	Aug. 8
100 days.	Aug. 9	Aug. 10	Aug. 11	Aug. 12	Aug. 13
1 month.	Jun. 1	June 2	June 3	June 4	June 5
2 months.	Jul. 1	July 2	Jul. 3	July 4	July 5
3 months.	Aug. 1	Aug. 2	Aug. 3	Aug. 4	Aug. 5
4 months.	Sep. 1	Sep. 2	Sep. 3	Sep. 4	Sep. 5
5 months.	Oct. 1	Oct. 2	Oct. 3	Oct. 4	Oct. 5
6 months.	Nov. 1	Nov. 2	Nov. 3	Nov. 4	Nov. 5
7 months.	Dec. 1	Dec. 2	Dec. 3	Dec. 4	Dec. 5
8 months.	Jan. 1	Jan. 2	Jan. 3	Jan. 4	Jan. 5
9 months.	Feb. 1	Feb. 2	Feb. 3	Feb. 4	Feb. 5
10 months.	Mar. 1	Mar. 2	Mar. 3	Mar. 4	Mar. 5
11 months.	Apr. 1	Apr. 2	Apr. 3	Apr. 4	Apr. 5
12 months.	May 1	May 2	May 3	May 4	May 5

The above Tables are for use in States where three days' grace are NOT allowed.

(WITHOUT GRACE.)

Time.	May 6.	May 7.	May 8.	May 9.	May 10.
5 days.	May 11	May 12	May 13	May 14	May 15
10 days.	May 16	May 17	May 18	May 19	May 20
15 days.	May 21	May 22	May 23	May 24	May 25
20 days.	May 26	May 27	May 28	May 29	May 30
25 days.	May 31	June 1	June 2	June 3	June 4
30 days.	June 5	June 6	June 7	June 8	June 9
35 days.	June 10	June 11	June 12	June 13	June 14
40 days.	June 15	June 16	June 17	June 18	June 19
45 days.	June 20	June 21	June 22	June 23	June 24
50 days.	June 25	June 26	June 27	June 28	June 29
55 days.	June 30	July 1	July 2	July 3	July 4
60 days.	July 5	July 6	July 7	July 8	July 9
65 days.	July 10	July 11	July 12	July 13	July 14
70 days.	July 15	July 16	July 17	July 18	July 19
75 days.	July 20	July 21	July 22	July 23	July 24
80 days.	July 25	July 26	July 27	July 28	July 29
85 days.	July 30	July 31	Aug. 1	Aug. 2	Aug. 3
90 days.	Aug. 4	Aug. 5	Aug. 6	Aug. 7	Aug. 8
95 days.	Aug. 9	Aug. 10	Aug. 11	Aug. 12	Aug. 13
100 days.	Aug. 14	Aug. 15	Aug. 16	Aug. 17	Aug. 18
1 month.	Jun. 6	June 7	June 8	June 9	June 10
2 months.	Jul. 6	July 7	Jul. 8	July 9	July 10
3 months.	Aug. 6	Aug. 7	Aug. 8	Aug. 9	Aug. 10
4 months.	Sep. 6	Sep. 7	Sep. 8	Sep. 9	Sep. 10
5 months.	Oct. 6	Oct. 7	Oct. 8	Oct. 9	Oct. 10
6 months.	Nov. 6	Nov. 7	Nov. 8	Nov. 9	Nov. 10
7 months.	Dec. 6	Dec. 7	Dec. 8	Dec. 9	Dec. 10
8 months.	Jan. 6	Jan. 7	Jan. 8	Jan. 9	Jan. 10
9 months.	Feb. 6	Feb. 7	Feb. 8	Feb. 9	Feb. 10
10 months.	Mar. 6	Mar. 7	Mar. 8	Mar. 9	Mar. 10
11 months.	Apr. 6	Apr. 7	Apr. 8	Apr. 9	Apr. 10
12 months.	May 6	May 7	May 8	May 9	May 10

The above Tables are for use in States where three days' grace are NOT allowed.

(WITHOUT GRACE.)

Time.	May 11.	May 12.	May 13.	May 14.	May 15.
5 days.	May 16	May 17	May 18	May 19	May 20
10 days.	May 21	May 22	May 23	May 24	May 25
15 days.	May 26	May 27	May 28	May 29	May 30
20 days.	May 31	June 1	June 2	June 3	June 4
25 days.	June 5	June 6	June 7	June 8	June 9
30 days.	June 10	June 11	June 12	June 13	June 14
35 days.	June 15	June 16	June 17	June 18	June 19
40 days.	June 20	June 21	June 22	June 23	June 24
45 days.	June 25	June 26	June 27	June 28	June 29
50 days.	June 30	July 1	July 2	July 3	July 4
55 days.	July 5	July 6	July 7	July 8	July 9
60 days.	July 10	July 11	July 12	July 13	July 14
65 days.	July 15	July 16	July 17	July 18	July 19
70 days.	July 20	July 21	July 22	July 23	July 24
75 days.	July 25	July 26	July 27	July 28	July 29
80 days.	July 30	July 31	Aug. 1	Aug. 2	Aug. 3
85 days.	Aug. 4	Aug. 5	Aug. 6	Aug. 7	Aug. 8
90 days.	Aug. 9	Aug. 10	Aug. 11	Aug. 12	Aug. 13
95 days.	Aug. 14	Aug. 15	Aug. 16	Aug. 17	Aug. 18
100 days.	Aug. 19	Aug. 20	Aug. 21	Aug. 22	Aug. 23
1 month.	Jun. 11	June 12	June 13	June 14	June 15
2 months.	Jul. 11	July 12	Jul. 13	July 14	July 15
3 months.	Aug. 11	Aug. 12	Aug. 13	Aug. 14	Aug. 15
4 months.	Sep. 11	Sep. 12	Sep. 13	Sep. 14	Sep. 15
5 months.	Oct. 11	Oct. 12	Oct. 13	Oct. 14	Oct. 15
6 months.	Nov. 11	Nov. 12	Nov. 13	Nov. 14	Nov. 15
7 months.	Dec. 11	Dec. 12	Dec. 13	Dec. 14	Dec. 15
8 months.	Jan. 11	Jan. 12	Jan. 13	Jan. 14	Jan. 15
9 months.	Feb. 11	Feb. 12	Feb. 13	Feb. 14	Feb. 15
10 months.	Mar. 11	Mar. 12	Mar. 13	Mar. 14	Mar. 15
11 months.	Apr. 11	Apr. 12	Apr. 13	Apr. 14	Apr. 15
12 months.	May 11	May 12	May 13	May 14	May 15

The above Tables are for use in States where three days' grace are NOT allowed.

(WITHOUT GRACE.)

Time.	May 16.	May 17.	May 18.	May 19.	May 20.
5 days.	May 21	May 22	May 23	May 24	May 25
10 days.	May 26	May 27	May 28	May 29	May 30
15 days.	May 31	June 1	June 2	June 3	June 4
20 days.	June 5	June 6	June 7	June 8	June 9
25 days.	June 10	June 11	June 12	June 13	June 14
30 days.	June 15	June 16	June 17	June 18	June 19
35 days.	June 20	June 21	June 22	June 23	June 24
40 days.	June 25	June 26	June 27	June 28	June 29
45 days.	June 30	July 1	July 2	July 3	July 4
50 days.	July 5	July 6	July 7	July 8	July 9
55 days.	July 10	July 11	July 12	July 13	July 14
60 days.	July 15	July 16	July 17	July 18	July 19
65 days.	July 20	July 21	July 22	July 23	July 24
70 days.	July 25	July 26	July 27	July 28	July 29
75 days.	July 30	July 31	Aug. 1	Aug. 2	Aug. 3
80 days.	Aug. 4	Aug. 5	Aug. 6	Aug. 7	Aug. 8
85 days.	Aug. 9	Aug. 10	Aug. 11	Aug. 12	Aug. 13
90 days.	Aug. 14	Aug. 15	Aug. 16	Aug. 17	Aug. 18
95 days.	Aug. 19	Aug. 20	Aug. 21	Aug. 22	Aug. 23
100 days.	Aug. 24	Aug. 25	Aug. 26	Aug. 27	Aug. 28
1 month.	June 16	June 17	June 18	June 19	June 20
2 months.	Jul. 16	July 17	Jul. 18	July 19	July 20
3 months.	Aug. 16	Aug. 17	Aug. 18	Aug. 19	Aug. 20
4 months.	Sep. 16	Sep. 17	Sep. 18	Sep. 19	Sep. 20
5 months.	Oct. 16	Oct. 17	Oct. 18	Oct. 19	Oct. 20
6 months.	Nov. 16	Nov. 17	Nov. 18	Nov. 19	Nov. 20
7 months.	Dec. 16	Dec. 17	Dec. 18	Dec. 19	Dec. 20
8 months.	Jan. 16	Jan. 17	Jan. 18	Jan. 19	Jan. 20
9 months.	Feb. 16	Feb. 17	Feb. 18	Feb. 19	Feb. 20
10 months.	Mar. 16	Mar. 17	Mar. 18	Mar. 19	Mar. 20
11 months.	Apr. 16	Apr. 17	Apr. 18	Apr. 19	Apr. 20
12 months.	May 16	May 17	May 18	May 19	May 20

The above Tables are for use in States where three days' grace are NOT allowed.

(WITHOUT GRACE.)

Time.	May 21.	May 22.	May 23.	May 24.	May 25.
5 days.	May 26	May 27	May 28	May 29	May 30
10 days.	May 31	June 1	June 2	June 3	June 4
15 days.	June 5	June 6	June 7	June 8	June 9
20 days.	June 10	June 11	June 12	June 13	June 14
25 days.	June 15	June 16	June 17	June 18	June 19
30 days.	June 20	June 21	June 22	June 23	June 24
35 days.	June 25	June 26	June 27	June 28	June 29
40 days.	June 30	July 1	July 2	July 3	July 4
45 days.	July 5	July 6	July 7	July 8	July 9
50 days.	July 10	July 11	July 12	July 13	July 14
55 days.	July 15	July 16	July 17	July 18	July 19
60 days.	July 20	July 21	July 22	July 23	July 24
65 days.	July 25	July 26	July 27	July 28	July 29
70 days.	July 30	July 31	Aug. 1	Aug. 2	Aug. 3
75 days.	Aug. 4	Aug. 5	Aug. 6	Aug. 7	Aug. 8
80 days.	Aug. 9	Aug. 10	Aug. 11	Aug. 12	Aug. 13
85 days.	Aug. 14	Aug. 15	Aug. 16	Aug. 17	Aug. 18
90 days.	Aug. 19	Aug. 20	Aug. 21	Aug. 22	Aug. 23
95 days.	Aug. 24	Aug. 25	Aug. 26	Aug. 27	Aug. 28
100 days.	Aug. 29	Aug. 30	Aug. 31	Sep. 1	Sep. 2
1 month.	Jun. 21	June 22	June 23	June 24	June 25
2 months.	Jul. 21	July 22	Jul. 23	July 24	July 25
3 months.	Aug. 21	Aug. 22	Aug. 23	Aug. 24	Aug. 25
4 months.	Sep. 21	Sep. 22	Sep. 23	Sep. 24	Sep. 25
5 months.	Oct. 21	Oct. 22	Oct. 23	Oct. 24	Oct. 25
6 months.	Nov. 21	Nov. 22	Nov. 23	Nov. 24	Nov. 25
7 months.	Dec. 21	Dec. 22	Dec. 23	Dec. 24	Dec. 25
8 months.	Jan. 21	Jan. 22	Jan. 23	Jan. 24	Jan. 25
9 months.	Feb. 21	Feb. 22	Feb. 23	Feb. 24	Feb. 25
10 months.	Mar. 21	Mar. 22	Mar. 23	Mar. 24	Mar. 25
11 months.	Apr. 21	Apr. 22	Apr. 23	Apr. 24	Apr. 25
12 months.	May 21	May 22	May 23	May 24	May 25

The above Tables are for use in States where three days' grace are NOT allowed.

Time.	May 26.	May 27.	May 28.	May 29.	May 30.
5 days.	May 31	June 1	June 2	June 3	June 4
10 days.	June 5	June 6	June 7	June 8	June 9
15 days.	June 10	June 11	June 12	June 13	June 14
20 days.	June 15	June 16	June 17	June 18	June 19
25 days.	June 20	June 21	June 22	June 23	June 24
30 days.	June 25	June 26	June 27	June 28	June 29
35 days.	June 30	July 1	July 2	July 3	July 4
40 days.	July 5	July 6	July 7	July 8	July 9
45 days.	July 10	July 11	July 12	July 13	July 14
50 days.	July 15	July 16	July 17	July 18	July 19
55 days.	July 20	July 21	July 22	July 23	July 24
60 days.	July 25	July 26	July 27	July 28	July 29
65 days.	July 30	July 31	Aug. 1	Aug. 2	Aug. 3
70 days.	Aug. 4	Aug. 5	Aug. 6	Aug. 7	Aug. 8
75 days.	Aug. 9	Aug. 10	Aug. 11	Aug. 12	Aug. 13
80 days.	Aug. 14	Aug. 15	Aug. 16	Aug. 17	Aug. 18
85 days.	Aug. 19	Aug. 20	Aug. 21	Aug. 22	Aug. 23
90 days.	Aug. 24	Aug. 25	Aug. 26	Aug. 27	Aug. 28
95 days.	Aug. 29	Aug. 30	Aug. 31	Sep. 1	Sep. 2
100 days.	Sep. 3	Sep. 4	Sep. 5	Sep. 6	Sep. 7
1 month.	Jun. 26	June 27	June 28	June 29	June 30
2 months.	Jul. 26	July 27	Jul. 28	July 29	July 30
3 months.	Aug. 26	Aug. 27	Aug. 28	Aug. 29	Aug. 30
4 months.	Sep. 26	Sep. 27	Sep. 28	Sep. 29	Sep. 30
5 months.	Oct. 26	Oct. 27	Oct. 28	Oct. 29	Oct. 30
6 months.	Nov. 26	Nov. 27	Nov. 28	Nov. 29	Nov. 30
7 months.	Dec. 26	Dec. 27	Dec. 28	Dec. 29	Dec. 30
8 months.	Jan. 26	Jan. 27	Jan. 28	Jan. 29	Jan. 30
9 months.	Feb. 26	Feb. 27	Feb. 28	Feb. 28	Feb. 28
*9 mo's, L.Y.	Feb. 26	Feb. 27	Feb. 28	Feb. 29	Feb. 29
10 months.	Mar. 26	Mar. 27	Mar. 28	Mar. 29	Mar. 30
11 months.	Apr. 26	Apr. 27	Apr. 28	Apr. 29	Apr. 30
12 months.	May 26	May 27	May 28	May 29	May 30

*Use this line for notes maturing in Leap Year.

The above Tables are for use in States where three days' grace are NOT allowed.

(WITHOUT GRACE.)

Time.	May 31.	June 1.	June 2.	June 3.	June 4.
5 days.	June 5	June 6	June 7	June 8	June 9
10 days.	June 10	June 11	June 12	June 13	June 14
15 days.	June 15	June 16	June 17	June 18	June 19
20 days.	June 20	June 21	June 22	June 23	June 24
25 days.	June 25	June 26	June 27	June 28	June 29
30 days.	June 30	July 1	July 2	July 3	July 4
35 days.	July 5	July 6	July 7	July 8	July 9
40 days.	July 10	July 11	July 12	July 13	July 14
45 days.	July 15	July 16	July 17	July 18	July 19
50 days.	July 20	July 21	July 22	July 23	July 24
55 days.	July 25	July 26	July 27	July 28	July 29
60 days.	July 30	July 31	Aug. 1	Aug. 2	Aug. 3
65 days.	Aug. 4	Aug. 5	Aug. 6	Aug. 7	Aug. 8
70 days.	Aug. 9	Aug. 10	Aug. 11	Aug. 12	Aug. 13
75 days.	Aug. 14	Aug. 15	Aug. 16	Aug. 17	Aug. 18
80 days.	Aug. 19	Aug. 20	Aug. 21	Aug. 22	Aug. 23
85 days.	Aug. 24	Aug. 25	Aug. 26	Aug. 27	Aug. 28
90 days.	Aug. 29	Aug. 30	Aug. 31	Sep. 1	Sep. 2
95 days.	Sep. 3	Sep. 4	Sep. 5	Sep. 6	Sep. 7
100 days.	Sep. 8	Sep. 9	Sep. 10	Sep. 11	Sep. 12
1 month.	Jun. 30	July 1	Jul. 2	July 3	July 4
2 months.	Jul. 31	Aug. 1	Aug. 2	Aug. 3	Aug. 4
3 months.	Aug. 31	Sep. 1	Sep. 2	Sep. 3	Sep. 4
4 months.	Sep. 30	Oct. 1	Oct. 2	Oct. 3	Oct. 4
5 months.	Oct. 31	Nov. 1	Nov. 2	Nov. 3	Nov. 4
6 months.	Nov. 30	Dec. 1	Dec. 2	Dec. 3	Dec. 4
7 months.	Dec. 31	Jan. 1	Jan. 2	Jan. 3	Jan. 4
8 months.	Jan. 31	Feb. 1	Feb. 2	Feb. 3	Feb. 4
9 months.	Feb. 28	Mar. 1	Mar. 2	Mar. 3	Mar. 4
*9 mo's, L.Y.	Feb. 29	Mar. 1	Mar. 2	Mar. 3	Mar. 4
10 months.	Mar. 31	Apr. 1	Apr. 2	Apr. 3	Apr. 4
11 months.	Apr. 30	May 1	May 2	May 3	May 4
12 months.	May 31	June 1	June 2	June 3	June 4

*Use this line for Notes maturing in Leap Year.

The above Tables are for use in States where three days' grace are NOT allowed.

Time.	June 5.	June 6.	June 7.	June 8.	June 9.
5 days.	June 10	June 11	June 12	June 13	June 14
10 days.	June 15	June 16	June 17	June 18	June 19
15 days.	June 20	June 21	June 22	June 23	June 24
20 days.	June 25	June 26	June 27	June 28	June 29
25 days.	June 30	July 1	July 2	July 3	July 4
30 days.	July 5	July 6	July 7	July 8	July 9
35 days.	July 10	July 11	July 12	July 13	July 14
40 days.	July 15	July 16	July 17	July 18	July 19
45 days.	July 20	July 21	July 22	July 23	July 24
50 days.	July 25	July 26	July 27	July 28	July 29
55 days.	July 30	July 31	Aug. 1	Aug. 2	Aug. 3
60 days.	Aug. 4	Aug. 5	Aug. 6	Aug. 7	Aug. 8
65 days.	Aug. 9	Aug. 10	Aug. 11	Aug. 12	Aug. 13
70 days.	Aug. 14	Aug. 15	Aug. 16	Aug. 17	Aug. 18
75 days.	Aug. 19	Aug. 20	Aug. 21	Aug. 22	Aug. 23
80 days.	Aug. 24	Aug. 25	Aug. 26	Aug. 27	Aug. 28
85 days.	Aug. 29	Aug. 30	Aug. 31	Sep. 1	Sep. 2
90 days.	Sep. 3	Sep. 4	Sep. 5	Sep. 6	Sep. 7
95 days.	Sep. 8	Sep. 9	Sep. 10	Sep. 11	Sep. 12
100 days.	Sep. 13	Sep. 14	Sep. 15	Sep. 16	Sep. 17
1 month.	Jul. 5	July 6	Jul. 7	July 8	July 9
2 months.	Aug. 5	Aug. 6	Aug. 7	Aug. 8	Aug. 9
3 months.	Sep. 5	Sep. 6	Sep. 7	Sep. 8	Sep. 9
4 months.	Oct. 5	Oct. 6	Oct. 7	Oct. 8	Oct. 9
5 months.	Nov. 5	Nov. 6	Nov. 7	Nov. 8	Nov. 9
6 months.	Dec. 5	Dec. 6	Dec. 7	Dec. 8	Dec. 9
7 months.	Jan. 5	Jan. 6	Jan. 7	Jan. 8	Jan. 9
8 months.	Feb. 5	Feb. 6	Feb. 7	Feb. 8	Feb. 9
9 months.	Mar. 5	Mar. 6	Mar. 7	Mar. 8	Mar. 9
10 months.	Apr. 5	Apr. 6	Apr. 7	Apr. 8	Apr. 9
11 months.	May 5	May 6	May 7	May 8	May 9
12 months.	Jun. 5	June 6	June 7	June 8	June 9

The above Tables are for use in States where three days' grace are NOT allowed.

(WITHOUT GRACE.)

Time.	June 10.	June 11.	June 12.	June 13.	June 14.
5 days.	June 15	June 16	June 17	June 18	June 19
10 days.	June 20	June 21	June 22	June 23	June 24
15 days.	June 25	June 26	June 27	June 28	June 29
20 days.	June 30	July 1	July 2	July 3	July 4
25 days.	July 5	July 6	July 7	July 8	July 9
30 days.	July 10	July 11	July 12	July 13	July 14
35 days.	July 15	July 16	July 17	July 18	July 19
40 days.	July 20	July 21	July 22	July 23	July 24
45 days.	July 25	July 26	July 27	July 28	July 29
50 days.	July 30	July 31	Aug. 1	Aug. 2	Aug. 3
55 days.	Aug. 4	Aug. 5	Aug. 6	Aug. 7	Aug. 8
60 days.	Aug. 9	Aug. 10	Aug. 11	Aug. 12	Aug. 13
65 days.	Aug. 14	Aug. 15	Aug. 16	Aug. 17	Aug. 18
70 days.	Aug. 19	Aug. 20	Aug. 21	Aug. 22	Aug. 23
75 days.	Aug. 24	Aug. 25	Aug. 26	Aug. 27	Aug. 28
80 days.	Aug. 29	Aug. 30	Aug. 31	Sep. 1	Sep. 2
85 days.	Sep. 3	Sep. 4	Sep. 5	Sep. 6	Sep. 7
90 days.	Sep. 8	Sep. 9	Sep. 10	Sep. 11	Sep. 12
95 days.	Sep. 13	Sep. 14	Sep. 15	Sep. 16	Sep. 17
100 days.	Sep. 18	Sep. 19	Sep. 20	Sep. 21	Sep. 22
1 month.	Jul. 10	July 11	Jul. 12	July 13	July 14
2 months.	Aug. 10	Aug. 11	Aug. 12	Aug. 13	Aug. 14
3 months.	Sep. 10	Sep. 11	Sep. 12	Sep. 13	Sep. 14
4 months.	Oct. 10	Oct. 11	Oct. 12	Oct. 13	Oct. 14
5 months.	Nov. 10	Nov. 11	Nov. 12	Nov. 13	Nov. 14
6 months.	Dec. 10	Dec. 11	Dec. 12	Dec. 13	Dec. 14
7 months.	Jan. 10	Jan. 11	Jan. 12	Jan. 13	Jan. 14
8 months.	Feb. 10	Feb. 11	Feb. 12	Feb. 13	Feb. 14
9 months.	Mar. 10	Mar. 11	Mar. 12	Mar. 13	Mar. 14
10 months.	Apr. 10	Apr. 11	Apr. 12	Apr. 13	Apr. 14
11 months.	May 10	May 11	May 12	May 13	May 14
12 months.	Jun. 10	June 11	June 12	June 13	June 14

The above Tables are for use in States where three days' grace are NOT allowed.

(WITHOUT GRACE.)

Time.	June 15.	June 16.	June 17.	June 18.	June 19.
5 days.	June 20	June 21	June 22	June 23	June 24
10 days.	June 25	June 26	June 27	June 28	June 29
15 days.	June 30	July 1	July 2	July 3	July 4
20 days.	July 5	July 6	July 7	July 8	July 9
25 days.	July 10	July 11	July 12	July 13	July 14
30 days.	July 15	July 16	July 17	July 18	July 19
35 days.	July 20	July 21	July 22	July 23	July 24
40 days.	July 25	July 26	July 27	July 28	July 29
45 days.	July 30	July 31	Aug. 1	Aug. 2	Aug. 3
50 days.	Aug. 4	Aug. 5	Aug. 6	Aug. 7	Aug. 8
55 days.	Aug. 9	Aug. 10	Aug. 11	Aug. 12	Aug. 13
60 days.	Aug. 14	Aug. 15	Aug. 16	Aug. 17	Aug. 18
65 days.	Aug. 19	Aug. 20	Aug. 21	Aug. 22	Aug. 23
70 days.	Aug. 24	Aug. 25	Aug. 26	Aug. 27	Aug. 28
75 days.	Aug. 29	Aug. 30	Aug. 31	Sep. 1	Sep. 2
80 days.	Sep. 3	Sep. 4	Sep. 5	Sep. 6	Sep. 7
85 days.	Sep. 8	Sep. 9	Sep. 10	Sep. 11	Sep. 12
90 days.	Sep. 13	Sep. 14	Sep. 15	Sep. 16	Sep. 17
95 days.	Sep. 18	Sep. 19	Sep. 20	Sep. 21	Sep. 22
100 days.	Sep. 23	Sep. 24	Sep. 25	Sep. 26	Sep. 27
1 month.	Jul. 15	July 16	Jul. 17	July 18	July 19
2 months.	Aug. 15	Aug. 16	Aug. 17	Aug. 18	Aug. 19
3 months.	Sep. 15	Sep. 16	Sep. 17	Sep. 18	Sep. 19
4 months.	Oct. 15	Oct. 16	Oct. 17	Oct. 18	Oct. 19
5 months.	Nov. 15	Nov. 16	Nov. 17	Nov. 18	Nov. 19
6 months.	Dec. 15	Dec. 16	Dec. 17	Dec. 18	Dec. 19
7 months.	Jan. 15	Jan. 16	Jan. 17	Jan. 18	Jan. 19
8 months.	Feb. 15	Feb. 16	Feb. 17	Feb. 18	Feb. 19
9 months.	Mar. 15	Mar. 16	Mar. 17	Mar. 18	Mar. 19
10 months.	Apr. 15	Apr. 16	Apr. 17	Apr. 18	Apr. 19
11 months.	May 15	May 16	May 17	May 18	May 19
12 months.	Jun. 15	June 16	June 17	June 18	June 19

The above Tables are for use in States where three days' grace are NOT allowed.

(WITHOUT GRACE.)

Time.	June 20.	June 21.	June 22.	June 23.	June 24.
5 days.	June 25	June 26	June 27	June 28	June 29
10 days.	June 30	July 1	July 2	July 3	July 4
15 days.	July 5	July 6	July 7	July 8	July 9
20 days.	July 10	July 11	July 12	July 13	July 14
25 days.	July 15	July 16	July 17	July 18	July 19
30 days.	July 20	July 21	July 22	July 23	July 24
35 days.	July 25	July 26	July 27	July 28	July 29
40 days.	July 30	July 31	Aug. 1	Aug. 2	Aug. 3
45 days.	Aug. 4	Aug. 5	Aug. 6	Aug. 7	Aug. 8
50 days.	Aug. 9	Aug. 10	Aug. 11	Aug. 12	Aug. 13
55 days.	Aug. 14	Aug. 15	Aug. 16	Aug. 17	Aug. 18
60 days.	Aug. 19	Aug. 20	Aug. 21	Aug. 22	Aug. 23
65 days.	Aug. 24	Aug. 25	Aug. 26	Aug. 27	Aug. 28
70 days.	Aug. 29	Aug. 30	Aug. 31	Sep. 1	Sep. 2
75 days.	Sep. 3	Sep. 4	Sep. 5	Sep. 6	Sep. 7
80 days.	Sep. 8	Sep. 9	Sep. 10	Sep. 11	Sep. 12
85 days.	Sep. 13	Sep. 14	Sep. 15	Sep. 16	Sep. 17
90 days.	Sep. 18	Sep. 19	Sep. 20	Sep. 21	Sep. 22
95 days.	Sep. 23	Sep. 24	Sep. 25	Sep. 26	Sep. 27
100 days.	Sep. 28	Sep. 29	Sep. 30	Oct. 1	Oct. 2
1 month.	Jul. 20	July 21	Jul. 22	July 23	July 24
2 months.	Aug. 20	Aug. 21	Aug. 22	Aug. 23	Aug. 24
3 months.	Sep. 20	Sep. 21	Sep. 22	Sep. 23	Sep. 24
4 months.	Oct. 20	Oct. 21	Oct. 22	Oct. 23	Oct. 24
5 months.	Nov. 20	Nov. 21	Nov. 22	Nov. 23	Nov. 24
6 months.	Dec. 20	Dec. 21	Dec. 22	Dec. 23	Dec. 24
7 months.	Jan. 20	Jan. 21	Jan. 22	Jan. 23	Jan. 24
8 months.	Feb. 20	Feb. 21	Feb. 22	Feb. 23	Feb. 24
9 months.	Mar. 20	Mar. 21	Mar. 22	Mar. 23	Mar. 24
10 months.	Apr. 20	Apr. 21	Apr. 22	Apr. 23	Apr. 24
11 months.	May 20	May 21	May 22	May 23	May 24
12 months.	Jun. 20	June 21	June 22	June 23	June 24

The above Tables are for use in States where three days' grace are NOT allowed.

(WITHOUT GRACE.)

Time.	June 25.	June 26.	June 27.	June 28.	June 29.
5 days.	June 30	July 1	July 2	July 3	July 4
10 days.	July 5	July 6	July 7	July 8	July 9
15 days.	July 10	July 11	July 12	July 13	July 14
20 days.	July 15	July 16	July 17	July 18	July 19
25 days.	July 20	July 21	July 22	July 23	July 24
30 days.	July 25	July 26	July 27	July 28	July 29
35 days.	July 30	July 31	Aug. 1	Aug. 2	Aug. 3
40 days.	Aug. 4	Aug. 5	Aug. 6	Aug. 7	Aug. 8
45 days.	Aug. 9	Aug. 10	Aug. 11	Aug. 12	Aug. 13
50 days.	Aug. 14	Aug. 15	Aug. 16	Aug. 17	Aug. 18
55 days.	Aug. 19	Aug. 20	Aug. 21	Aug. 22	Aug. 23
60 days.	Aug. 24	Aug. 25	Aug. 26	Aug. 27	Aug. 28
65 days.	Aug. 29	Aug. 30	Aug. 31	Sep. 1	Sep. 2
70 days.	Sep. 3	Sep. 4	Sep. 5	Sep. 6	Sep. 7
75 days.	Sep. 8	Sep. 9	Sep. 10	Sep. 11	Sep. 12
80 days.	Sep. 13	Sep. 14	Sep. 15	Sep. 16	Sep. 17
85 days.	Sep. 18	Sep. 19	Sep. 20	Sep. 21	Sep. 22
90 days.	Sep. 23	Sep. 24	Sep. 25	Sep. 26	Sep. 27
95 days.	Sep. 28	Sep. 29	Sep. 30	Oct. 1	Oct. 2
100 days.	Oct. 3	Oct. 4	Oct. 5	Oct. 6	Oct. 7
1 month.	Jul. 25	July 26	Jul. 27	July 28	July 29
2 months.	Aug. 25	Aug. 26	Aug. 27	Aug. 28	Aug. 29
3 months.	Sep. 25	Sep. 26	Sep. 27	Sep. 28	Sep. 29
4 months.	Oct. 25	Oct. 26	Oct. 27	Oct. 28	Oct. 29
5 months.	Nov. 25	Nov. 26	Nov. 27	Nov. 28	Nov. 29
6 months.	Dec. 25	Dec. 26	Dec. 27	Dec. 28	Dec. 29
7 months.	Jan. 25	Jan. 26	Jan. 27	Jan. 28	Jan. 29
8 months.	Feb. 25	Feb. 26	Feb. 27	Feb. 28	Feb. 28
*8 mo's, L.Y.	Feb. 25	Feb. 26	Feb. 27	Feb. 28	Feb. 29
9 months.	Mar. 25	Mar. 26	Mar. 27	Mar. 28	Mar. 29
10 months.	Apr. 25	Apr. 26	Apr. 27	Apr. 28	Apr. 29
11 months.	May 25	May 26	May 27	May 28	May 29
12 months.	Jun. 25	June 26	June 27	June 28	June 29

*Use this line for Notes maturing in Leap Year.

The above Tables are for use in States where three days' grace are NOT allowed.

(WITHOUT GRACE.)

Time.	June 30.	July 1.	July 2.	July 3.	July 4.
5 days.	July 5	July 6	July 7	July 8	July 9
10 days.	July 10	July 11	July 12	July 13	July 14
15 days.	July 15	July 16	July 17	July 18	July 19
20 days.	July 20	July 21	July 22	July 23	July 24
25 days.	July 25	July 26	July 27	July 28	July 29
30 days.	July 30	July 31	Aug. 1	Aug. 2	Aug. 3
35 days.	Aug. 4	Aug. 5	Aug. 6	Aug. 7	Aug. 8
40 days.	Aug. 9	Aug. 10	Aug. 11	Aug. 12	Aug. 13
45 days.	Aug. 14	Aug. 15	Aug. 16	Aug. 17	Aug. 18
50 days.	Aug. 19	Aug. 20	Aug. 21	Aug. 22	Aug. 23
55 days.	Aug. 24	Aug. 25	Aug. 26	Aug. 27	Aug. 28
60 days.	Aug. 29	Aug. 30	Aug. 31	Sep. 1	Sep. 2
65 days.	Sep. 3	Sep. 4	Sep. 5	Sep. 6	Sep. 7
70 days.	Sep. 8	Sep. 9	Sep. 10	Sep. 11	Sep. 12
75 days.	Sep. 13	Sep. 14	Sep. 15	Sep. 16	Sep. 17
80 days.	Sep. 18	Sep. 19	Sep. 20	Sep. 21	Sep. 22
85 days.	Sep. 23	Sep. 24	Sep. 25	Sep. 26	Sep. 27
90 days.	Sep. 28	Sep. 29	Sep. 30	Oct. 1	Oct. 2
95 days.	Oct. 3	Oct. 4	Oct. 5	Oct. 6	Oct. 7
100 days.	Oct. 8	Oct. 9	Oct. 10	Oct. 11	Oct. 12
1 month.	Jul. 30	Aug. 1	Aug. 2	Aug. 3	Aug. 4
2 months.	Aug. 30	Sep. 1	Sep. 2	Sep. 3	Sep. 4
3 months.	Sep. 30	Oct. 1	Oct. 2	Oct. 3	Oct. 4
4 months.	Oct. 30	Nov. 1	Nov. 2	Nov. 3	Nov. 4
5 months.	Nov. 30	Dec. 1	Dec. 2	Dec. 3	Dec. 4
6 months.	Dec. 30	Jan. 1	Jan. 2	Jan. 3	Jan. 4
7 months.	Jan. 30	Feb. 1	Feb. 2	Feb. 3	Feb. 4
8 months.	Feb. 28	Mar. 1	Mar. 2	Mar. 3	Mar. 4
*8 mo's, L.Y.	Feb. 29	Mar. 1	Mar. 2	Mar. 3	Mar. 4
9 months.	Mar. 30	Apr. 1	Apr. 2	Apr. 3	Apr. 4
10 months.	Apr. 30	May 1	May 2	May 3	May 4
11 months.	May 30	June 1	June 2	June 3	June 4
12 months.	Jun. 30	July 1	Jul. 2	July 3	July 4

*Use this line for Notes maturing in Leap Year.

The above Tables are for use in States where three days'
grace are NOT allowed.

Time.	July 5.	July 6.	July 7.	July 8.	July 9.
5 days.	July 10	July 11	July 12	July 13	July 14
10 days.	July 15	July 16	July 17	July 18	July 19
15 days.	July 20	July 21	July 22	July 23	July 24
20 days.	July 25	July 26	July 27	July 28	July 29
25 days.	July 30	July 31	Aug. 1	Aug. 2	Aug. 3
30 days.	Aug. 4	Aug. 5	Aug. 6	Aug. 7	Aug. 8
35 days.	Aug. 9	Aug. 10	Aug. 11	Aug. 12	Aug. 13
40 days.	Aug. 14	Aug. 15	Aug. 16	Aug. 17	Aug. 18
45 days.	Aug. 19	Aug. 20	Aug. 21	Aug. 22	Aug. 23
50 days.	Aug. 24	Aug. 25	Aug. 26	Aug. 27	Aug. 28
55 days.	Aug. 29	Aug. 30	Aug. 31	Sep. 1	Sep. 2
60 days.	Sep. 3	Sep. 4	Sep. 5	Sep. 6	Sep. 7
65 days.	Sep. 8	Sep. 9	Sep. 10	Sep. 11	Sep. 12
70 days.	Sep. 13	Sep. 14	Sep. 15	Sep. 16	Sep. 17
75 days.	Sep. 18	Sep. 19	Sep. 20	Sep. 21	Sep. 22
80 days.	Sep. 23	Sep. 24	Sep. 25	Sep. 26	Sep. 27
85 days.	Sep. 28	Sep. 29	Sep. 30	Oct. 1	Oct. 2
90 days.	Oct. 3	Oct. 4	Oct. 5	Oct. 6	Oct. 7
95 days.	Oct. 8	Oct. 9	Oct. 10	Oct. 11	Oct. 12
100 days.	Oct. 13	Oct. 14	Oct. 15	Oct. 16	Oct. 17
1 month.	Aug. 5	Aug. 6	Aug. 7	Aug. 8	Aug. 9
2 months.	Sep. 5	Sep. 6	Sep. 7	Sep. 8	Sep. 9
3 months.	Oct. 5	Oct. 6	Oct. 7	Oct. 8	Oct. 9
4 months.	Nov. 5	Nov. 6	Nov. 7	Nov. 8	Nov. 9
5 months.	Dec. 5	Dec. 6	Dec. 7	Dec. 8	Dec. 9
6 months.	Jan. 5	Jan. 6	Jan. 7	Jan. 8	Jan. 9
7 months.	Feb. 5	Feb. 6	Feb. 7	Feb. 8	Feb. 9
8 months.	Mar. 5	Mar. 6	Mar. 7	Mar. 8	Mar. 9
9 months.	Apr. 5	Apr. 6	Apr. 7	Apr. 8	Apr. 9
10 months.	May 5	May 6	May 7	May 8	May 9
11 months.	Jun. 5	June 6	June 7	June 8	June 9
12 months.	Jul. 5	July 6	Jul. 7	July 8	July 9

The above Tables are for use in States where three days' grace are NOT allowed.

WITHOUT GRACE.
For Leap Year changes, see next page.

Time.	July 10.	July 11.	July 12.	July 13.	July 14.
5 days.	July 15	July 16	July 17	July 18	July 19
10 days.	July 20	July 21	July 22	July 23	July 24
15 days.	July 25	July 26	July 27	July 28	July 29
20 days.	July 30	July 31	Aug 1	Aug 2	Aug 3
25 days.	Aug 4	Aug 5	Aug 6	Aug 7	Aug 8
30 days.	Aug 9	Aug 10	Aug 11	Aug 12	Aug 13
35 days.	Aug 14	Aug 15	Aug 16	Aug 17	Aug 18
40 days.	Aug 19	Aug 20	Aug 21	Aug 22	Aug 23
45 days.	Aug 24	Aug 25	Aug 26	Aug 27	Aug 28
50 days.	Aug 29	Aug 30	Aug 31	Sept 1	Sept 2
55 days.	Sept 3	Sept 4	Sept 5	Sept 6	Sept 7
60 days.	Sept 8	Sept 9	Sept 10	Sept 11	Sept 12
65 days.	Sept 13	Sept 14	Sept 15	Sept 16	Sept 17
70 days.	Sept 18	Sept 19	Sept 20	Sept 21	Sept 22
75 days.	Sept 23	Sept 24	Sept 25	Sept 26	Sept 27
80 days.	Sept 28	Sept 29	Sept 30	Oct 1	Oct 2
85 days.	Oct 3	Oct 4	Oct 5	Oct 6	Oct 7
90 days.	Oct 8	Oct 9	Oct 10	Oct 11	Oct 12
95 days.	Oct 13	Oct 14	Oct 15	Oct 16	Oct 17
100 days.	Oct 18	Oct 19	Oct 20	Oct 21	Oct 22
1 month.	Aug. 10	Aug. 11	Aug. 12	Aug. 13	Aug. 14
2 months.	Sep. 10	Sep. 11	Sep. 12	Sept. 13	Sep. 14
3 months.	Oct. 10	Oct. 11	Oct. 12	Oct. 13	Oct. 14
4 months.	Nov. 10	Nov. 11	Nov. 12	Nov. 13	Nov. 14
5 months.	Dec. 10	Dec. 11	Dec. 12	Dec. 13	Dec. 14
6 months.	Jan. 10	Jan. 11	Jan. 12	Jan. 13	Jan. 14
7 months.	Feb. 10	Feb. 11	Feb. 12	Feb. 13	Feb. 14
8 months.	Mar. 10	Mar. 11	Mar. 12	Mar. 13	Mar. 14
9 months.	Apr. 10	Apr. 11	Apr. 12	Apr. 13	Apr. 14
10 months.	May 10	May 11	May 12	May 13	May 14
11 months.	Jun. 10	Jun. 11	Jun. 12	June 13	Jun. 14
12 months.	Jul. 10	Jul. 11	Jul. 12	July 13	July 14

The above Tables are WITHOUT three days' grace.

WITHOUT GRACE.

For Leap Year changes, see next page.

Time.	July 15.	July 16.	July 17.	July 18.	July 19.
5 days.	July 20	July 21	July 22	July 23	July 24
10 days.	July 25	July 26	July 27	July 28	July 29
15 days.	July 30	July 31	Aug 1	Aug 2	Aug 3
20 days.	Aug 4	Aug 5	Aug 6	Aug 7	Aug 8
25 days.	Aug 9	Aug 10	Aug 11	Aug 12	Aug 13
30 days.	Aug 14	Aug 15	Aug 16	Aug 17	Aug 18
35 days.	Aug 19	Aug 20	Aug 21	Aug 22	Aug 23
40 days.	Aug 24	Aug 25	Aug 26	Aug 27	Aug 28
45 days.	Aug 29	Aug 30	Aug 31	Sept 1	Sept 2
50 days.	Sept 3	Sept 4	Sept 5	Sept 6	Sept 7
55 days.	Sept 8	Sept 9	Sept 10	Sept 11	Sept 12
60 days.	Sept 13	Sept 14	Sept 15	Sept 16	Sept 17
65 days.	Sept 18	Sept 19	Sept 20	Sept 21	Sept 22
70 days.	Sept 23	Sept 24	Sept 25	Sept 26	Sept 27
75 days.	Sept 28	Sept 29	Sept 30	Oct 1	Oct 2
80 days.	Oct 3	Oct 4	Oct 5	Oct 6	Oct 7
85 days.	Oct 8	Oct 9	Oct 10	Oct 11	Oct 12
90 days.	Oct 13	Oct 14	Oct 15	Oct 16	Oct 17
95 days.	Oct 18	Oct 19	Oct 20	Oct 21	Oct 22
100 days.	Oct 23	Oct 24	Oct 25	Oct 26	Oct 27
1 month.	Aug. 15	Aug. 16	Aug. 17	Aug. 18	Aug. 19
2 months.	Sep. 15	Sep. 16	Sep. 17	Sept. 18	Sep. 19
3 months.	Oct. 15	Oct. 16	Oct. 17	Oct. 18	Oct. 19
4 months.	Nov. 15	Nov. 16	Nov. 17	Nov. 18	Nov. 19
5 months.	Dec. 15	Dec. 16	Dec. 17	Dec. 18	Dec. 19
6 months.	Jan. 15	Jan. 16	Jan. 17	Jan. 18	Jan. 19
7 months.	Feb. 15	Feb. 16	Feb. 17	Feb. 18	Feb. 19
8 months.	Mar. 15	Mar. 16	Mar. 17	Mar. 18	Mar. 19
9 months.	Apr. 15	Apr. 16	Apr. 17	Apr. 18	Apr. 19
10 months.	May 15	May 16	May 17	May 18	May 19
11 months.	Jun. 15	Jun. 16	Jun. 17	June 18	Jun. 19
12 months.	Jul. 15	Jul. 16	Jul. 17	July 18	July 19

The above Tables are WITHOUT three days' grace.

(WITHOUT GRACE.)

Time.	July 20.	July 21.	July 22.	July 23.	July 24.
5 days.	July 25	July 26	July 27	July 28	July 29
10 days.	July 30	July 31	Aug 1	Aug 2	Aug 3
15 days.	Aug 4	Aug 5	Aug 6	Aug 7	Aug 8
20 days.	Aug 9	Aug 10	Aug 11	Aug 12	Aug 13
25 days.	Aug 14	Aug 15	Aug 16	Aug 17	Aug 18
30 days.	Aug 19	Aug 20	Aug 21	Aug 22	Aug 23
35 days.	Aug 24	Aug 25	Aug 26	Aug 27	Aug 28
40 days.	Aug 29	Aug 30	Aug 31	Sept. 1	Sept. 2
45 days.	Sept. 3	Sept. 4	Sept. 5	Sept. 6	Sept. 7
50 days.	Sept. 8	Sept. 9	Sept. 10	Sept. 11	Sept. 12
55 days.	Sept. 13	Sept. 14	Sept. 15	Sept. 16	Sept. 17
60 days.	Sept. 18	Sept. 19	Sept. 20	Sept. 21	Sept. 22
65 days.	Sept. 23	Sept. 24	Sept. 25	Sept. 26	Sept. 27
70 days.	Sept. 28	Sept. 29	Sept. 30	Oct. 1	Oct. 2
75 days.	Oct. 3	Oct. 4	Oct. 5	Oct. 6	Oct. 7
80 days.	Oct. 8	Oct. 9	Oct. 10	Oct. 11	Oct. 12
85 days.	Oct. 13	Oct. 14	Oct. 15	Oct. 16	Oct. 17
90 days.	Oct. 18	Oct. 19	Oct. 20	Oct. 21	Oct. 22
95 days.	Oct. 23	Oct. 24	Oct. 25	Oct. 26	Oct. 27
100 days.	Oct. 28	Oct. 29	Oct. 30	Oct. 31	Nov. 1
1 month.	Aug. 20	Aug. 21	Aug. 22	Aug 23	Aug 24
2 months.	Sept. 20	Sept. 21	Sept. 22	Sept. 23	Sept. 24
3 months.	Oct. 20	Oct. 21	Oct. 22	Oct. 23	Oct. 24
4 months.	Nov. 20	Nov. 21	Nov. 22	Nov. 23	Nov. 24
5 months.	Dec. 20	Dec. 21	Dec. 22	Dec. 23	Dec. 24
6 months.	Jan. 20	Jan. 21	Jan. 22	Jan. 23	Jan. 24
7 months.	Feb. 20	Feb. 21	Feb. 22	Feb. 23	Feb. 24
8 months.	Mch 20	Mar. 21	Mar. 22	Mar. 23	Mar. 24
9 months.	Apr. 20	Apr. 21	Apr. 22	Apr. 23	Apr. 24
10 months.	May 20	May 21	May 22	May 23	May 24
11 months.	June 20	June 21	June 22	June 23	June 24
12 months.	July 20	July 21	July 22	July 23	July 25

The above Tables are WITHOUT three days' grace.

Time.	July 25.	July 26.	July 27.	July 28.	July 29.
5 days.	July 30	July 31	Aug. 1	Aug. 2	Aug. 3
10 days.	Aug. 4	Aug. 5	Aug. 6	Aug. 7	Aug. 8
15 days.	Aug. 9	Aug. 10	Aug. 11	Aug. 12	Aug. 13
20 days.	Aug. 14	Aug. 15	Aug. 16	Aug. 17	Aug. 18
25 days.	Aug. 19	Aug. 20	Aug. 21	Aug. 22	Aug. 23
30 days.	Aug. 24	Aug. 25	Aug. 26	Aug. 27	Aug. 28
35 days.	Aug. 29	Aug. 30	Aug. 31	Sept. 1	Sept. 2
40 days.	Sept. 3	Sept. 4	Sept. 5	Sept. 6	Sept. 7
45 days.	Sept. 8	Sept. 9	Sept. 10	Sept. 11	Sept. 12
50 days.	Sept. 13	Sept. 14	Sept. 15	Sept. 16	Sept. 17
55 days.	Sept. 18	Sept. 19	Sept. 20	Sept. 21	Sept. 22
60 days.	Sept. 23	Sept. 24	Sept. 25	Sept. 26	Sept. 27
65 days.	Sept. 28	Sept. 29	Sept. 30	Oct. 1	Oct. 2
70 days.	Oct. 3	Oct. 4	Oct. 5	Oct. 6	Oct. 7
75 days.	Oct. 8	Oct. 9	Oct. 10	Oct. 11	Oct. 12
80 days.	Oct. 13	Oct. 14	Oct. 15	Oct. 16	Oct. 17
85 days.	Oct. 18	Oct. 19	Oct. 20	Oct. 21	Oct. 22
90 days.	Oct. 23	Oct. 24	Oct. 25	Oct. 26	Oct. 27
95 days.	Oct. 28	Oct. 29	Oct. 30	Oct. 31	Nov. 1
100 days.	Nov. 2	Nov. 3	Nov. 4	Nov. 5	Nov. 6
1 month.	Aug. 25	Aug. 26	Aug. 27	Aug. 28	Aug. 29
2 months.	Sep. 25	Sep. 26	Sep. 27	Sep. 28	Sep. 29
3 months.	Oct. 25	Oct. 26	Oct. 27	Oct. 28	Oct. 29
4 months.	Nov. 25	Nov. 26	Nov. 27	Nov. 28	Nov. 29
5 months.	Dec. 25	Dec. 26	Dec. 27	Dec. 28	Dec. 29
6 months.	Jan. 25	Jan. 26	Jan. 27	Jan. 28	Jan. 29
7 months.	Feb. 25	Feb. 26	Feb. 27	Feb. 28	Feb. 28
*7 mo's, L.Y	Feb. 25	Feb. 26	Feb. 27	Feb. 28	Feb. 29
8 months.	Mch 25	Mch 26	Mch 27	Mch 28	Mch 29
9 months.	Apr. 25	Apr. 26	Apr. 27	Apr. 28	Apr. 29
10 months.	May 25	May 26	May 27	May 28	May 29
11 months.	June 25	June 26	June 27	June 28	June 29
12 months.	July 25	July 26	July 27	July 28	July 29

*Use this line for Notes maturing in Leap-Year.

The above tables are WITHOUT three days' grace.

(WITHOUT GRACE.)

Time.	July 30.	July 31.	August 1.	August 2.	August 3.
5 days.	Aug. 4	Aug. 5	Aug. 6	Aug. 7	Aug. 8
10 days.	Aug 9	Aug 10	Aug 11	Aug 12	Aug 13
15 days.	Aug 14	Aug 15	Aug 16	Aug 17	Aug 18
20 days.	Aug 19	Aug 20	Aug 21	Aug 22	Aug 23
25 days.	Aug 24	Aug 25	Aug 26	Aug 27	Aug 28
30 days.	Aug 29	Aug 30	Aug 31	Sept 1	Sept 2
35 days.	Sept 3	Sept 4	Sept 5	Sept 6	Sept 7
40 days.	Sept 8	Sept 9	Sept 10	Sept 11	Sept 12
45 days.	Sept 13	Sept 14	Sept 15	Sept 16	Sept 17
50 days.	Sept 18	Sept 19	Sept 20	Sept 21	Sept 22
55 days.	Sept 23	Sept 24	Sept 25	Sept 26	Sept 27
60 days.	Sept 28	Sept 29	Sept 30	Oct 1	Oct 2
65 days.	Oct 3	Oct 4	Oct 5	Oct 6	Oct 7
70 days.	Oct 8	Oct 9	Oct 10	Oct 11	Oct 12
75 days.	Oct 13	Oct 14	Oct 15	Oct 16	Oct 17
80 days.	Oct 18	Oct 19	Oct 20	Oct 21	Oct 22
85 days.	Oct 23	Oct 24	Oct 25	Oct 26	Oct 27
90 days.	Oct 28	Oct 29	Oct 30	Oct 31	Nov 1
95 days.	Nov 2	Nov 3	Nov 4	Nov 5	Nov 6
100 days.	Nov 7	Nov 8	Nov 9	Nov 10	Nov 11
1 month.	Aug. 30	Aug. 31	Sep. 1	Sep. 2	Sep. 3
2 months.	Sep. 30	Sep. 30	Oct. 1	Oct. 2	Oct. 3
3 months.	Oct. 30	Oct. 31	Nov. 1	Nov. 2	Nov. 3
4 months.	Nov. 30	Nov. 30	Dec. 1	Dec. 2	Dec. 3
5 months.	Dec. 30	Dec. 31	Jan. 1	Jan. 2	Jan. 3
6 months.	Jan. 30	Jan. 31	Feb. 1	Feb. 2	Feb. 3
7 months.	Feb. 28	Feb. 28	Mar. 1	Mar. 2	Mar. 3
*7 mo's, L.Y.	Feb. 29	Feb. 29	Mar. 1	Mar. 2	Mar. 3
8 months.	Mar. 30	Mar. 31	Apr. 1	Apr. 2	Apr. 3
9 months.	Apr. 30	Apr. 30	May 1	May 2	May 3
10 months.	May 30	May 31	June 1	June 2	June 3
11 months.	June 30	June 30	July 1	July 2	July 3
12 months.	July 30	July 31	Aug. 1	Aug. 2	Aug. 3

*Use this line for notes maturing in Leap Year.

The above Tables are for use in States where three days' grace are NOT allowed.

Time.	August 4.	August 5.	August 6.	August 7.	August 8.
5 days.	Aug 9	Aug 10	Aug 11	Aug 12	Aug 13
10 days.	Aug 14	Aug 15	Aug 16	Aug 17	Aug 18
15 days.	Aug 19	Aug 20	Aug 21	Aug 22	Aug 23
20 days.	Aug 24	Aug 25	Aug 26	Aug 27	Aug 28
25 days.	Aug 29	Aug 30	Aug 31	Sept 1	Sept 2
30 days.	Sept 3	Sept 4	Sept 5	Sept 6	Sept 7
35 days.	Sept 8	Sept 9	Sept 10	Sept 11	Sept 12
40 days.	Sept 13	Sept 14	Sept 15	Sept 16	Sept 17
45 days.	Sept 18	Sept 19	Sept 20	Sept 21	Sept 22
50 days.	Sept 23	Sept 24	Sept 25	Sept 26	Sept 27
55 days.	Sept 28	Sept 29	Sept 30	Oct 1	Oct 2
60 days.	Oct 3	Oct 4	Oct 5	Oct 6	Oct 7
65 days.	Oct 8	Oct 9	Oct 10	Oct 11	Oct 12
70 days.	Oct 13	Oct 14	Oct 15	Oct 16	Oct 17
75 days.	Oct 18	Oct 19	Oct 20	Oct 21	Oct 22
80 days.	Oct 23	Oct 24	Oct 25	Oct 26	Oct 27
85 days.	Oct 28	Oct 29	Oct 30	Oct 31	Nov 1
90 days.	Nov 2	Nov 3	Nov 4	Nov 5	Nov 6
95 days.	Nov 7	Nov 8	Nov 9	Nov 10	Nov 11
100 days.	Nov. 12	Nov. 13	Nov. 14	Nov. 15	Nov. 16
1 month.	Sep. 4	Sep. 5	Sep. 6	Sep. 7	Sep. 8
2 months.	Oct. 4	Oct. 5	Oct. 6	Oct. 7	Oct. 8
3 months.	Nov. 4	Nov. 5	Nov. 6	Nov. 7	Nov. 8
4 months.	Dec. 4	Dec. 5	Dec. 6	Dec. 7	Dec. 8
5 months.	Jan. 4	Jan. 5	Jan. 6	Jan. 7	Jan. 8
6 months.	Feb. 4	Feb. 5	Feb. 6	Feb. 7	Feb. 8
7 months.	Mar. 4	Mar. 5	Mar. 6	Mar. 7	Mar. 8
8 months.	Apr. 4	Apr. 5	Apr. 6	Apr. 7	Apr. 8
9 months.	May 4	May 5	May 6	May 7	May 8
10 months.	June 4	June 5	June 6	June 7	June 8
11 months.	July 4	July 5	July 6	July 7	July 8
12 months.	Aug. 4	Aug. 5	Aug. 6	Aug. 7	Aug. 8

The above Tables are for use in States where three days' grace are NOT allowed.

(WITHOUT GRACE.)

Time.	August 9.	August 10.	August 11.	August 12.	August 13.
5 days.	Aug 14	Aug 15	Aug 16	Aug 17	Aug 18
10 days.	Aug 19	Aug 20	Aug 21	Aug 22	Aug 23
15 days.	Aug 24	Aug 25	Aug 26	Aug 27	Aug 28
20 days.	Aug 29	Aug 30	Aug 31	Sept 1	Sept 2
25 days.	Sept 3	Sept 4	Sept 5	Sept 6	Sept 7
30 days.	Sept 8	Sept 9	Sept 10	Sept 11	Sept 12
35 days.	Sept 13	Sept 14	Sept 15	Sept 16	Sept 17
40 days.	Sept 18	Sept 19	Sept 20	Sept 21	Sept 22
45 days.	Sept 23	Sept 24	Sept 25	Sept 26	Sept 27
50 days.	Sept 28	Sept 29	Sept 30	Oct 1	Oct 2
55 days.	Oct 3	Oct 4	Oct 5	Oct 6	Oct 7
60 days.	Oct 8	Oct 9	Oct 10	Oct 11	Oct 12
65 days.	Oct 13	Oct 14	Oct 15	Oct 16	Oct 17
70 days.	Oct 18	Oct 19	Oct 20	Oct 21	Oct 22
75 days.	Oct 23	Oct 24	Oct 25	Oct 26	Oct 27
80 days.	Oct 28	Oct 29	Oct 30	Oct 31	Nov 1
85 days.	Nov 2	Nov 3	Nov 4	Nov 5	Nov 6
90 days.	Nov 7	Nov 8	Nov 9	Nov 10	Nov 11
95 days.	Nov. 12	Nov. 13	Nov. 14	Nov. 15	Nov. 16
100 days.	Nov 17	Nov 18	Nov 19	Nov 20	Nov 21
1 month.	Sep. 9	Sep. 10	Sep. 11	Sep. 12	Sep. 13
2 months.	Oct. 9	Oct. 10	Oct. 11	Oct. 12	Oct. 13
3 months.	Nov. 9	Nov. 10	Nov. 11	Nov. 12	Nov. 13
4 months.	Dec. 9	Dec. 10	Dec. 11	Dec. 12	Dec. 13
5 months.	Jan. 9	Jan. 10	Jan. 11	Jan. 12	Jan. 13
6 months.	Feb. 9	Feb. 10	Feb. 11	Feb. 12	Feb. 13
7 months.	Mar. 9	Mar. 10	Mar. 11	Mar. 12	Mar. 13
8 months.	Apr. 9	Apr. 10	Apr. 11	Apr. 12	Apr. 13
9 months.	May 9	May 10	May 11	May 12	May 13
10 months.	June 9	June 10	June 11	June 12	June 13
11 months.	July 9	July 10	July 11	July 12	July 13
12 months.	Aug. 9	Aug. 10	Aug. 11	Aug. 12	Aug. 13

The above Tables are for use in States where three days' grace are NOT allowed.

Time.	August 14.	August 15.	August 16.	August 17.	August 18.
5 days.	Aug 19	Aug 20	Aug 21	Aug 22	Aug 23
10 days.	Aug 24	Aug 25	Aug 26	Aug 27	Aug 28
15 days.	Aug 29	Aug 30	Aug 31	Sept 1	Sept 2
20 days.	Sept 3	Sept 4	Sept 5	Sept 6	Sept 7
25 days.	Sept 8	Sept 9	Sept 10	Sept 11	Sept 12
30 days.	Sept 13	Sept 14	Sept 15	Sept 16	Sept 17
35 days.	Sept 18	Sept 19	Sept 20	Sept 21	Sept 22
40 days.	Sept 23	Sept 24	Sept 25	Sept 26	Sept 27
45 days.	Sept 28	Sept 29	Sept 30	Oct 1	Oct 2
50 days.	Oct 3	Oct 4	Oct 5	Oct 6	Oct 7
55 days.	Oct 8	Oct 9	Oct 10	Oct 11	Oct 12
60 days.	Oct 13	Oct 14	Oct 15	Oct 16	Oct 17
65 days.	Oct 18	Oct 19	Oct 20	Oct 21	Oct 22
70 days.	Oct 23	Oct 24	Oct 25	Oct 26	Oct 27
75 days.	Oct 28	Oct 29	Oct 30	Oct 31	Nov 1
80 days.	Nov 2	Nov 3	Nov 4	Nov 5	Nov 6
85 days.	Nov 7	Nov 8	Nov 9	Nov 10	Nov 11
90 days.	Nov 12	Nov 13	Nov 14	Nov 15	Nov 16
95 days.	Nov 17	Nov 18	Nov 19	Nov 20	Nov 21
100 days.	Nov 22	Nov 23	Nov 24	Nov 25	Nov 26
1 month.	Sep. 14	Sep. 15	Sep. 16	Sep. 17	Sep. 18
2 months.	Oct. 14	Oct. 15	Oct. 16	Oct. 17	Oct. 18
3 months.	Nov. 14	Nov. 15	Nov. 16	Nov. 17	Nov. 18
4 months.	Dec. 14	Dec. 15	Dec. 16	Dec. 17	Dec. 18
5 months.	Jan. 14	Jan. 15	Jan. 16	Jan. 17	Jan. 18
6 months.	Feb. 14	Feb. 15	Feb. 16	Feb. 17	Feb. 18
7 months.	Mar. 14	Mar. 15	Mar. 16	Mar. 17	Mar. 18
8 months.	Apr. 14	Apr. 15	Apr. 16	Apr. 17	Apr. 18
9 months.	May 14	May 15	May 16	May 17	May 18
10 months.	June 14	June 15	June 16	June 17	June 18
11 months.	July 14	July 15	July 16	July 17	July 18
12 months.	Aug. 14	Aug. 15	Aug. 16	Aug. 17	Aug. 18

The above Tables are for use in States where three days' grace are NOT allowed.

(WITHOUT GRACE.)

Time.	August 19.	August 20.	August 21.	August 22.	August 23.
5 days.	Aug 24	Aug 25	Aug 26	Aug 27	Aug 28
10 days.	Aug 29	Aug 30	Aug 31	Sept 1	Sept 2
15 days.	Sept 3	Sept 4	Sept 5	Sept 6	Sept 7
20 days.	Sept 8	Sept 9	Sept 10	Sept 11	Sept 12
25 days.	Sept 13	Sept 14	Sept 15	Sept 16	Sept 17
30 days.	Sept 18	Sept 19	Sept 20	Sept 21	Sept 22
35 days.	Sept 23	Sept 24	Sept 25	Sept 26	Sept 27
40 days.	Sept 28	Sept 29	Sept 30	Oct 1	Oct 2
45 days.	Oct 3	Oct 4	Oct 5	Oct 6	Oct 7
50 days.	Oct 8	Oct 9	Oct 10	Oct 11	Oct 12
55 days.	Oct 13	Oct 14	Oct 15	Oct 16	Oct 17
60 days.	Oct 18	Oct 19	Oct 20	Oct 21	Oct 22
65 days.	Oct 23	Oct 24	Oct 25	Oct 26	Oct 27
70 days.	Oct 28	Oct 29	Oct 30	Oct 31	Nov 1
75 days.	Nov 2	Nov 3	Nov 4	Nov 5	Nov 6
80 days.	Nov 7	Nov 8	Nov 9	Nov 10	Nov 11
85 days.	Nov 12	Nov 13	Nov 14	Nov 15	Nov 16
90 days.	Nov 17	Nov 18	Nov 19	Nov 20	Nov 21
95 days.	Nov 22	Nov 23	Nov 24	Nov 25	Nov 26
100 days.	Nov 27	Nov 28	Nov 29	Nov 30	Dec 1
1 month.	Sep. 19	Sep. 20	Sep. 21	Sep. 22	Sep. 23
2 months.	Oct. 19	Oct. 20	Oct. 21	Oct. 22	Oct. 23
3 months.	Nov. 19	Nov. 20	Nov. 21	Nov. 22	Nov. 23
4 months.	Dec. 19	Dec. 20	Dec. 21	Dec. 22	Dec. 23
5 months.	Jan. 19	Jan. 20	Jan. 21	Jan. 22	Jan. 23
6 months.	Feb. 19	Feb. 20	Feb. 21	Feb. 22	Feb. 23
7 months.	Mar. 19	Mar. 20	Mar. 21	Mar. 22	Mar. 23
8 months.	Apr. 19	Apr. 20	Apr. 21	Apr. 22	Apr. 23
9 months.	May 19	May 20	May 21	May 22	May 23
10 months.	June 19	June 20	June 21	June 22	June 23
11 months.	July 19	July 20	July 21	July 22	July 23
12 months.	Aug. 19	Aug. 20	Aug. 21	Aug. 22	Aug. 23

The above Tables are for use in States where three days' grace are NOT allowed.

(WITHOUT GRACE.)

Time.	August 24.	August 25.	August 26.	August 27.	August 28.
5 days.	Aug 29	Aug 30	Aug 31	Sept 1	Sept 2
10 days.	Sept 3	Sept 4	Sept 5	Sept 6	Sept 7
15 days.	Sept 8	Sept 9	Sept 10	Sept 11	Sept 12
20 days.	Sept 13	Sept 14	Sept 15	Sept 16	Sept 17
25 days.	Sept 18	Sept 19	Sept 20	Sept 21	Sept 22
30 days.	Sept 23	Sept 24	Sept 25	Sept 26	Sept 27
35 days.	Sept 28	Sept 29	Sept 30	Oct 1	Oct 2
40 days.	Oct 3	Oct 4	Oct 5	Oct 6	Oct 7
45 days.	Oct 8	Oct 9	Oct 10	Oct 11	Oct 12
50 days.	Oct 13	Oct 14	Oct 15	Oct 16	Oct 17
55 days.	Oct 18	Oct 19	Oct 20	Oct 21	Oct 22
60 days.	Oct 23	Oct 24	Oct 25	Oct 26	Oct 27
65 days.	Oct 28	Oct 29	Oct 30	Oct 31	Nov 1
70 days.	Nov 2	Nov 3	Nov 4	Nov 5	Nov 6
75 days.	Nov 7	Nov 8	Nov 9	Nov 10	Nov 11
80 days.	Nov 12	Nov 13	Nov 14	Nov 15	Nov 16
85 days.	Nov 17	Nov 18	Nov 19	Nov 20	Nov 21
90 days.	Nov 22	Nov 23	Nov 24	Nov 25	Nov 26
95 days.	Nov 27	Nov 28	Nov 29	Nov 30	Dec 1
100 days.	Dec 2	Dec 3	Dec 4	Dec 5	Dec 6
1 month.	Sep. 24	Sep. 25	Sep. 26	Sep. 27	Sep. 28
2 months.	Oct. 24	Oct. 25	Oct. 26	Oct. 27	Oct. 28
3 months.	Nov. 24	Nov. 25	Nov. 26	Nov. 27	Nov. 28
4 months.	Dec. 24	Dec. 25	Dec. 26	Dec. 27	Dec. 28
5 months.	Jan. 24	Jan. 25	Jan. 26	Jan. 27	Jan. 28
6 months.	Feb. 24	Feb. 25	Feb. 26	Feb. 27	Feb. 28
7 months.	Mar. 24	Mar. 25	Mar. 26	Mar. 27	Mar. 28
8 months.	Apr. 24	Apr. 25	Apr. 26	Apr. 27	Apr. 28
9 months.	May 24	May 25	May 26	May 27	May 28
10 months.	June 24	June 25	June 26	June 27	June 28
11 months.	July 24	July 25	July 26	July 27	July 28
12 months.	Aug. 24	Aug. 25	Aug. 26	Aug. 27	Aug. 28

The above Tables are for use in States where three days'
grace are NOT allowed.

(WITHOUT GRACE.)

Time.	August 29.	August 30.	August 31.	Sept'r 1.	Sept'r 2.
5 days.	Sept 3	Sept 4	Sept 5	Sept 6	Sept 7
10 days.	Sept 8	Sept 9	Sept 10	Sept 11	Sept 12
15 days.	Sept 13	Sept 14	Sept 15	Sept 16	Sept 17
20 days.	Sept 18	Sept 19	Sept 20	Sept 21	Sept 22
25 days.	Sept 23	Sept 24	Sept 25	Sept 26	Sept 27
30 days.	Sept 28	Sept 29	Sept 30	Oct 1	Oct 2
35 days.	Oct 3	Oct 4	Oct 5	Oct 6	Oct 7
40 days.	Oct 8	Oct 9	Oct 10	Oct 11	Oct 12
45 days.	Oct 13	Oct 14	Oct 15	Oct 16	Oct 17
50 days.	Oct 18	Oct 19	Oct 20	Oct 21	Oct 22
55 days.	Oct 23	Oct 24	Oct 25	Oct 26	Oct 27
60 days.	Oct 28	Oct 29	Oct 30	Oct 31	Nov 1
65 days.	Nov 2	Nov 3	Nov 4	Nov 5	Nov 6
70 days.	Nov 7	Nov 8	Nov 9	Nov 10	Nov 11
75 days.	Nov 12	Nov 13	Nov 14	Nov 15	Nov 16
80 days.	Nov 17	Nov 18	Nov 19	Nov 20	Nov 21
85 days.	Nov 22	Nov 23	Nov 24	Nov 25	Nov 26
90 days.	Nov 27	Nov 28	Nov 29	Nov 30	Dec 1
95 days.	Dec 2	Dec 3	Dec 4	Dec 5	Dec 6
100 days.	Dec 7	Dec 8	Dec 9	Dec 10	Dec 11
1 month.	Sep. 29	Sep. 30	Sep. 30	Oct. 1	Oct. 2
2 months.	Oct. 29	Oct. 30	Oct. 31	Nov. 1	Nov. 2
3 months.	Nov. 29	Nov. 30	Nov. 30	Dec. 1	Dec. 2
4 months.	Dec. 29	Dec. 30	Dec. 31	Jan. 1	Jan. 2
5 months.	Jan. 29	Jan. 30	Jan. 31	Feb. 1	Feb. 2
6 months.	Feb. 28	Feb. 28	Feb. 28	Mar. 1	Mar. 2
*6 mo's, L.Y.	Feb. 29	Feb. 29	Feb. 29	Mar. 1	Mar. 2
7 months.	Mar. 29	Mar. 30	Mar. 31	Apr. 1	Apr. 2
8 months.	Apr. 29	Apr. 30	Apr. 30	May 1	May 2
9 months.	May 29	May 30	May 31	June 1	June 2
10 months.	June 29	June 30	June 30	July 1	July 2
11 months.	July 29	July 30	July 31	Aug. 1	Aug. 2
12 months.	Aug. 29	Aug. 30	Aug. 31	Sep. 1	Sep. 2

*Use this line for Notes maturing in Leap Year.

The above Tables are for use in States where three days' grace are NOT allowed.

(WITHOUT GRACE.)

Time.	Sept'r 3.	Sept'r 4.	Sept'r 5.	Sept'r 6.	Sept'r 7.
5 days.	Sept 8	Sept 9	Sept 10	Sept 11	Sept 12
10 days.	Sept 13	Sept 14	Sept 15	Sept 16	Sept 17
15 days.	Sept 18	Sept 19	Sept 20	Sept 21	Sept 22
20 days.	Sept 23	Sept 24	Sept 25	Sept 26	Sept 27
25 days.	Sept 28	Sept 29	Sept 30	Oct 1	Oct 2
30 days.	Oct 3	Oct 4	Oct 5	Oct 6	Oct 7
35 days.	Oct 8	Oct 9	Oct 10	Oct 11	Oct 12
40 days.	Oct 13	Oct 14	Oct 15	Oct 16	Oct 17
45 days.	Oct 18	Oct 19	Oct 20	Oct 21	Oct 22
50 days.	Oct 23	Oct 24	Oct 25	Oct 26	Oct 27
55 days.	Oct 28	Oct 29	Oct 30	Oct 31	Nov 1
60 days.	Nov 2	Nov 3	Nov 4	Nov 5	Nov 6
65 days.	Nov 7	Nov 8	Nov 9	Nov 10	Nov 11
70 days.	Nov 12	Nov 13	Nov 14	Nov 15	Nov 16
75 days.	Nov 17	Nov 18	Nov 19	Nov 20	Nov 21
80 days.	Nov 22	Nov 23	Nov 24	Nov 25	Nov 26
85 days.	Nov 27	Nov 28	Nov 29	Nov 30	Dec 1
90 days.	Dec 2	Dec 3	Dec 4	Dec 5	Dec 6
95 days.	Dec 7	Dec 8	Dec 9	Dec 10	Dec 11
100 days.	Dec 12	Dec 13	Dec 14	Dec 15	Dec 16
1 month.	Oct. 3	Oct. 4	Oct. 5	Oct. 6	Oct. 7
2 months.	Nov. 3	Nov. 4	Nov. 5	Nov. 6	Nov. 7
3 months.	Dec. 3	Dec. 4	Dec. 5	Dec. 6	Dec. 7
4 months.	Jan. 3	Jan. 4	Jan. 5	Jan. 6	Jan. 7
5 months.	Feb. 3	Feb. 4	Feb. 5	Feb. 6	Feb. 7
6 months.	Mar. 3	Mar. 4	Mar. 5	Mar. 6	Mar. 7
7 months.	Apr. 3	Apr. 4	Apr. 5	Apr. 6	Apr. 7
8 months.	May 3	May 4	May 5	May 6	May 7
9 months.	June 3	June 4	June 5	June 6	June 7
10 months.	July 3	July 4	July 5	July 6	July 7
11 months.	Aug. 3	Aug. 4	Aug. 5	Aug. 6	Aug. 7
12 months.	Sep. 3	Sep. 4	Sep. 5	Sep. 6	Sep. 7

The above Tables are for use in States where three days' grace are NOT allowed.

(WITHOUT GRACE.)

Time.	Sept'r 8.	Sept'r 9.	Sept'r 10.	Sept'r 11.	Sept'r 12.
5 days.	Sept 13	Sept 14	Sept 15	Sept 16	Sept 17
10 days.	Sept 18	Sept 19	Sept 20	Sept 21	Sept 22
15 days.	Sept 23	Sept 24	Sept 25	Sept 26	Sept 27
20 days.	Sept 28	Sept 29	Sept 30	Oct 1	Oct 2
25 days.	Oct 3	Oct 4	Oct 5	Oct 6	Oct 7
30 days.	Oct 8	Oct 9	Oct 10	Oct 11	Oct 12
35 days.	Oct 13	Oct 14	Oct 15	Oct 16	Oct 17
40 days.	Oct 18	Oct 19	Oct 20	Oct 21	Oct 22
45 days.	Oct 23	Oct 24	Oct 25	Oct 26	Oct 27
50 days.	Oct 28	Oct 29	Oct 30	Oct 31	Nov 1
55 days.	Nov 2	Nov 3	Nov 4	Nov 5	Nov 6
60 days.	Nov 7	Nov 8	Nov 9	Nov 10	Nov 11
65 days.	Nov 12	Nov 13	Nov 14	Nov 15	Nov 16
70 days.	Nov 17	Nov 18	Nov 19	Nov 20	Nov 21
75 days.	Nov 22	Nov 23	Nov 24	Nov 25	Nov 26
80 days.	Nov 27	Nov 28	Nov 29	Nov 30	Dec 1
85 days.	Dec 2	Dec 3	Dec 4	Dec 5	Dec 6
90 days.	Dec 7	Dec 8	Dec 9	Dec 10	Dec 11
95 days.	Dec 12	Dec 13	Dec 14	Dec 15	Dec 16
100 days.	Dec. 17	Dec. 18	Dec. 19	Dec. 20	Dec. 21
1 month.	Oct. 8	Oct. 9	Oct. 10	Oct. 11	Oct. 12
2 months.	Nov. 8	Nov. 9	Nov. 10	Nov. 11	Nov. 12
3 months.	Dec. 8	Dec. 9	Dec. 10	Dec. 11	Dec. 12
4 months.	Jan. 8	Jan. 9	Jan. 10	Jan. 11	Jan. 12
5 months.	Feb. 8	Feb. 9	Feb. 10	Feb. 11	Feb. 12
6 months.	Mar. 8	Mar. 9	Mar. 10	Mar. 11	Mar. 12
7 months.	Apr. 8	Apr. 9	Apr. 10	Apr. 11	Apr. 12
8 months.	May 8	May 9	May 10	May 11	May 12
9 months.	June 8	June 9	June 10	June 11	June 12
10 months.	July 8	July 9	July 10	July 11	July 12
11 months.	Aug. 8	Aug. 9	Aug. 10	Aug. 11	Aug. 12
12 months.	Sep. 8	Sep. 9	Sep. 10	Sep. 11	Sep. 12

The above Tables are for use in States where three days' grace are NOT allowed.

(WITHOUT GRACE.)

Time.	Sept'r 13.	Sept'r 14.	Sept'r 15.	Sept'r 16.	Sept'r 17.
5 days.	Sep. 18	Sep. 19	Sep. 20	Sep. 21	Sep. 22
10 days.	Sep. 23	Sep. 24	Sep. 25	Sep. 26	Sep. 27
15 days.	Sep. 28	Sep. 29	Sep. 30	Oct. 1	Oct. 2
20 days.	Oct. 3	Oct. 4	Oct. 5	Oct. 6	Oct. 7
25 days.	Oct. 8	Oct. 9	Oct. 10	Oct. 11	Oct. 12
30 days.	Oct. 13	Oct. 14	Oct. 15	Oct. 16	Oct. 17
35 days.	Oct. 18	Oct. 19	Oct. 20	Oct. 21	Oct. 22
40 days.	Oct. 23	Oct. 24	Oct. 25	Oct. 26	Oct. 27
45 days.	Oct. 28	Oct. 29	Oct. 30	Oct. 31	Nov. 1
50 days.	Nov. 2	Nov. 3	Nov. 4	Nov. 5	Nov. 6
55 days.	Nov. 7	Nov. 8	Nov. 9	Nov. 10	Nov. 11
60 days.	Nov. 12	Nov. 13	Nov. 14	Nov. 15	Nov. 16
65 days.	Nov. 17	Nov. 18	Nov. 19	Nov. 20	Nov. 21
70 days.	Nov. 22	Nov. 23	Nov. 24	Nov. 25	Nov. 26
75 days.	Nov. 27	Nov. 28	Nov. 29	Nov. 30	Dec. 1
80 days.	Dec. 2	Dec. 3	Dec. 4	Dec. 5	Dec. 6
85 days.	Dec. 7	Dec. 8	Dec. 9	Dec. 10	Dec. 11
90 days.	Dec. 12	Dec. 13	Dec. 14	Dec. 15	Dec. 16
95 days.	Dec. 17	Dec. 18	Dec. 19	Dec. 20	Dec. 21
100 days.	Dec. 22	Dec. 23	Dec. 24	Dec. 25	Dec. 26
1 month.	Oct. 13	Oct. 14	Oct. 15	Oct. 16	Oct. 17
2 months.	Nov. 13	Nov. 14	Nov. 15	Nov. 16	Nov. 17
3 months.	Dec. 13	Dec. 14	Dec. 15	Dec. 16	Dec. 17
4 months.	Jan. 13	Jan. 14	Jan 15	Jan. 16	Jan. 17
5 months.	Feb. 13	Feb. 14	Feb. 15	Feb. 16	Feb. 17
6 months.	Mar. 13	Mar. 14	Mar. 15	Mar. 16	Mar. 17
7 months.	Apr. 13	Apr. 14	Apr. 15	Apr. 16	Apr. 17
8 months.	May 13	May 14	May 15	May 16	May 17
9 months.	June 13	June 14	June 15	June 16	June 17
10 months.	July 13	July 14	July 15	July 16	July 17
11 months.	Aug. 13	Aug. 14	Aug. 15	Aug. 16	Aug. 17
12 months.	Sep. 13	Sep. 14	Sep. 15	Sep. 16	Sep. 17

The above Tables are WITHOUT three days' grace.

(WITHOUT GRACE.)

Time.	Sept'r 18.	Sept'r 19.	Sept'r 20.	Sept'r 21.	Sept'r 22.
5 days.	Sep. 23	Sep. 24	Sep. 25	Sep. 26	Sep. 27
10 days.	Sep. 28	Sep. 29	Sep. 30	Oct. 1	Oct. 2
15 days.	Oct. 3	Oct. 4	Oct. 5	Oct. 6	Oct. 7
20 days.	Oct. 8	Oct. 9	Oct. 10	Oct. 11	Oct. 12
25 days.	Oct. 13	Oct. 14	Oct. 15	Oct. 16	Oct. 17
30 days.	Oct. 18	Oct. 19	Oct. 20	Oct. 21	Oct. 22
35 days.	Oct. 23	Oct. 24	Oct. 25	Oct. 26	Oct. 27
40 days.	Oct. 28	Oct. 29	Oct. 30	Oct. 31	Nov. 1
45 days.	Nov. 2	Nov. 3	Nov. 4	Nov. 5	Nov. 6
50 days.	Nov. 7	Nov. 8	Nov. 9	Nov. 10	Nov. 11
55 days.	Nov. 12	Nov. 13	Nov. 14	Nov. 15	Nov. 16
60 days.	Nov. 17	Nov. 18	Nov. 19	Nov. 20	Nov. 21
65 days.	Nov. 22	Nov. 23	Nov. 24	Nov. 25	Nov. 26
70 days.	Nov. 27	Nov. 28	Nov. 29	Nov. 30	Dec. 1
75 days.	Dec. 2	Dec. 3	Dec. 4	Dec. 5	Dec. 6
80 days.	Dec. 7	Dec. 8	Dec. 9	Dec. 10	Dec. 11
85 days.	Dec. 12	Dec. 13	Dec. 14	Dec. 15	Dec. 16
90 days.	Dec. 17	Dec. 18	Dec. 19	Dec. 20	Dec. 21
95 days.	Dec. 22	Dec. 23	Dec. 24	Dec. 25	Dec. 26
100 days.	Dec. 27	Dec. 28	Dec. 29	Dec. 30	Dec. 31
1 month.	Oct. 18	Oct. 19	Oct. 20	Oct. 21	Oct. 22
2 months.	Nov. 18	Nov. 19	Nov. 20	Nov. 21	Nov. 22
3 months.	Dec. 18	Dec. 19	Dec. 20	Dec. 21	Dec. 22
4 months.	Jan. 18	Jan. 19	Jan 20	Jan. 21	Jan. 22
5 months.	Feb. 18	Feb. 19	Feb. 20	Feb. 21	Feb. 22
6 months.	Mar. 18	Mar. 19	Mar. 20	Mar. 21	Mar. 22
7 months.	Apr. 18	Apr. 19	Apr. 20	Apr. 21	Apr. 22
8 months.	May 18	May 19	May 20	May 21	May 22
9 months.	June 18	June 19	June 20	June 21	June 22
10 months.	July 18	July 19	July 20	July 21	July 22
11 months.	Aug. 18	Aug. 19	Aug. 20	Aug. 21	Aug. 22
12 months.	Sep. 18	Sep. 19	Sep. 20	Sep. 21	Sep. 22

The above Tables are WITHOUT three days' grace.

Time.	Sept'r 23.	Sept'r 24.	Sept'r 25.	Sept'r 26.	Sept'r 27.
5 days.	Sep. 28	Sep. 29	Sep. 30	Oct. 1	Oct. 2
10 days.	Oct. 3	Oct. 4	Oct. 5	Oct. 6	Oct. 7
15 days.	Oct. 8	Oct. 9	Oct. 10	Oct. 11	Oct. 12
20 days.	Oct. 13	Oct. 14	Oct. 15	Oct. 16	Oct. 17
25 days.	Oct. 18	Oct. 19	Oct. 20	Oct. 21	Oct. 22
30 days.	Oct. 23	Oct. 24	Oct. 25	Oct. 26	Oct. 27
35 days.	Oct. 28	Oct. 29	Oct. 30	Oct. 31	Nov. 1
40 days.	Nov. 2	Nov. 3	Nov. 4	Nov. 5	Nov. 6
45 days.	Nov. 7	Nov. 8	Nov. 9	Nov. 10	Nov. 11
50 days.	Nov. 12	Nov. 13	Nov. 14	Nov. 15	Nov. 16
55 days.	Nov. 17	Nov. 18	Nov. 19	Nov. 20	Nov. 21
60 days.	Nov. 22	Nov. 23	Nov. 24	Nov. 25	Nov. 26
65 days.	Nov. 27	Nov. 28	Nov. 29	Nov. 30	Dec. 1
70 days.	Dec. 2	Dec. 3	Dec. 4	Dec. 5	Dec. 6
75 days.	Dec. 7	Dec. 8	Dec. 9	Dec. 10	Dec. 11
80 days.	Dec. 12	Dec. 13	Dec. 14	Dec. 15	Dec. 16
85 days.	Dec. 17	Dec. 18	Dec. 19	Dec. 20	Dec. 21
90 days.	Dec. 22	Dec. 23	Dec. 24	Dec. 25	Dec. 26
95 days.	Dec. 27	Dec. 28	Dec. 29	Dec. 30	Dec. 31
100 days.	Jan. 1	Jan. 2	Jan. 3	Jan. 4	Jan. 5
1 month.	Oct. 23	Oct. 24	Oct. 25	Oct. 26	Oct. 27
2 months.	Nov. 23	Nov. 24	Nov. 25	Nov. 26	Nov. 27
3 months.	Dec. 23	Dec. 24	Dec. 25	Dec. 26	Dec. 27
4 months.	Jan. 23	Jan. 24	Jan 25	Jan. 26	Jan. 27
5 months.	Feb. 23	Feb. 24	Feb. 25	Feb. 26	Feb. 27
6 months.	Mar. 23	Mar. 24	Mar. 25	Mar. 26	Mar. 27
7 months.	Apr. 23	Apr. 24	Apr. 25	Apr. 26	Apr. 27
8 months.	May 23	May 24	May 25	May 26	May 27
9 months.	June 23	June 24	June 25	June 26	June 27
10 months.	July 23	July 24	July 25	July 26	July 27
11 months.	Aug. 23	Aug. 24	Aug. 25	Aug. 26	Aug. 27
12 months.	Sep. 23	Sep. 24	Sep. 25	Sep. 26	Sep. 27

The above Tables are WITHOUT three days' grace.

Time.	Sept'r 28.	Sept'r 29.	Sept'r 30.	October 1.	October 2.
5 days.	Oct. 3	Oct. 4	Oct. 5	Oct. 6	Oct. 7
10 days.	Oct. 8	Oct. 9	Oct. 10	Oct. 11	Oct. 12
15 days.	Oct. 13	Oct. 14	Oct. 15	Oct. 16	Oct. 17
20 days.	Oct. 18	Oct. 19	Oct. 20	Oct. 21	Oct. 22
25 days.	Oct. 23	Oct. 24	Oct. 25	Oct. 26	Oct. 27
30 days.	Oct. 28	Oct. 29	Oct. 30	Oct. 31	Nov. 1
35 days.	Nov. 2	Nov. 3	Nov. 4	Nov. 5	Nov. 6
40 days.	Nov. 7	Nov. 8	Nov. 9	Nov. 10	Nov. 11
45 days.	Nov. 12	Nov. 13	Nov. 14	Nov. 15	Nov. 16
50 days.	Nov. 17	Nov. 18	Nov. 19	Nov. 20	Nov. 21
55 days.	Nov. 22	Nov. 23	Nov. 24	Nov. 25	Nov. 26
60 days.	Nov. 27	Nov. 28	Nov. 29	Nov. 30	Dec. 1
65 days.	Dec. 2	Dec. 3	Dec. 4	Dec. 5	Dec. 6
70 days.	Dec. 7	Dec. 8	Dec. 9	Dec. 10	Dec. 11
75 days.	Dec. 12	Dec. 13	Dec. 14	Dec. 15	Dec. 16
80 days.	Dec. 17	Dec. 18	Dec. 19	Dec. 20	Dec. 21
85 days.	Dec. 22	Dec. 23	Dec. 24	Dec. 25	Dec. 26
90 days.	Dec. 27	Dec. 28	Dec. 29	Dec. 30	Dec. 31
95 days.	Jan. 1	Jan. 2	Jan. 3	Jan. 4	Jan. 5
100 days.	Jan. 6	Jan. 7	Jan. 8	Jan. 9	Jan. 10
1 month.	Oct. 28	Oct. 29	Oct. 30	Nov. 1	Nov. 2
2 months.	Nov. 28	Nov. 29	Nov. 30	Dec. 1	Dec. 2
3 months.	Dec. 28	Dec. 29	Dec. 30	Jan. 1	Jan. 2
4 months.	Jan. 28	Jan. 29	Jan 30	Feb. 1	Feb. 2
5 months.	Feb. 28	Feb. 28	Feb. 28	Mar. 1	Mar. 2
*5 mos, L.Y.	Feb. 28	Feb. 29	Feb. 29	Mch 1	Mch 2
6 months.	Mar. 28	Mar. 29	Mar. 30	Apr. 1	Apr. 2
7 months.	Apr. 28	Apr. 29	Apr. 30	May 1	May 2
8 months.	May 28	May 29	May 30	June 1	June 2
9 months.	June 28	June 29	June 30	July 1	July 2
10 months.	July 28	July 29	July 30	Aug. 1	Aug. 2
11 months.	Aug. 28	Aug. 29	Aug. 30	Sep. 1	Sep. 2
12 months.	Sep. 28	Sep. 29	Sep. 30	Oct. 1	Oct. 2

*Use this line for Notes maturing in Leap Year.

The above Tables are WITHOUT three days' grace.

(WITHOUT GRACE.)

Time.	October 3.	October 4.	October 5.	October 6.	October 7.
5 days.	Oct. 8	Oct. 9	Oct. 10	Oct. 11	Oct. 12
10 days.	Oct. 13	Oct. 14	Oct. 15	Oct. 16	Oct. 17
15 days.	Oct. 18	Oct. 19	Oct. 20	Oct. 21	Oct. 22
20 days.	Oct. 23	Oct. 24	Oct. 25	Oct. 26	Oct. 27
25 days.	Oct. 28	Oct. 29	Oct. 30	Oct. 31	Nov. 1
30 days.	Nov. 2	Nov. 3	Nov. 4	Nov. 5	Nov. 6
35 days.	Nov. 7	Nov. 8	Nov. 9	Nov. 10	Nov. 11
40 days.	Nov. 12	Nov. 13	Nov. 14	Nov. 15	Nov. 16
45 days.	Nov. 17	Nov. 18	Nov. 19	Nov. 20	Nov. 21
50 days.	Nov. 22	Nov. 23	Nov. 24	Nov. 25	Nov. 26
55 days.	Nov. 27	Nov. 28	Nov. 29	Nov. 30	Dec. 1
60 days.	Dec. 2	Dec. 3	Dec. 4	Dec. 5	Dec. 6
65 days.	Dec. 7	Dec. 8	Dec. 9	Dec. 10	Dec. 11
70 days.	Dec. 12	Dec. 13	Dec. 14	Dec. 15	Dec. 16
75 days.	Dec. 17	Dec. 18	Dec. 19	Dec. 20	Dec. 21
80 days.	Dec. 22	Dec. 23	Dec. 24	Dec. 25	Dec. 26
85 days.	Dec. 27	Dec. 28	Dec. 29	Dec. 30	Dec. 31
90 days.	Jan. 1	Jan. 2	Jan. 3	Jan. 4	Jan. 5
95 days.	Jan. 6	Jan. 7	Jan. 8	Jan. 9	Jan. 10
100 days.	Jan. 11	Jan. 12	Jan. 13	Jan. 14	Jan. 15
1 month.	Nov. 3	Nov. 4	Nov. 5	Nov. 6	Nov. 7
2 months.	Dec. 3	Dec. 4	Dec. 5	Dec. 6	Dec. 7
3 months.	Jan. 3	Jan. 4	Jan 5	Jan. 6	Jan. 7
4 months.	Feb. 3	Feb. 4	Feb. 5	Feb. 6	Feb. 7
5 months.	Mar. 3	Mar. 4	Mar. 5	Mar. 6	Mar. 7
6 months.	Apr. 3	Apr. 4	Apr. 5	Apr. 6	Apr. 7
7 months.	May 3	May 4	May 5	May 6	May 7
8 months.	June 3	June 4	June 5	June 6	June 7
9 months.	July 3	July 4	July 5	July 6	July 7
10 months.	Aug. 3	Aug. 4	Aug. 5	Aug. 6	Aug. 7
11 months.	Sep. 3	Sep. 4	Sep. 5	Sep. 6	Sep. 7
12 months.	Oct. 3	Oct. 4	Oct. 5	Oct. 6	Oct. 7

The above Tables are WITHOUT three days' grace.

(WITHOUT GRACE.)

Time.	October 8.	October 9.	October 10.	October 11.	October 12.
5 days.	Oct. 13	Oct. 14	Oct. 15	Oct. 16	Oct. 17
10 days.	Oct. 18	Oct. 19	Oct. 20	Oct. 21	Oct. 22
15 days.	Oct. 23	Oct. 24	Oct. 25	Oct. 26	Oct. 27
20 days.	Oct. 28	Oct. 29	Oct. 30	Oct. 31	Nov. 1
25 days.	Nov. 2	Nov. 3	Nov. 4	Nov. 5	Nov. 6
30 days.	Nov. 7	Nov. 8	Nov. 9	Nov. 10	Nov. 11
35 days.	Nov. 12	Nov. 13	Nov. 14	Nov. 15	Nov. 16
40 days.	Nov. 17	Nov. 18	Nov. 19	Nov. 20	Nov. 21
45 days.	Nov. 22	Nov. 23	Nov. 24	Nov. 25	Nov. 26
50 days.	Nov. 27	Nov. 28	Nov. 29	Nov. 30	Dec. 1
55 days.	Dec. 2	Dec. 3	Dec. 4	Dec. 5	Dec. 6
60 days.	Dec. 7	Dec. 8	Dec. 9	Dec. 10	Dec. 11
65 days.	Dec. 12	Dec. 13	Dec. 14	Dec. 15	Dec. 16
70 days.	Dec. 17	Dec. 18	Dec. 19	Dec. 20	Dec. 21
75 days.	Dec. 22	Dec. 23	Dec. 24	Dec. 25	Dec. 26
80 days.	Dec. 27	Dec. 28	Dec. 29	Dec. 30	Dec. 31
85 days.	Jan. 1	Jan. 2	Jan. 3	Jan. 4	Jan. 5
90 days.	Jan. 6	Jan. 7	Jan. 8	Jan. 9	Jan. 10
95 days.	Jan. 11	Jan. 12	Jan. 13	Jan. 14	Jan. 15
100 days.	Jan. 16	Jan. 17	Jan. 18	Jan. 19	Jan. 20
1 month.	Nov. 8	Nov. 9	Nov. 10	Nov. 11	Nov. 12
2 months.	Dec. 8	Dec. 9	Dec. 10	Dec. 11	Dec. 12
3 months.	Jan. 8	Jan. 9	Jan. 10	Jan. 11	Jan. 12
4 months.	Feb. 8	Feb. 9	Feb. 10	Feb. 11	Feb. 12
5 months.	Mar. 8	Mar. 9	Mar. 10	Mar. 11	Mar. 12
6 months.	Apr. 8	Apr. 9	Apr. 10	Apr. 11	Apr. 12
7 months.	May 8	May 9	May 10	May 11	May 12
8 months.	June 8	June 9	June 10	June 11	June 12
9 months.	July 8	July 9	July 10	July 11	July 12
10 months.	Aug. 8	Aug. 9	Aug. 10	Aug. 11	Aug. 12
11 months.	Sep. 8	Sep. 9	Sep. 10	Sep. 11	Sep. 12
12 months.	Oct. 8	Oct. 9	Oct. 10	Oct. 11	Oct. 12

The above Tables are WITHOUT three days' grace.

Time.	October 13.	October 14.	October 15.	October 16.	October 17.
5 days.	Oct. 18	Oct. 19	Oct. 20	Oct. 21	Oct. 22
10 days.	Oct. 23	Oct. 24	Oct. 25	Oct. 26	Oct. 27
15 days.	Oct. 28	Oct. 29	Oct. 30	Oct. 31	Nov. 1
20 days.	Nov. 2	Nov. 3	Nov. 4	Nov. 5	Nov. 6
25 days.	Nov. 7	Nov. 8	Nov. 9	Nov. 10	Nov. 11
30 days.	Nov. 12	Nov. 13	Nov. 14	Nov. 15	Nov. 16
35 days.	Nov. 17	Nov. 18	Nov. 19	Nov. 20	Nov. 21
40 days.	Nov. 22	Nov. 23	Nov. 24	Nov. 25	Nov. 26
45 days.	Nov. 27	Nov. 28	Nov. 29	Nov. 30	Dec. 1
50 days.	Dec. 2	Dec. 3	Dec. 4	Dec. 5	Dec. 6
55 days.	Dec. 7	Dec. 8	Dec. 9	Dec. 10	Dec. 11
60 days.	Dec. 12	Dec. 13	Dec. 14	Dec. 15	Dec. 16
65 days.	Dec. 17	Dec. 18	Dec. 19	Dec. 20	Dec. 21
70 days.	Dec. 22	Dec. 23	Dec. 24	Dec. 25	Dec. 26
75 days.	Dec. 27	Dec. 28	Dec. 29	Dec. 30	Dec. 31
80 days.	Jan. 1	Jan. 2	Jan. 3	Jan. 4	Jan. 5
85 days.	Jan. 6	Jan. 7	Jan. 8	Jan. 9	Jan. 10
90 days.	Jan. 11	Jan. 12	Jan. 13	Jan. 14	Jan. 15
95 days.	Jan. 16	Jan. 17	Jan. 18	Jan. 19	Jan. 20
100 days.	Jan. 21	Jan. 22	Jan. 23	Jan. 24	Jan. 25
1 month.	Nov. 13	Nov. 14	Nov. 15	Nov. 16	Nov. 17
2 months.	Dec. 13	Dec. 14	Dec. 15	Dec. 16	Dec. 17
3 months.	Jan. 13	Jan. 14	Jan 15	Jan. 16	Jan. 17
4 months.	Feb. 13	Feb. 14	Feb. 15	Feb. 16	Feb. 17
5 months.	Mar. 13	Mar. 14	Mar. 15	Mar. 16	Mar. 17
6 months.	Apr. 13	Apr. 14	Apr. 15	Apr. 16	Apr. 17
7 months.	May 13	May 14	May 15	May 16	May 17
8 months.	June 13	June 14	June 15	June 16	June 17
9 months.	July 13	July 14	July 15	July 16	July 17
10 months.	Aug. 13	Aug. 14	Aug. 15	Aug. 16	Aug. 17
11 months.	Sep. 13	Sep. 14	Sep. 15	Sep. 16	Sep. 17
12 months.	Oct. 13	Oct. 14	Oct. 15	Oct. 16	Oct. 17

The above Tables are WITHOUT three days' grace.

(WITHOUT GRACE.)

Time.	October 18.	October 19.	October 20.	October 21.	October 22.
5 days.	Oct. 23	Oct. 24	Oct. 25	Oct. 26	Oct. 27
10 days.	Oct. 28	Oct. 29	Oct. 30	Oct. 31	Nov. 1
15 days.	Nov. 2	Nov. 3	Nov. 4	Nov. 5	Nov. 6
20 days.	Nov. 7	Nov. 8	Nov. 9	Nov. 10	Nov. 11
25 days.	Nov. 12	Nov. 13	Nov. 14	Nov. 15	Nov. 16
30 days.	Nov. 17	Nov. 18	Nov. 19	Nov. 20	Nov. 21
35 days.	Nov. 22	Nov. 23	Nov. 24	Nov. 25	Nov. 26
40 days.	Nov. 27	Nov. 28	Nov. 29	Nov. 30	Dec. 1
45 days.	Dec. 2	Dec. 3	Dec. 4	Dec. 5	Dec. 6
50 days.	Dec. 7	Dec. 8	Dec. 9	Dec. 10	Dec. 11
55 days.	Dec. 12	Dec. 13	Dec. 14	Dec. 15	Dec. 16
60 days.	Dec. 17	Dec. 18	Dec. 19	Dec. 20	Dec. 21
65 days.	Dec. 22	Dec. 23	Dec. 24	Dec. 25	Dec. 26
70 days.	Dec. 27	Dec. 28	Dec. 29	Dec. 30	Dec. 31
75 days.	Jan. 1	Jan. 2	Jan. 3	Jan. 4	Jan. 5
80 days.	Jan. 6	Jan. 7	Jan. 8	Jan. 9	Jan. 10
85 days.	Jan. 11	Jan. 12	Jan. 13	Jan. 14	Jan. 15
90 days.	Jan. 16	Jan. 17	Jan. 18	Jan. 19	Jan. 20
95 days.	Jan. 21	Jan. 22	Jan. 23	Jan. 24	Jan. 25
100 days.	Jan. 26	Jan. 27	Jan. 28	Jan. 29	Jan. 30
1 month.	Nov. 18	Nov. 19	Nov. 20	Nov. 21	Nov. 22
2 months.	Dec. 18	Dec. 19	Dec. 20	Dec. 21	Dec. 22
3 months.	Jan. 18	Jan. 19	Jan 20	Jan. 21	Jan. 22
4 months.	Feb. 18	Feb. 19	Feb. 20	Feb. 21	Feb. 22
5 months.	Mar. 18	Mar. 19	Mar. 20	Mar. 21	Mar. 22
6 months.	Apr. 18	Apr. 19	Apr. 20	Apr. 21	Apr. 22
7 months.	May 18	May 19	May 20	May 21	May 22
8 months.	June 18	June 19	June 20	June 21	June 22
9 months.	July 18	July 19	July 20	July 21	July 22
10 months.	Aug. 18	Aug. 19	Aug. 20	Aug. 21	Aug. 22
11 months.	Sep. 18	Sep. 19	Sep. 20	Sep. 21	Sep. 22
12 mouths.	Oct. 18	Oct. 19	Oct. 20	Oct. 21	Oct. 22

The above Tables are WITHOUT three days' grace.

(WITHOUT GRACE.)

Time.	October 23.	October 24.	October 25.	October 26.	October 27.
5 days.	Oct. 28	Oct. 29	Oct. 30	Oct. 31	Nov. 1
10 days.	Nov. 2	Nov. 3	Nov. 4	Nov. 5	Nov. 6
15 days.	Nov. 7	Nov. 8	Nov. 9	Nov. 10	Nov. 11
20 days.	Nov. 12	Nov. 13	Nov. 14	Nov. 15	Nov. 16
25 days.	Nov. 17	Nov. 18	Nov. 19	Nov. 20	Nov. 21
30 days.	Nov. 22	Nov. 23	Nov. 24	Nov. 25	Nov. 26
35 days.	Nov. 27	Nov. 28	Nov. 29	Nov. 30	Dec. 1
40 days.	Dec. 2	Dec. 3	Dec. 4	Dec. 5	Dec. 6
45 days.	Dec. 7	Dec. 8	Dec. 9	Dec. 10	Dec. 11
50 days.	Dec. 12	Dec. 13	Dec. 14	Dec. 15	Dec. 16
55 days.	Dec. 17	Dec. 18	Dec. 19	Dec. 20	Dec. 21
60 days.	Dec. 22	Dec. 23	Dec. 24	Dec. 25	Dec. 26
65 days.	Dec. 27	Dec. 28	Dec. 29	Dec. 30	Dec. 31
70 days.	Jan. 1	Jan. 2	Jan. 3	Jan. 4	Jan. 5
75 days.	Jan. 6	Jan. 7	Jan. 8	Jan. 9	Jan. 10
80 days.	Jan. 11	Jan. 12	Jan. 13	Jan. 14	Jan. 15
85 days.	Jan. 16	Jan. 17	Jan. 18	Jan. 19	Jan. 20
90 days.	Jan. 21	Jan. 22	Jan. 23	Jan. 24	Jan. 25
95 days.	Jan. 26	Jan. 27	Jan. 28	Jan. 29	Jan. 30
100 days.	Jan. 31	Feb. 1	Feb. 2	Feb. 3	Feb. 4
1 month.	Nov. 23	Nov. 24	Nov. 25	Nov. 26	Nov. 27
2 months.	Dec. 23	Dec. 24	Dec. 25	Dec. 26	Dec. 27
3 months.	Jan. 23	Jan. 24	Jan 25	Jan. 26	Jan. 27
4 months.	Feb. 23	Feb. 24	Feb. 25	Feb. 26	Feb. 27
5 months.	Mar. 23	Mar. 24	Mar. 25	Mar. 26	Mar. 27
6 months.	Apr. 23	Apr. 24	Apr. 25	Apr. 26	Apr. 27
7 months.	May 23	May 24	May 25	May 26	May 27
8 months.	June 23	June 24	June 25	June 26	June 27
9 months.	July 23	July 24	July 25	July 26	July 27
10 months.	Aug. 23	Aug. 24	Aug. 25	Aug. 26	Aug. 27
11 months.	Sep. 23	Sep. 24	Sep. 25	Sep. 26	Sep. 27
12 months.	Oct. 23	Oct. 24	Oct. 25	Oct. 26	Oct. 27

The above Tables are WITHOUT three days' grace.

Time.	October 28.	October 29.	October 30.	October 31.	Nov'm'r 1.
5 days.	Nov. 2	Nov. 3	Nov. 4	Nov. 5	Nov. 6
10 days.	Nov. 7	Nov. 8	Nov. 9	Nov. 10	Nov. 11
15 days.	Nov. 12	Nov. 13	Nov. 14	Nov. 15	Nov. 16
20 days.	Nov. 17	Nov. 18	Nov. 19	Nov. 20	Nov. 21
25 days.	Nov. 22	Nov. 23	Nov. 24	Nov. 25	Nov. 26
30 days.	Nov. 27	Nov. 28	Nov. 29	Nov. 30	Dec. 1
35 days.	Dec. 2	Dec. 3	Dec. 4	Dec. 5	Dec. 6
40 days.	Dec. 7	Dec. 8	Dec. 9	Dec. 10	Dec. 11
45 days.	Dec. 12	Dec. 13	Dec. 14	Dec. 15	Dec. 16
50 days.	Dec. 17	Dec. 18	Dec. 19	Dec. 20	Dec. 21
55 days.	Dec. 22	Dec. 23	Dec. 24	Dec. 25	Dec. 26
60 days.	Dec. 27	Dec. 28	Dec. 29	Dec. 30	Dec. 31
65 days.	Jan. 1	Jan. 2	Jan. 3	Jan. 4	Jan. 5
70 days.	Jan. 6	Jan. 7	Jan. 8	Jan. 9	Jan. 10
75 days.	Jan. 11	Jan. 12	Jan. 13	Jan. 14	Jan. 15
80 days.	Jan. 16	Jan. 17	Jan. 18	Jan. 19	Jan. 20
85 days.	Jan. 21	Jan. 22	Jan. 23	Jan. 24	Jan. 25
90 days.	Jan. 26	Jan. 27	Jan. 28	Jan. 29	Jan. 30
95 days.	Jan. 31	Feb. 1	Feb. 2	Feb. 3	Feb. 4
100 days.	Feb. 5	Feb. 6	Feb. 7	Feb. 8	Feb. 9
1 month.	Nov. 28	Nov. 29	Nov. 30	Nov. 30	Dec. 1
2 months.	Dec. 28	Dec. 29	Dec. 30	Dec. 31	Jan. 1
3 months.	Jan. 28	Jan. 29	Jan 30	Jan. 31	Feb. 1
4 months.	Feb. 28	Feb. 28	Feb. 28	Feb. 28	Mar. 1
*4 mo's, L.Y.	Feb. 28	Feb. 29	Feb. 29	Feb. 29	Mar. 1
5 months.	Mar. 28	Mar. 29	Mar. 30	Mar. 31	Apr. 1
6 months.	Apr. 28	Apr. 29	Apr. 30	Apr. 30	May 1
7 months.	May 28	May 29	May 30	May 31	June 1
8 months.	June 28	June 29	June 30	June 30	July 1
9 months.	July 28	July 29	July 30	July 31	Aug. 1
10 months.	Aug. 28	Aug. 29	Aug. 30	Aug. 31	Sep. 1
11 months.	Sep. 28	Sep. 29	Sep. 30	Sep. 30	Oct. 1
12 months.	Oct. 28	Oct. 29	Oct. 30	Oct. 31	Nov. 1

*Use this line for Notes maturing in Leap Year.

The above Tables are WITHOUT three days' grace.

(WITHOUT GRACE.)

Time.	Nov'm'r 2.	Nov'm'r 3.	Nov'm'r 4.	Nov'm'r 5.	Nov'm'r 6.
5 days.	Nov. 7	Nov. 8	Nov. 9	Nov. 10	Nov. 11
10 days.	Nov. 12	Nov. 13	Nov. 14	Nov. 15	Nov. 16
15 days.	Nov. 17	Nov. 18	Nov. 19	Nov. 20	Nov. 21
20 days.	Nov. 22	Nov. 23	Nov. 24	Nov. 25	Nov. 26
25 days.	Nov. 27	Nov. 28	Nov. 29	Nov. 30	Dec. 1
30 days.	Dec. 2	Dec. 3	Dec. 4	Dec. 5	Dec. 6
35 days.	Dec. 7	Dec. 8	Dec. 9	Dec. 10	Dec. 11
40 days.	Dec. 12	Dec. 13	Dec. 14	Dec. 15	Dec. 16
45 days.	Dec. 17	Dec. 18	Dec. 19	Dec. 20	Dec. 21
50 days.	Dec. 22	Dec. 23	Dec. 24	Dec. 25	Dec. 26
55 days.	Dec. 27	Dec. 28	Dec. 29	Dec. 30	Dec. 31
60 days.	Jan. 1	Jan. 2	Jan. 3	Jan. 4	Jan. 5
65 days.	Jan. 6	Jan. 7	Jan. 8	Jan. 9	Jan. 10
70 days.	Jan. 11	Jan. 12	Jan. 13	Jan. 14	Jan. 15
75 days.	Jan. 16	Jan. 17	Jan. 18	Jan. 19	Jan. 20
80 days.	Jan. 21	Jan. 22	Jan. 23	Jan. 24	Jan. 25
85 days.	Jan. 26	Jan. 27	Jan. 28	Jan. 29	Jan. 30
90 days.	Jan. 31	Feb. 1	Feb. 2	Feb. 3	Feb. 4
95 days.	Feb. 5	Feb. 6	Feb. 7	Feb. 8	Feb. 9
100 days.	Feb. 10	Feb. 11	Feb. 12	Feb. 13	Feb. 14
1 month.	Dec. 2	Dec. 3	Dec. 4	Dec. 5	Dec. 6
2 months.	Jan. 2	Jan. 3	Jan 4	Jan. 5	Jan. 6
3 months.	Feb. 2	Feb. 3	Feb. 4	Feb. 5	Feb. 6
4 months.	Mar. 2	Mar. 3	Mar. 4	Mar. 5	Mar. 6
5 months.	Apr. 2	Apr. 3	Apr. 4	Apr. 5	Apr. 6
6 months.	May 2	May 3	May 4	May 5	May 6
7 months.	June 2	June 3	June 4	June 5	June 6
8 months.	July 2	July 3	July 4	July 5	July 6
9 months.	Aug. 2	Aug. 3	Aug. 4	Aug. 5	Aug. 6
10 months.	Sep. 2	Sep. 3	Sep. 4	Sep. 5	Sep. 6
11 months.	Oct. 2	Oct. 3	Oct. 4	Oct. 5	Oct. 6
12 months.	Nov. 2	Nov. 3	Nov. 4	Nov. 5	Nov. 6

The above Tables are WITHOUT three days' grace.

(WITHOUT GRACE.)

Time.	Nov'm'r 7.	Nov'm'r 8.	Nov'm'r 9.	Nov'm'r 10.	Nov'm'r 11.
5 days.	Nov. 12	Nov. 13	Nov. 14	Nov. 15	Nov. 16
10 days.	Nov. 17	Nov. 18	Nov. 19	Nov. 20	Nov. 21
15 days.	Nov. 22	Nov. 23	Nov. 24	Nov. 25	Nov. 26
20 days.	Nov. 27	Nov. 28	Nov. 29	Nov. 30	Dec. 1
25 days.	Dec. 2	Dec. 3	Dec. 4	Dec. 5	Dec. 6
30 days.	Dec. 7	Dec. 8	Dec. 9	Dec. 10	Dec. 11
35 days.	Dec. 12	Dec. 13	Dec. 14	Dec. 15	Dec. 16
40 days.	Dec. 17	Dec. 18	Dec. 19	Dec. 20	Dec. 21
45 days.	Dec. 22	Dec. 23	Dec. 24	Dec. 25	Dec. 26
50 days.	Dec. 27	Dec. 28	Dec. 29	Dec. 30	Dec. 31
55 days.	Jan. 1	Jan. 2	Jan. 3	Jan. 4	Jan. 5
60 days.	Jan. 6	Jan. 7	Jan. 8	Jan. 9	Jan. 10
65 days.	Jan. 11	Jan. 12	Jan. 13	Jan. 14	Jan. 15
70 days.	Jan. 16	Jan. 17	Jan. 18	Jan. 19	Jan. 20
75 days.	Jan. 21	Jan. 22	Jan. 23	Jan. 24	Jan. 25
80 days.	Jan. 26	Jan. 27	Jan. 28	Jan. 29	Jan. 30
85 days.	Jan. 31	Feb. 1	Feb. 2	Feb. 3	Feb. 4
90 days.	Feb. 5	Feb. 6	Feb. 7	Feb. 8	Feb. 9
95 days.	Feb. 10	Feb. 11	Feb. 12	Feb. 13	Feb. 14
100 days.	Feb. 15	Feb. 16	Feb. 17	Feb. 18	Feb. 19
1 month.	Dec. 7	Dec. 8	Dec. 9	Dec. 10	Dec. 11
2 months.	Jan. 7	Jan. 8	Jan 9	Jan. 10	Jan. 11
3 months.	Feb. 7	Feb. 8	Feb. 9	Feb. 10	Feb. 11
4 months.	Mar. 7	Mar. 8	Mar. 9	Mar. 10	Mar. 11
5 months.	Apr. 7	Apr. 8	Apr. 9	Apr. 10	Apr. 11
6 months.	May 7	May 8	May 9	May 10	May 11
7 months.	June 7	June 8	June 9	June 10	June 11
8 months.	July 7	July 8	July 9	July 10	July 11
9 months.	Aug. 7	Aug. 8	Aug. 9	Aug. 10	Aug. 11
10 months.	Sep. 7	Sep. 8	Sep. 9	Sep. 10	Sep. 11
11 months.	Oct. 7	Oct. 8	Oct. 9	Oct. 10	Oct. 11
12 months.	Nov. 7	Nov. 8	Nov. 9	Nov. 10	Nov. 11

The above Tables are WITHOUT three days' grace.

(WITHOUT GRACE.)

Time.	Nov'm'r 12.	Nov'm'r 13.	Nov'm'r 14.	Nov'm'r 15.	Nov'm'r 16.
5 days.	Nov. 17	Nov. 18	Nov. 19	Nov. 20	Nov. 21
10 days.	Nov. 22	Nov. 23	Nov. 24	Nov. 25	Nov. 26
15 days.	Nov. 27	Nov. 28	Nov. 29	Nov. 30	Dec. 1
20 days.	Dec. 2	Dec. 3	Dec. 4	Dec. 5	Dec. 6
25 days.	Dec. 7	Dec. 8	Dec. 9	Dec. 10	Dec. 11
30 days.	Dec. 12	Dec. 13	Dec. 14	Dec. 15	Dec. 16
35 days.	Dec. 17	Dec. 18	Dec. 19	Dec. 20	Dec. 21
40 days.	Dec. 22	Dec. 23	Dec. 24	Dec. 25	Dec. 26
45 days.	Dec. 27	Dec. 28	Dec. 29	Dec. 30	Dec. 31
50 days.	Jan. 1	Jan. 2	Jan. 3	Jan. 4	Jan. 5
55 days.	Jan. 6	Jan. 7	Jan. 8	Jan. 9	Jan. 10
60 days.	Jan. 11	Jan. 12	Jan. 13	Jan. 14	Jan. 15
65 days.	Jan. 16	Jan. 17	Jan. 18	Jan. 19	Jan. 20
70 days.	Jan. 21	Jan. 22	Jan. 23	Jan. 24	Jan. 25
75 days.	Jan. 26	Jan. 27	Jan. 28	Jan. 29	Jan. 30
80 days.	Jan. 31	Feb. 1	Feb. 2	Feb. 3	Feb. 4
85 days.	Feb. 5	Feb. 6	Feb. 7	Feb. 8	Feb. 9
90 days.	Feb. 10	Feb. 11	Feb. 12	Feb. 13	Feb. 14
95 days.	Feb. 15	Feb. 16	Feb. 17	Feb. 18	Feb. 19
100 days.	Feb. 20	Feb. 21	Feb. 22	Feb. 23	Feb. 24
1 month.	Dec. 12	Dec. 13	Dec. 14	Dec. 15	Dec. 16
2 months.	Jan. 12	Jan. 13	Jan 14	Jan. 15	Jan. 16
3 months.	Feb. 12	Feb. 13	Feb. 14	Feb. 15	Feb. 16
4 months.	Mar. 12	Mar. 13	Mar. 14	Mar. 15	Mar. 16
5 months.	Apr. 12	Apr. 13	Apr. 14	Apr. 15	Apr. 16
6 months.	May 12	May 13	May 14	May 15	May 16
7 months.	June 12	June 13	June 14	June 15	June 16
8 months.	July 12	July 13	July 14	July 15	July 16
9 months.	Aug. 12	Aug. 13	Aug. 14	Aug. 15	Aug. 16
10 months.	Sep. 12	Sep. 13	Sep. 14	Sep. 15	Sep. 16
11 months.	Oct. 12	Oct. 13	Oct. 14	Oct. 15	Oct. 16
12 months.	Nov. 12	Nov. 13	Nov. 14	Nov. 15	Nov. 16

The above Tables are WITHOUT three days' grace.

(WITHOUT GRACE.)
For Leap-Year changes, see next page.

Time.	Nov'm'r 17.	Nov'm'r 18.	Nov'm'r 19.	Nov'm'r 20.	Nov'm'r 21.
5 days.	Nov. 22	Nov. 23	Nov. 24	Nov. 25	Nov. 26
10 days.	Nov. 27	Nov. 28	Nov. 29	Nov. 30	Dec. 1
15 days.	Dec. 2	Dec. 3	Dec. 4	Dec. 5	Dec. 6
20 days.	Dec. 7	Dec. 8	Dec. 9	Dec. 10	Dec. 11
25 days.	Dec. 12	Dec. 13	Dec. 14	Dec. 15	Dec. 16
30 days.	Dec. 17	Dec. 18	Dec. 19	Dec. 20	Dec. 21
35 days.	Dec. 22	Dec. 23	Dec. 24	Dec. 25	Dec. 26
40 days.	Dec. 27	Dec. 28	Dec. 29	Dec. 30	Dec. 31
45 days.	Jan. 1	Jan. 2	Jan. 3	Jan. 4	Jan. 5
50 days.	Jan. 6	Jan. 7	Jan. 8	Jan. 9	Jan. 10
55 days.	Jan. 11	Jan. 12	Jan. 13	Jan. 14	Jan. 15
60 days.	Jan. 16	Jan. 17	Jan. 18	Jan. 19	Jan. 20
65 days.	Jan. 21	Jan. 22	Jan. 23	Jan. 24	Jan. 25
70 days.	Jan. 26	Jan. 27	Jan. 28	Jan. 29	Jan. 30
75 days.	Jan. 31	Feb. 1	Feb. 2	Feb. 3	Feb. 4
80 days.	Feb. 5	Feb. 6	Feb. 7	Feb. 8	Feb. 9
85 days.	Feb. 10	Feb. 11	Feb. 12	Feb. 13	Feb. 14
90 days.	Feb. 15	Feb. 16	Feb. 17	Feb. 18	Feb. 19
95 days.	Feb. 20	Feb. 21	Feb. 22	Feb. 23	Feb. 24
100 days.	Feb. 25	Feb. 26	Feb. 27	Feb. 28	Mar. 1
1 month.	Dec. 17	Dec. 18	Dec. 19	Dec. 20	Dec. 21
2 months.	Jan. 17	Jan. 18	Jan. 19	Jan. 20	Jan. 21
3 months.	Feb. 17	Feb. 18	Feb. 19	Feb. 20	Feb. 21
4 months.	Mar. 17	Mar. 18	Mar. 19	Mar. 20	Mar. 21
5 months.	Apr. 17	Apr. 18	Apr. 19	Apr. 20	Apr. 21
6 months.	May 17	May 18	May 19	May 20	May 21
7 months.	June 17	June 18	June 19	June 20	June 21
8 months.	July 17	July 18	July 19	July 20	July 21
9 months.	Aug. 17	Aug. 18	Aug. 19	Aug. 20	Aug. 21
10 months.	Sep. 17	Sep. 18	Sep. 19	Sep. 20	Sep. 21
11 months.	Oct. 17	Oct. 18	Oct. 19	Oct. 20	Oct. 21
12 months.	Nov. 17	Nov. 18	Nov. 19	Nov. 20	Nov. 21

The above Tables are WITHOUT three days' grace.

(WITHOUT GRACE.)

Changes when Notes mature in Leap-Year.

Time.	Nov'r 17.	Nov'r 18.	Nov'r 19.	Nov'r 20.	Nov'r 21.
100 days.	Feb. 25	Feb. 26	Feb. 27	Feb. 28	Feb. 29

The above Tables are for use in States where three days' grace are NOT allowed.

(WITHOUT GRACE.)

For Leap-Year changes, see next page.

Time.	Nov'r 22.	Nov'r 23.	Nov'r 24.	Nov'r 25.	Nov'r 26.
5 days.	Nov. 27	Nov. 28	Nov. 29	Nov. 30	Dec. 1
10 days.	Dec. 2	Dec. 3	Dec. 4	Dec. 5	Dec. 6
15 days.	Dec. 7	Dec. 8	Dec. 9	Dec. 10	Dec. 11
20 days.	Dec. 12	Dec. 13	Dec. 14	Dec. 15	Dec. 16
25 days.	Dec. 17	Dec. 18	Dec. 19	Dec. 20	Dec. 21
30 days.	Dec. 22	Dec. 23	Dec. 24	Dec. 25	Dec. 26
35 days.	Dec. 27	Dec. 28	Dec. 29	Dec. 30	Dec. 31
40 days.	Jan. 1	Jan. 2	Jan. 3	Jan. 4	Jan. 5
45 days.	Jan. 6	Jan. 7	Jan. 8	Jan. 9	Jan. 10
50 days.	Jan. 11	Jan. 12	Jan. 13	Jan. 14	Jan. 15
55 days.	Jan. 16	Jan. 17	Jan. 18	Jan. 19	Jan. 20
60 days.	Jan. 21	Jan. 22	Jan. 23	Jan. 24	Jan. 25
65 days.	Jan. 26	Jan. 27	Jan. 28	Jan. 29	Jan. 30
70 days.	Jan. 31	Feb. 1	Feb. 2	Feb. 3	Feb. 4
75 days.	Feb. 5	Feb. 6	Feb. 7	Feb. 8	Feb. 9
80 days.	Feb. 10	Feb. 11	Feb. 12	Feb. 13	Feb. 14
85 days.	Feb. 15	Feb. 16	Feb. 17	Feb. 18	Feb. 19
90 days.	Feb. 20	Feb. 21	Feb. 22	Feb. 23	Feb. 24
95 days.	Feb. 25	Feb. 26	Feb. 27	Feb. 28	Mar. 1
100 days.	Mar. 2	Mar. 3	Mar. 4	Mar. 5	Mar. 6
1 month.	Dec. 22	Dec. 23	Dec. 24	Dec. 25	Dec. 26
2 months.	Jan. 22	Jan. 23	Jan. 24	Jan. 25	Jan. 26
3 months.	Feb. 22	Feb. 23	Feb. 24	Feb. 25	Feb. 26
4 months.	Mar. 22	Mar. 23	Mar. 24	Mar. 25	Mar. 26
5 months.	Apr. 22	Apr. 23	Apr. 24	Apr. 25	Apr. 26
6 months.	May 22	May 23	May 24	May 25	May 26
7 months.	June 22	June 23	June 24	June 25	June 26
8 months.	July 22	July 23	July 24	July 25	July 26
9 months.	Aug. 22	Aug. 23	Aug. 24	Aug. 25	Aug. 26
10 months.	Sep. 22	Sep. 23	Sep. 24	Sep. 25	Sep. 26
11 months.	Oct. 22	Oct. 23	Oct. 24	Oct. 25	Oct. 26
12 months.	Nov. 22	Nov. 23	Nov. 24	Nov. 25	Nov. 26

The above Tables are for use in States where three days' grace are NOT allowed.

(WITHOUT GRACE.)

Changes when Notes mature in Leap-Year.

Time.	Nov'r 22.	Nov'r 23.	Nov'r 24.	Nov'r 25.	Nov'r 26.
95 days.	Feb. 25	Feb. 26	Feb. 27	Feb. 28	Feb. 29
100 days.	Mar. 1	Mar. 2	Mar. 3	Mar. 4	Mar. 5

The above Tables are for use in States where three days' grace are NOT allowed.

(WITHOUT GRACE.)
For Leap-Year changes, see next page.

Time.	Nov'r 27.	Nov'r 28.	Nov'r 29.	Nov'r 30.	Dec'm'r 1.
5 days.	Dec. 2	Dec. 3	Dec. 4	Dec. 5	Dec. 6
10 days.	Dec. 7	Dec. 8	Dec. 9	Dec. 10	Dec. 11
15 days.	Dec. 12	Dec. 13	Dec. 14	Dec. 15	Dec. 16
20 days.	Dec. 17	Dec. 18	Dec. 19	Dec. 20	Dec. 21
25 days.	Dec. 22	Dec. 23	Dec. 24	Dec. 25	Dec. 26
30 days.	Dec. 27	Dec. 28	Dec. 29	Dec. 30	Dec. 31
35 days.	Jan. 1	Jan. 2	Jan. 3	Jan. 4	Jan. 5
40 days.	Jan. 6	Jan. 7	Jan. 8	Jan. 9	Jan. 10
45 days.	Jan. 11	Jan. 12	Jan. 13	Jan. 14	Jan. 15
50 days.	Jan. 16	Jan. 17	Jan. 18	Jan. 19	Jan. 20
55 days.	Jan. 21	Jan. 22	Jan. 23	Jan. 24	Jan. 25
60 days.	Jan. 26	Jan. 27	Jan. 28	Jan. 29	Jan. 30
65 days.	Jan. 31	Feb. 1	Feb. 2	Feb. 3	Feb. 4
70 days.	Feb. 5	Feb. 6	Feb. 7	Feb. 8	Feb. 9
75 days.	Feb. 10	Feb. 11	Feb. 12	Feb. 13	Feb. 14
80 days.	Feb. 15	Feb. 16	Feb. 17	Feb. 18	Feb. 19
85 days.	Feb. 20	Feb. 21	Feb. 22	Feb. 23	Feb. 24
90 days.	Feb. 25	Feb. 26	Feb. 27	Feb. 28	Mar. 1
95 days.	Mar. 2	Mar. 3	Mar. 4	Mar. 5	Mar. 6
100 days.	Mar. 7	Mar. 8	Mar. 9	Mar. 10	Mar. 11
1 month.	Dec. 27	Dec. 28	Dec. 29	Dec. 30	Jan. 1
2 months.	Jan. 27	Jan. 28	Jan. 29	Jan. 30	Feb. 1
3 months.	Feb. 27	Feb. 28	Feb. 28	Feb. 28	Mar. 1
4 months.	Mar. 27	Mar. 28	Mar. 29	Mar. 30	Apr. 1
5 months.	Apr. 27	Apr. 28	Apr. 29	Apr. 30	May 1
6 months.	May 27	May 28	May 29	May 30	June 1
7 months.	June 27	June 28	June 29	June 30	July 1
8 months.	July 27	July 28	July 29	July 30	Aug. 1
9 months.	Aug. 27	Aug. 28	Aug. 29	Aug. 30	Sep. 1
10 months.	Sep. 27	Sep. 28	Sep. 29	Sep. 30	Oct. 1
11 months.	Oct. 27	Oct. 28	Oct. 29	Oct. 30	Nov. 1
12 months.	Nov. 27	Nov. 28	Nov. 29	Nov. 30	Dec. 1

The above Tables are for use in States where three days' grace are NOT allowed.

(WITHOUT GRACE.)
Changes when Notes mature in Leap-Year.

Time.	Nov'r 27.	Nov'r 28.	Nov'r 29.	Nov'r 30.	Dec'm'r 1.
90 days.	Feb. 25	Feb. 26	Feb. 27	Feb. 28	Feb. 29
95 days.	Mar. 1	Mar. 2	Mar. 3	Mar. 4	Mar. 5
100 days.	Mar. 6	Mar, 7	Mar. 8	Mar. 9	Mar. 10
3 months.	Feb. 27	Feb. 28	Feb. 29	Feb. 29	Mar. 1

The above Tables are for use in States where three days' grace are NOT allowed.

NOTE-MATURITY TABLES.
(WITHOUT GRACE.)
For Leap-Year changes, see next page.

Time.	Dec'm'r 2.	Dec'm'r 3.	Dec'm'r 4.	Dec'm'r 5.	Dec'm'r 6.
5 days.	Dec. 7	Dec. 8	Dec. 9	Dec. 10	Dec. 11
10 days.	Dec. 12	Dec. 13	Dec. 14	Dec. 15	Dec. 16
15 days.	Dec. 17	Dec. 18	Dec. 19	Dec. 20	Dec. 21
20 days.	Dec. 22	Dec. 23	Dec. 24	Dec. 25	Dec. 26
25 days.	Dec. 27	Dec. 28	Dec. 29	Dec. 30	Dec. 31
30 days.	Jan. 1	Jan. 2	Jan. 3	Jan. 4	Jan. 5
35 days.	Jan. 6	Jan. 7	Jan. 8	Jan. 9	Jan. 10
40 days.	Jan. 11	Jan. 12	Jan. 13	Jan. 14	Jan. 15
45 days.	Jan. 16	Jan. 17	Jan. 18	Jan. 19	Jan. 20
50 days.	Jan. 21	Jan. 22	Jan. 23	**Jan. 24**	Jan. 25
55 days.	Jan. 26	Jan. 27	Jan. 28	**Jan. 29**	Jan. 30
60 days.	Jan. 31	Feb. 1	Feb. 2	**Feb. 3**	Feb. 4
65 days.	Feb. 5	Feb. 6	Feb. 7	Feb. 8	Feb. 9
70 days.	Feb. 10	Feb. 11	Feb. 12	Feb. 13	Feb. 14
75 days.	Feb. 15	Feb. 16	Feb. 17	Feb. 18	Feb. 19
80 days.	Feb. 20	Feb. 21	Feb. 22	Feb. 23	Feb. 24
85 days.	Feb. 25	Feb. 26	Feb. 27	Feb. 28	Mar. 1
90 days.	Mar. 2	Mar. 3	Mar. 4	Mar. 5	Mar. 6
95 days.	Mar. 7	Mar. 8	Mar. 9	Mar. 10	Mar. 11
100 days.	Mar. 12	Mar. 13	Mar. 14	Mar. 15	Mar. 16
1 month.	Jan. 2	Jan. 3	Jan. 4	Jan. 5	Jan. 6
2 months.	Feb. 2	Feb. 3	Feb. 4	Feb. 5	Feb. 6
3 months.	Mar. 2	Mar. 3	Mar. 4	Mar. 5	Mar. 6
4 months.	Apr. 2	Apr. 3	Apr. 4	Apr. 5	Apr. 6
5 months.	May 2	May 3	May 4	May 5	May 6
6 months.	June 2	June 3	June 4	June 5	June 6
7 months.	July 2	July 3	July 4	July 5	July 6
8 months.	Aug. 2	Aug. 3	Aug. 4	Aug. 5	Aug. 6
9 months.	Sep. 2	Sep. 3	Sep. 4	Sep. 5	Sep. 6
10 months.	Oct. 2	Oct. 3	Oct. 4	Oct. 5	Oct. 6
11 months.	Nov. 2	Nov. 3	Nov. 4	Nov. 5	Nov. 6
12 months.	Dec. 2	Dec. 3	Dec. 4	Dec. 5	Dec. 6

The above Tables are for use in States where three days' grace are NOT allowed.

(WITHOUT GRACE.)

Changes when Notes mature in Leap-Year.

Time.	Dec'm'r 2.	Dec'm'r 3.	Dec'm'r 4.	Dec'm'r 5.	Dec'm'r 6.
85 days.	Feb. 25	Feb. 26	Feb. 27	Feb. 28	Feb. 29
90 days.	Mar. 1	Mar. 2	Mar. 3	Mar. 4	Mar. 5
95 days.	Mar. 6	Mar. 7	Mar. 8	Mar. 9	Mar. 10
100 days.	Mar. 11	Mar. 12	Mar. 13	Mar. 14	Mar. 15

The above Tables are for use in States where three days' grace are NOT allowed.

(WITHOUT GRACE.)

For Leap-Year changes, see next page.

Time.	Dec'm'r 7.	Dec'm'r 8.	Dec'm'r 9.	Dec'm'r 10.	Dec'm'r 11.
5 days.	Dec. 12	Dec. 13	Dec. 14	Dec. 15	Dec. 16
10 days.	Dec. 17	Dec. 18	Dec. 19	Dec. 20	Dec. 21
15 days.	Dec. 22	Dec. 23	Dec. 24	Dec. 25	Dec. 26
20 days.	Dec. 27	Dec. 28	Dec. 29	Dec. 30	Dec. 31
25 days.	Jan. 1	Jan. 2	Jan. 3	Jan. 4	Jan. 5
30 days.	Jan. 6	Jan. 7	Jan. 8	Jan. 9	Jan. 10
35 days.	Jan. 11	Jan. 12	Jan. 13	Jan. 14	Jan. 15
40 days.	Jan. 16	Jan. 17	Jan. 18	Jan. 19	Jan. 20
45 days.	Jan. 21	Jan. 22	Jan. 23	Jan. 24	Jan. 25
50 days.	Jan. 26	Jan. 27	Jan. 28	Jan. 29	Jan. 30
55 days.	Jan. 31	Feb. 1	Feb. 2	Feb. 3	Feb. 4
60 days.	Feb. 5	Feb. 6	Feb. 7	Feb. 8	Feb. 9
65 days.	Feb. 10	Feb. 11	Feb. 12	Feb. 13	Feb. 14
70 days.	Feb. 15	Feb. 16	Feb. 17	Feb. 18	Feb. 19
75 days.	Feb. 20	Feb. 21	Feb. 22	Feb. 23	Feb. 24
80 days.	Feb. 25	Feb. 26	Feb. 27	Feb. 28	Mar. 1
85 days.	Mar. 2	Mar. 3	Mar. 4	Mar. 5	Mar. 6
90 days.	Mar. 7	Mar. 8	Mar. 9	Mar. 10	Mar. 11
95 days.	Mar. 12	Mar. 13	Mar. 14	Mar. 15	Mar. 16
100 days.	Mch 17	Mch 18	Mch 19	Mch 20	Mch 21
1 month.	Jan. 7	Jan. 8	Jan. 9	Jan. 10	Jan. 11
2 months.	Feb. 7	Feb. 8	Feb. 9	Feb. 10	Feb. 11
3 months.	Mar. 7	Mar. 8	Mar. 9	Mar. 10	Mar. 11
4 months.	Apr. 7	Apr. 8	Apr. 9	Apr. 10	Apr. 11
5 months.	May 7	May 8	May 9	May 10	May 11
6 months.	June 7	June 8	June 9	June 10	June 11
7 months.	July 7	July 8	July 9	July 10	July 11
8 months.	Aug. 7	Aug. 8	Aug. 9	Aug. 10	Aug. 11
9 months.	Sep. 7	Sep. 8	Sep. 9	Sep. 10	Sep. 11
10 months.	Oct. 7	Oct. 8	Oct. 9	Oct. 10	Oct. 11
11 months.	Nov. 7	Nov. 8	Nov. 9	Nov. 10	Nov. 11
12 months.	Dec. 7	Dec. 8	Dec. 9	Dec. 10	Dec. 11

The above Tables are for use in States where three days' grace are NOT allowed.

(WITHOUT GRACE.)

Changes when Notes mature in Leap-Year.

Time.	Dec'm'r 7.	Dec'm'r 8.	Dec'm'r 9.	Dec'm'r 10.	Dec'm'r 11.
80 days.	Feb. 25	Feb. 26	Feb. 27	Feb. 28	Feb. 29
85 days.	Mar. 1	Mar. 2	Mar. 3	Mar. 4	Mar. 5
90 days.	Mar. 6	Mar. 7	Mar. 8	Mar. 9	Mar. 10
95 days.	Mar. 11	Mar. 12	Mar. 13	Mar. 14	Mar. 15
100 days.	Mch 16	Mch 17	Mch 18	Mch 19	Mch 20

The above Tables are for use in States where three days' grace are NOT allowed.

(WITHOUT GRACE.)

For Leap-Year changes, see next page.

Time.	Dec'm'r 12.	Dec'm'r 13.	Dec'm'r 14.	Dec'm'r 15.	Dec'm'r 16.
5 days.	Dec. 17	Dec. 18	Dec. 19	Dec. 20	Dec. 21
10 days.	Dec. 22	Dec. 23	Dec. 24	Dec. 25	Dec. 26
15 days.	Dec. 27	Dec. 28	Dec. 29	Dec. 30	Dec. 31
20 days.	Jan. 1	Jan. 2	Jan. 3	Jan. 4	Jan. 5
25 days.	Jan. 6	Jan. 7	Jan. 8	Jan. 9	Jan. 10
30 days.	Jan. 11	Jan. 12	Jan. 13	Jan. 14	Jan. 15
35 days.	Jan. 16	Jan. 17	Jan. 18	Jan. 19	Jan. 20
40 days.	Jan. 21	Jan. 22	Jan. 23	Jan. 24	Jan. 25
45 days.	Jan. 26	Jan. 27	Jan. 28	Jan. 29	Jan. 30
50 days.	Jan. 31	Feb. 1	Feb. 2	Feb. 3	Feb. 4
55 days.	Feb. 5	Feb. 6	Feb. 7	Feb. 8	Feb. 9
60 days.	Feb. 10	Feb. 11	Feb. 12	Feb. 13	Feb. 14
65 days.	Feb. 15	Feb. 16	Feb. 17	Feb. 18	Feb. 19
70 days.	Feb. 20	Feb. 21	Feb. 22	Feb. 23	Feb. 24
75 days.	Feb. 25	Feb. 26	Feb. 27	Feb. 28	Mar. 1
80 days.	Mar. 2	Mar. 3	Mar. 4	Mar. 5	Mar. 6
85 days.	Mar. 7	Mar. 8	Mar. 9	Mar. 10	Mar. 11
90 days.	Mar. 12	Mar. 13	Mar. 14	Mar. 15	Mar. 16
95 days.	Mch 17	Mch 18	Mch 19	Mch 20	Mch 21
100 days.	Mch 22	Mch 23	Mch 24	Mch 25	Mch 26
1 month.	Jan. 12	Jan. 13	Jan. 14	Jan. 15	Jan. 16
2 months.	Feb. 12	Feb. 13	Feb. 14	Feb. 15	Feb. 16
3 months.	Mar. 12	Mar. 13	Mar. 14	Mar. 15	Mar. 16
4 months.	Apr. 12	Apr. 13	Apr. 14	Apr. 15	Apr. 16
5 months.	May 12	May 13	May 14	May 15	May 16
6 months.	June 12	June 13	June 14	June 15	June 16
7 months.	July 12	July 13	July 14	July 15	July 16
8 months.	Aug. 12	Aug. 13	Aug. 14	Aug. 15	Aug. 16
9 months.	Sep. 12	Sep. 13	Sep. 14	Sep. 15	Sep. 16
10 months.	Oct. 12	Oct. 13	Oct. 14	Oct. 15	Oct. 16
11 months.	Nov. 12	Nov. 13	Nov. 14	Nov. 15	Nov. 16
12 months.	Dec. 12	Dec. 13	Dec. 14	Dec. 15	Dec. 16

The above Tables are for use in States where three days' grace are NOT allowed.

(WITHOUT GRACE.)

Changes when Notes mature in Leap-Year.

Time.	Dec'm'r 12.	Dec'm'r 13.	Dec'm'r 14.	Dec'm'r 15.	Dec'm'r 16.
75 days.	Feb. 25	Feb. 26	Feb. 27	Feb. 28	Feb. 29
80 days.	Mar. 1	Mar. 2	Mar. 3	Mar. 4	Mar. 5
85 days.	Mar. 6	Mar. 7	Mar. 8	Mar. 9	Mar. 10
90 days.	Mar. 11	Mar. 12	Mar. 13	Mar. 14	Mar. 15
95 days.	Mch 16	Mch 17	Mch 18	Mch 19	Mch 20
100 days.	Mar. 21	Mar. 22	Mar. 23	Mar. 24	Mar. 25

The above Tables are for use in States where three days' grace are NOT allowed.

(WITHOUT GRACE.)
For Leap-Year changes, see next page.

Time.	Dec'm'r 17.	Dec'm'r 18.	Dec'm'r 19.	Dec'm'r 20.	Dec'm'r 21.
5 days.	Dec. 22	Dec. 23	Dec. 24	Dec. 25	Dec. 26
10 days.	Dec. 27	Dec. 28	Dec. 29	Dec. 30	Dec. 31
15 days.	Jan. 1	Jan. 2	Jan. 3	Jan. 4	Jan. 5
20 days.	Jan. 6	Jan. 7	Jan. 8	Jan. 9	Jan. 10
25 days.	Jan. 11	Jan. 12	Jan. 13	Jan. 14	Jan. 15
30 days.	Jan. 16	Jan. 17	Jan. 18	Jan. 19	Jan. 20
35 days.	Jan. 21	Jan. 22	Jan. 23	Jan. 24	Jan. 25
40 days.	Jan. 26	Jan. 27	Jan. 28	Jan. 29	Jan. 30
45 days.	Jan. 31	Feb. 1	Feb. 2	Feb. 3	Feb. 4
50 days.	Feb. 5	Feb. 6	Feb. 7	Feb. 8	Feb. 9
55 days.	Feb. 10	Feb. 11	Feb. 12	Feb. 13	Feb. 14
60 days.	Feb. 15	Feb. 16	Feb. 17	Feb. 18	Feb. 19
65 days.	Feb. 20	Feb. 21	Feb. 22	Feb. 23	Feb. 24
70 days.	Feb. 25	Feb. 26	Feb. 27	Feb. 28	Mar. 1
75 days.	Mar. 2	Mar. 3	Mar. 4	Mar. 5	Mar. 6
80 days.	Mar. 7	Mar. 8	Mar. 9	Mar. 10	Mar. 11
85 days.	Mar. 12	Mar. 13	Mar. 14	Mar. 15	Mar. 16
90 days.	Mch 17	Mch 18	Mch 19	Mch 20	Mch 21
95 days.	Mch 22	Mch 23	Mch 24	Mch 25	Mch 26
100 days.	Mch 27	Mch 28	Mch 29	Mch 30	Mch 31
1 month.	Jan. 17	Jan. 18	Jan. 19	Jan. 20	Jan. 21
2 months.	Feb. 17	Feb. 18	Feb. 19	Feb. 20	Feb. 21
3 months.	Mar. 17	Mar. 18	Mar. 19	Mar. 20	Mar. 21
4 months.	Apr. 17	Apr. 18	Apr. 19	Apr. 20	Apr. 21
5 months.	May 17	May 18	May 19	May 20	May 21
6 months.	June 17	June 18	June 19	June 20	June 21
7 months.	July 17	July 18	July 19	July 20	July 21
8 months.	Aug. 17	Aug. 18	Aug. 19	Aug. 20	Aug. 21
9 months.	Sep. 17	Sep. 18	Sep. 19	Sep. 20	Sep. 21
10 months.	Oct. 17	Oct. 18	Oct. 19	Oct. 20	Oct. 21
11 months.	Nov. 17	Nov. 18	Nov. 19	Nov. 20	Nov. 21
12 months.	Dec. 17	Dec. 18	Dec. 19	Dec. 20	Dec. 21

The above Tables are for use in States where three days'
grace are NOT allowed.

(WITHOUT GRACE.)

Changes when Notes mature in Leap-Year.

Time.	Dec'm'r 17.	Dec'm'r 18.	Dec'm'r 19.	Dec'm'r 20.	Dec'm'r 21.
70 days.	Feb. 25	Feb. 26	Feb. 27	Feb. 28	Feb. 29
75 days.	Mar. 1	Mar. 2	Mar. 3	Mar. 4	Mar. 5
80 days.	Mar. 6	Mar, 7	Mar. 8	Mar. 9	Mar. 10
85 days.	Mar. 11	Mar. 12	Mar. 13	Mar. 14	Mar. 15
90 days.	Mch 16	Mch 17	Mch 18	Mch 19	Mch 20
95 days.	Mar. 21	Mar. 22	Mar. 23	Mar. 24	Mar. 25
100 days.	Mar. 26	Mar. 27	Mar. 28	Mar. 29	Mar. 30

The above Tables are for use in States where three days' grace are NOT allowed.

(WITHOUT GRACE.)

For Leap-Year changes, see next page.

Time.	Dec'm'r 22.	Dec'm'r 23.	Dec'm'r 24.	Dec'm'r 25.	Dec'm'r 26.
5 days.	Dec. 27	Dec. 28	Dec. 29	Dec. 30	Dec. 31
10 days.	Jan. 1	Jan. 2	Jan. 3	Jan. 4	Jan. 5
15 days.	Jan. 6	Jan. 7	Jan. 8	Jan. 9	Jan. 10
20 days.	Jan. 11	Jan. 12	Jan. 13	Jan. 14	Jan. 15
25 days.	Jan. 16	Jan. 17	Jan. 18	Jan. 19	Jan. 20
30 days.	Jan. 21	Jan. 22	Jan. 23	Jan. 24	Jan. 25
35 days.	Jan. 26	Jan. 27	Jan. 28	Jan. 29	Jan. 30
40 days.	Jan. 31	Feb. 1	Feb. 2	Feb. 3	Feb. 4
45 days.	Feb. 5	Feb. 6	Feb. 7	Feb. 8	Feb. 9
50 days.	Feb. 10	Feb. 11	Feb. 12	Feb. 13	Feb. 14
55 days.	Feb. 15	Feb. 16	Feb. 17	Feb. 18	Feb. 19
60 days.	Feb. 20	Feb. 21	Feb. 22	Feb. 23	Feb. 24
65 days.	Feb. 25	Feb. 26	Feb. 27	Feb. 28	Mar. 1
70 days.	Mar. 2	Mar. 3	Mar. 4	Mar. 5	Mar. 6
75 days.	Mar. 7	Mar. 8	Mar. 9	Mar. 10	Mar. 11
80 days.	Mar. 12	Mar. 13	Mar. 14	Mar. 15	Mar. 16
85 days.	Mch 17	Mch 18	Mch 19	Mch 20	Mch 21
90 days.	Mch 22	Mch 23	Mch 24	Mch 25	Mch 26
95 days.	Mch 27	Mch 28	Mch 29	Mch 30	Mch 31
100 days.	Apr. 1	Apr. 2	Apr. 3	Apr. 4	Apr. 5
1 month.	Jan. 22	Jan. 23	Jan. 24	Jan. 25	Jan. 26
2 months.	Feb. 22	Feb. 23	Feb. 24	Feb. 25	Feb. 26
3 months.	Mar. 22	Mar. 23	Mar. 24	Mar. 25	Mar. 26
4 months.	Apr. 22	Apr. 23	Apr. 24	Apr. 25	Apr. 26
5 months.	May 22	May 23	May 24	May 25	May 26
6 months.	June 22	June 23	June 24	June 25	June 26
7 months.	July 22	July 23	July 24	July 25	July 26
8 months.	Aug. 22	Aug. 23	Aug. 24	Aug. 25	Aug. 26
9 months.	Sep. 22	Sep. 23	Sep. 24	Sep. 25	Sep. 26
10 months.	Oct. 22	Oct. 23	Oct. 24	Oct. 25	Oct. 26
11 months.	Nov. 22	Nov. 23	Nov. 24	Nov. 25	Nov. 26
12 months.	Dec. 22	Dec. 23	Dec. 24	Dec. 25	Dec. 26

The above Tables are for use in States where three days' grace are NOT allowed.

(WITHOUT GRACE.)

Changes when Notes mature in Leap-Year.

Time.	Dec'm'r 22.	Dec'm'r 23.	Dec'm'r 24.	Dec'm'r 25.	Dec'm'r 26.
65 days.	Feb. 25	Feb. 26	Feb. 27	Feb. 28	Feb. 29
70 days.	Mar. 1	Mar. 2	Mar. 3	Mar. 4	Mar. 5
75 days.	Mar. 6	Mar. 7	Mar. 8	Mar. 9	Mar. 10
80 days.	Mar. 11	Mar. 12	Mar. 13	Mar. 14	Mar. 15
85 days.	Mch 16	Mch 17	Mch 18	Mch 19	Mch 20
90 days.	Mar. 21	Mar. 22	Mar. 23	Mar. 24	Mar. 25
95 days.	Mar. 26	Mar. 27	Mar. 28	Mar. 29	Mar. 30
100 days.	Mar. 31	Apr. 1	Apr. 2	Apr. 3	Apr. 4

The above Tables are for use in States where three days' grace are NOT allowed.

WITHOUT GRACE.

For Leap Year changes, see next page.

Time.	Dec'm'r 27.	Dec'm'r 28.	Dec'm'r 29.	Dec'm'r 30.	Dec'm'r 31.
5 days.	Jan. 1	Jan. 2	Jan. 3	Jan. 4	Jan. 5
10 days.	Jan. 6	Jan. 7	Jan. 8	Jan. 9	Jan. 10
15 days.	Jan. 11	Jan. 12	Jan. 13	Jan. 14	Jan. 15
20 days.	Jan. 16	Jan. 17	Jan. 18	Jan. 19	Jan. 20
25 days.	Jan. 21	Jan. 22	Jan. 23	Jan. 24	Jan. 25
30 days.	Jan. 26	Jan. 27	Jan. 28	Jan. 29	Jan. 30
35 days.	Jan. 31	Feb. 1	Feb. 2	Feb. 3	Feb. 4
40 days.	Feb. 5	Feb. 6	Feb. 7	Feb. 8	Feb. 9
45 days.	Feb. 10	Feb. 11	Feb. 12	Feb. 13	Feb. 14
50 days.	Feb. 15	Feb. 16	Feb. 17	Feb. 18	Feb. 19
55 days.	Feb. 20	Feb. 21	Feb. 22	Feb. 23	Feb. 24
60 days.	Feb. 25	Feb. 26	Feb. 27	Feb. 28	Mar. 1
65 days.	Mar. 2	Mar. 3	Mar. 4	Mar. 5	Mar. 6
70 days.	Mar. 7	Mar. 8	Mar. 9	Mar. 10	Mar. 11
75 days.	Mar. 12	Mar. 13	Mar. 14	Mar. 15	Mar. 16
80 days.	Mar. 17	Mar. 18	Mar. 19	Mar. 20	Mar. 21
85 days.	Mar. 22	Mar. 23	Mar. 24	Mar. 25	Mar. 26
90 days.	Mar. 27	Mar. 28	Mar. 29	Mar. 30	Mar. 31
95 days.	Apr. 1	Apr. 2	Apr. 3	Apr. 4	Apr. 5
100 days.	Apr. 6	Apr. 7	Apr. 8	Apr. 9	Apr. 10
1 month.	Jan. 27	Jan. 28	Jan. 29	Jan. 30	Jan. 31
2 months.	Feb. 27	Feb. 28	Feb. 28	Feb. 28	Feb. 28
3 months.	Mar. 27	Mar. 28	Mar. 29	Mar. 30	Mar. 31
4 months.	Apr. 27	Apr. 28	Apr. 29	Apr. 30	Apr. 31
5 months.	May 27	May 28	May 29	May 30	May 31
6 months.	Jun. 27	Jun. 28	Jun. 29	June 30	Jun. 31
7 months.	Jul. 27	Jul. 28	Jul. 29	July 30	July 31
8 months.	Aug. 27	Aug. 28	Aug. 29	Aug. 30	Aug. 31
9 months.	Sep. 27	Sep. 28	Sep. 29	Sept. 30	Sep. 31
10 months.	Oct. 27	Oct. 28	Oct. 29	Oct. 30	Oct. 31
11 months.	Nov. 27	Nov. 28	Nov. 29	Nov. 30	Nov. 31
12 months.	Dec. 27	Dec. 28	Dec. 29	Dec. 30	Dec. 31

The above Tables are WITHOUT three days' grace.

(WITHOUT GRACE.)
Changes when Notes mature in Leap-Year.

Time.	Dec'm'r 27.	Dec'm'r 28.	Dec'm'r 29.	Dec'm'r 30.	Dec'm'r 31.
60 days.	Feb. 25	Feb. 26	Feb. 27	Feb. 28	Feb. 29
65 days.	Mar. 1	Mar. 2	Mar. 3	Mar. 4	Mar. 5
70 days.	Mar. 6	Mar, 7	Mar. 8	Mar. 9	Mar. 10
75 days.	Mar. 11	Mar. 12	Mar. 13	Mar. 14	Mar. 15
80 days.	Mch 16	Mch 17	Mch 18	Mch 19	Mch 20
85 days.	Mar. 21	Mar. 22	Mar. 23	Mar. 24	Mar. 25
90 days.	Mar. 26	Mar. 27	Mar. 28	Mar. 29	Mar. 30
95 days.	Mar. 31	Apr. 1	Apr. 2	Apr. 3	Apr. 4
100 days.	Apr. 5	Apr. 6	Apr. 7	Apr. 8	Apr. 9
2 months.	Feb. 27	Feb. 28	Feb. 29	Feb. 29	Feb. 29

The above Tables are for use in States where three days' grace are NOT allowed.

www.ingramcontent.com/pod-product-compliance
Lightning Source LLC
Chambersburg PA
CBHW030825270326
41928CB00007B/898